THE VIRTUES OF UNDERWEAR

The VIRTUES of UNDERWEAR

Modesty, Flamboyance and Filth

NINA EDWARDS

REAKTION BOOKS

To Josie

Published by
REAKTION BOOKS LTD
Unit 32, Waterside
44–48 Wharf Road
London N1 7UX, UK
www.reaktionbooks.co.uk

First published 2024
Copyright © Nina Edwards 2024

Printed and bound in Great Britain by
TJ Books Ltd, Padstow, Cornwall

A catalogue record for this book is available from the British Library

ISBN 978 1 78914 956 2

Contents

Underwear stall at a street market in Kyiv, 2023.

Introduction

O'erstep not the modesty of nature
HAMLET TO THE PLAYERS, *Hamlet* (III.2)

U nderwear is comforting, embarrassing and comical, sometimes saucy, but seldom all at the same time. We tend to
cover our more intimate parts, that is, our genitals, buttocks and
the female breast. Underwear both protects and hides certain
parts of the body from others. It can cause embarrassment when
exposed to public view, even when the wearer's private parts
remain hidden – such as when trouser flies are accidentally left
undone – because underwear reminds us of what lies beneath.
At the same time, a glimpse of underwear can be playful. Ideas
about modesty and hygiene, and what should or should not be
concealed, fluctuate over time. Bra straps and boxer short elastic
are largely acceptable, but an escaping testicle is generally
frowned upon.

There is a difference in the nature of ridicule apportioned
to a woman compared to a man regarding the embarrassment
or shame felt when underwear comes astray or fails to do its job.
A sign in the public lavatories behind the National Portrait
Gallery in London in the late 1970s comes to mind: 'Gentlemen
Please Adjust Your Clothing Before Emerging'. The statement
is a suggestion, nothing more. Such an accident of undress
might be compared to a woman unaware that her skirt is tucked
into her knickers. In a novel by Curtis Sittenfeld, a fictionalized

Hillary Clinton introduces herself to a class of students, and wonders why they seem distracted:

> Horrifyingly, I understood. I reached around and, though I couldn't see it, I could feel it. After I'd used the bathroom before class, I had tucked the back of my skirt into my pantyhose. I had just taught my first class, in its entirety, with my underwear and upper thighs exposed. 'Oh God,' I said.[1]

Clinton muses that at least the incident gained her a place in history, for it turned out to be the 'first time the word "pantyhose" had been used onstage at a presidential debate'.[2] In the German language such an embarrassment, which might derive from something as minor as having a petticoat showing beneath the hem of a skirt, is referred to as *es blitzt* (it flashes), like a flash of lightning, in that it catches the attention, but the question is why it matters to us. The classical scholar Kerry Olson provides a parallel with the ancient Roman world by quoting the poet Martial, who describes, with some force, a problem with women's flowing skirts, particularly in humid weather: 'Whenever you get up from your chair (I have noticed it again and again), your unfortunate tunics sodomize you, Lesbia. You try and try to pluck them out with your left hand and your right, till you extract them with tears and groans, so firmly are they constrained.'[3]

This book sets out to examine the history and meaning of clothing that is, by definition, though not always, hidden from view, by comparing its varying styles and the attitudes they have brought about. Oddly, much of what is termed 'underwear' today is clothing that is neither under- nor outerwear, but serves both functions, as in a sports bra worn as a summer top. What is more strictly termed 'underwear' is clothing which goes unnoticed by others except in the most intimate of circumstances, such as when removing clothing or dressing in a shared changing room. Underwear plays a significant role in sex work, pornography and at times when our state of dress or undress is not under our control, as with a prisoner or enslaved person.

Underwear comes into close contact with our most sensitive regions and replacing it with freshly laundered garments can make us feel that it is possible to be both human *and* hygienic and sweet smelling. Fresh from a hot bath or shower, clean underwear can make us feel brand new, dissatisfactions with our body and life in general set aside. We put on underwear in order to keep outer clothing from the various excretions and rub of our bodies, and to protect tender skin from rougher textured clothing. Thus it is that in many Slavic languages the word for 'underwear' is synonymous with whiteness. Freshly washed underwear can represent cleanliness even when the body beneath remains dirty.

Underwear's associated vocabulary forms a range of metaphor often so commonplace that we may hardly notice it as such. Some garments or aspects thereof, throughout history and in many cultures, have seemed too ordinary or simply too private to be given formal attention. Yet such apparel is closely tied to individual preference as well as to our shared needs and desires, and has the potential to reveal aspects of what underlies a society as a whole. As with the bustle or the thong, particular underwear can come to signify an era. Sometimes the adoption of a bygone style of underwear seems to represent a longing to return to former values – for what is imagined to be the greater dignity of the past, perhaps. The male buttoned fly and sock suspender are both awkward and unreliable features, yet retain for some a fogeyish and reassuring charm. Female stockings and suspenders are similarly impractical and have become highly sexually suggestive items of dress.

In Imperial China women are reputed to have covered their bound feet first when discovered naked, masking from view what was considered the most intimate and private part of their bodies.[4] We are sometimes advised when preparing for a job interview to imagine the interviewer dressed in only their

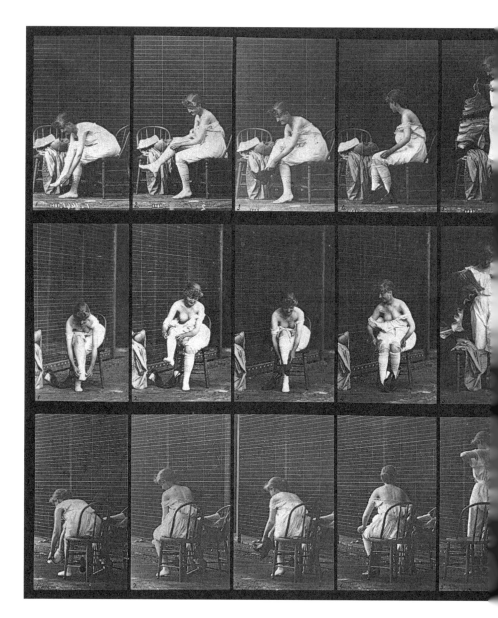

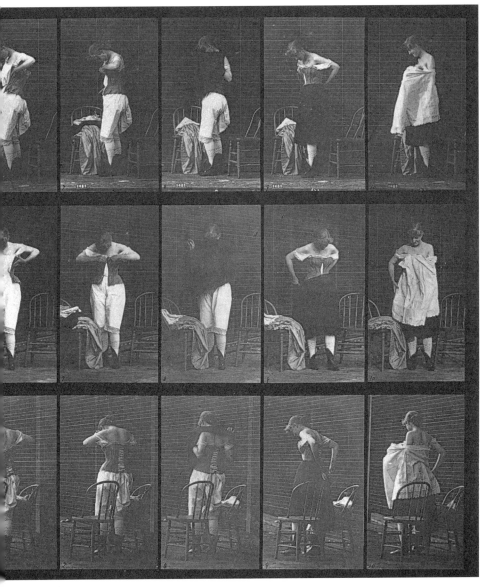

Eadweard Muybridge, *Woman Puts on Clothing over Her Undergarments*, from the series 'Animal Locomotion', 1887 collotype.

undergarments, or perhaps wearing no clothes at all, to puncture the potential power they have over us. The imagined tired bra or droopy Y-fronts of an apparently formidable boss, possibly exposing their none-too-buff physique, can help us keep our nerve. The poor old emperor is unaware of the foolish figure he cuts.

Stripped of our clothing, we may cower and attempt somehow to hide our most private parts from view. Even in more welcome circumstances, it is not uncommon for us to feel vulnerable when exposed to another in our underthings alone. We are led to believe by encounters in rom-com films that romantic attraction breeds relaxed self-confidence in our bodies, but this is far less common in reality. When we are seen without our outer clothing we may stagger backwards, seeking the cover of a duvet. We fear the laughable wobble and dangle or possible evidence of arousal, shamed by our animal self being exposed to view. We are regularly prompted to embrace and accept our bodies as they are, to learn to show them off boldly, declaring that our warts and all form has intrinsic value. Some find that the idea of wearing would-be sexy underwear to heighten their attractions is far more problematic than simply being naked. We may fear to suggest that we rate our bodies too highly, gilding what may be rather less lovely than the lily. There are those for whom the right lingerie heightens their confidence, but a sexual encounter always has the potential to be embarrassing. Underwear, when too obviously sexy, can easily make things far, far worse.

This conundrum is neatly expressed in the advice given by a publisher to writers of soft-core pornography in the 1930s. It seems that both sexes have to be careful about being seen entirely naked . . . at least when they are not playing the part of a corpse:

> Whenever possible, avoid complete nudity of the
> female characters. You can have a girl strip to her
> underwear, or transparent negligée, or nightgown,

or the thin torn shred of her garments, but while the
girl is alive and in contact with a man, we do not want
complete nudity. A nude female corpse is allowable,
of course . . . Do not have men in underwear in scenes
with women, and no nude men at all.[5]

There remain limitations to the zipless encounter even in
a modern, more liberal climate. The publisher initially refers to
'girls' and 'men', with the male role relying on outer clothing
being maintained, whereas female desirability requires merely
some underwear remaining, and of the flimsiest kind. However,
the writer hastily reverts to the use of 'women' rather than 'girls'
in the final sentence, when he advises that men should never be
seen in their underwear, still less buck naked. The switch implies
the re-establishment of a more formal relationship between the
sexes.

Advertising from the late nineteenth century onwards has
increasingly relied on models in underwear to sell a variety of
products. Recent examples include the many video advertisements sited on the sides of bus shelters or in supermarket windows. People going about the ordinary business of shopping on
the high street or perhaps commuting are suddenly confronted
with larger-than-life beautiful models, dressed in scanty underwear. There are many only distantly related items that underwear
is called upon to sell, from deodorants to cars. An Austrian wine
firm, as a means initially of deflecting attention from the sullied
reputation of the Austrian wine industry – caused by an adulter-
ation scandal in the 1980s when an ingredient of anti-freeze was
used by several wineries to improve the flavour of their wines –
has since 2000 been publishing a promotional calendar, *Jung
Winzerinnen* (Young Female Winemakers). Nubile young women
are shown hard at work in their underthings: 'Twelve months
and twelve women means that the calendar captures a year in
the life of the scantily clad winemaker in some detail. Pruning,
harvesting, cleaning tanks, lying awkwardly on some stairs

The Jolly Widdower:

OR,

A Warning for BATCHELORS.

Left they marry with a Shrow, and so become impatient under the pain and punishment of a Hornified Head-piece.

| Now he that marrys with a shrow, believe me this is true, | {} | Over her Husband she will crow, ay, and cornute him too. |

To the Tune of, Caper and ferkit.

Underclothing can be the cause of marital discord, as in this early modern English ballad depicting a couple fighting over who wears the drawers: 'The Jolly Widdower; or, A Warning for Batchelors', c. 1664–1703.

Young Men and Batchelors, pray attend
unto my doleful Tale,
It is to you that these lines I send,
in hopes they may prevail
With you, to take a special care,
when ever you mean to wed,
For if that a Shrow, should over you crow,
then, then all thy joys are fled.

Alas! by woful experience now,
I know this too be true,
I am forced for to cringe and bow,

For being married unto a Scold,
my joys they are fully fled,
Which makes me to cry so sorrowfully,
I wou'd I had ne'r been wed.

When I was single i'de rant and roar,
and court the charming bowl,
Both Silver and Gold I had good store,
and none could me controul:
But now the case is altered quite,
I now am to ruine led,
The Horns that I wear, doth make me dispair.

clutching a carafe of Grüner Veltliner: it has been laid bare for the public to see.'[6]

Autopsies in film and television dramas customarily conceal the genitals of the deceased with a small piece of white cloth. In reality, however, such a gesture is unlikely, with a corpse receiving less ritualized respect of this kind in a pathology laboratory. Given the increasing lack of boundaries in both fictional and documentary accounts, in which viewers are shown the handling of inner organs outside the body, brains being weighed and eyeballs dissected and so on, the stand-in underwear of the white napkin is provided as if to satisfy the finer feelings of the audience. The covering serves to heighten the curious appeal of almost seeing what we feel we should not see.

Underwear plays a role that has both practical and psychological significance for wearer and onlooker alike. Clothing in general speaks of time and place but also of character, and so it follows that its underlying linings and foundations, its many hidden layers (sometimes only partly hidden from view), may be especially noteworthy. You may consider that you wear only what is sensibly comfortable and practical, particularly in relation to underwear, which, generally speaking, few get the opportunity to judge. Surely we should be able to put functionality first and largely ignore fashion? And we may, for instance, be motivated to wear certain clothing not necessarily in the hopes of looking attractive to another, but by feelings of nostalgia that have nothing whatsoever to do with comfort and protection. It is not uncommon for a hidden designer label, even when languishing unseen, to nonetheless boost the confidence of the wearer. Take, as an example, an exquisite and expensive Empreinte Cassiopee bra, which might make the wearer feel pampered and privileged. The brand is presumably derived from the Cassiopeia of Greek mythology, a vain and arrogant queen who ended up in chains in the heavens as punishment for her boasts of beauty – so a bold name for lingerie. At times we seek what makes us feel more powerful and appealing, sexy, slender or maybe generously endowed.

The first time we are intimate with a new sexual partner can be embarrassing. No wonder that many rely on alcohol or murky lighting to give them courage. Jarvis Cocker, frontman and lyricist for the English rock band Pulp, suggests how daunting it can be, in the song 'Underwear' (1995), when removing the last remaining clothing before the naked body is exposed. It can be both a panicky and wondrous moment.

The manner in which we remove our underwear may reveal our attitudes to our bodies. In a swimming pool changing room, for example, there are those who opt for the privacy of a cubicle; younger people, especially those with gym-toned bodies, often appear more relaxed in such a communal setting. Some, whatever their age, may prefer the cover of a large towel to shield their dignity. New freedoms for trans people challenge previous distinctions and can make the designation of changing areas a problem. It is said that cis men are far more likely to feel at ease when naked compared to cis women, whatever their sexual preference might be. In Germany and some Scandinavian countries gender-neutral changing rooms, certainly for sporting activities, are commonplace, but for some, the problem of an appropriate place to undress remains. Some people prefer to change in spaces that have an assigned gender, even if they are in the process of transitioning. Others claim that whether or not there are separated-off booths, mixed gender changing areas can easily become 'a hunting ground for predatory or exhibitionist men' and a source of 'traumatic encounters'.[7] After consultation with LGBTQ+ groups, UK stores such as Primark, H&M, John Lewis and M&S have recently agreed to provide gender-neutral facilities, but it seems unlikely that these measures can satisfy all viewpoints.

Terms such as restroom, comfort room or cloakroom suggest that women's public lavatories have also provided a safe, private space. Since the nineteenth century, in both Britain and America, they offered women provision for washing and changing theirs and their infants' clothing. At Morgan State University in Baltimore, America, when a transgender student who had begun to wear women's clothes decided to use female rather than male restrooms, some found it disturbing.[8] Where we feel comfortable to be seen in our underwear is salient – and we may even feel strongly about where others should be permitted to undress. How to negotiate transgender concerns about the freedom of individual expression and issues of privacy and security seem to be increasingly fraught. But this in itself is nothing new. Attitudes to undress and underwear have long been contentious matters.

When underwear is worn in part or even wholly as outer clothing then its meaning can become difficult to unravel. It may be merely an unthinking nod to the fashion of the moment, or it can be a deliberate attempt to suggest ideas that are pornographic or fetishistic. Underwear worn in this way often requires an audience capable of understanding the meaning of what is being worn. Sexy underwear may be worn to excite lust, but also to arouse envy in those who would not have the figure or confidence to carry it off. It surely follows, in both cases, that the wearer's intimate clothing needs to be seen by others.

Underwear can evoke *Carry On* film naughtiness as well as more serious issues of uniformity and weaselly appropriateness. It can also have a medical function, tackling menstruation and incontinence issues for example, and serve to aid those with disabilities or deformities, and so on. Clerical underwear, like much of its outerwear, often follows otherwise outdated styles. Some religious views hold to the idea that underclothing masks and protects us from our potential sinfulness. Because of long-held proscriptions concerning ethical dress it can be hard to examine such underwear and interrogate why it continues to be worn. Enquiries can seem in themselves to represent irreligious prurience, or choices may be so long established that it appears to be unthinkable to question them. However, on occasion what is worn hidden from view can reveal aspects of past centuries' attitudes to dress, suggesting what was meant and may still be meant by continuing to wear such garments.

In the field of lingerie, many an elegant dresser may secretly be wearing items that are surprisingly shabby under cover of their fashion-conscious chic. It may well be true that much can be learned about a person from the contents of their underwear drawer. The underwear of childhood, of vests and underpants, pristine whites and pale-coloured fabrics and all the fuss of laundered frills and furbelows, may be evidence of care, and possibly of affluence. Undergarments that appear to be merely utilitarian may still reveal minute distinctions, for example in the context of poverty, where it can be no mean feat to acquire and launder them. Female versus male distinctions fluctuate. Some items of underwear cater to all categories of gender. Apparel marketed distinctly as male or female underwear may be worn by both cross-gender and non-binary people to express their individual, non-gender-defined preferences.

The history of underwear from ancient to modern times reveals its variety as well as elements of common ground, regarding our bodily form and functions and also its range of requirements over time. Whereas outer clothing is more obviously subject to fashion, some of what is worn unseen can seem relatively constant in design. Foundation garments transform the silhouette from, for example, a 'buxom, voluptuous, and ... rotund' standard of female beauty to that of a prepubescent waif,[9] or from the corseted, codpieced courtier to the unremittingly sensible white jersey combinations of the apparently classless Western male of over two hundred years ago. Only the occasional flourish of colour and fine feathers appears to remain into the twentieth century. The following chapters set out to examine underwear's conflicting concerns regarding warmth and comfort and the need for protection and cleanliness, and our recurring desire for flattering display. An appetite for erotic suggestiveness is more often expressed in female rather than male dress in the West, but this feature is again in a state of flux. The eighteenth-century dandy has returned, with men just as aware of issues concerning the figure and what underwear can achieve. The details of our underclothing and the sentiments the items may elicit betray the nuanced, dynamic distinctions of class and means; because of its sometime invisibility, underwear can also allow an individual to express tastes peculiar to them alone.

I

What Is Underwear For?

Thou woldest make me kisse thyn olde breech,
And swere it were a relyk of a seint,
Though it were with thy fundement depeint.

Why, you would have me kissing your old breeches,
And swear they were the relics of a saint,
Though with your excrement 'twere dabbed like paint.

GEOFFREY CHAUCER, *The Pardoner's Tale* [1]

In Hilary Mantel's *Wolf Hall* (2009) Thomas Cromwell is advised by Cardinal Wolsey, 'Try always . . . to learn what people wear under their clothes.'[2] Let us begin at the beginning, which is to say, at the bottom, a place where we might be overcome by disgust or encounter the pull of attraction, for they are so closely interwoven that they can hardly be said to be opposites at all. We enter the land of pratfall sniggers, of children nudging each other and stifling giggles in response to the ludicrous business of our vain attempts to disguise the evidence of our true base corporality. What lies beneath a Roman toga or a Scottish kilt? Why was it that late fourteenth-century *pandos*, or loose-legged drawers, an early form of trousers, were sometimes deliberately cut so short as to reveal the genitals?[3]

Samuel Pepys, ashamed to find himself doubting his wife's fidelity, admitted in his diary in May 1663 that he would nevertheless have felt more than justified had he ascertained that she had gone out without wearing any underwear: 'I am ashamed

A FASHIONABLE LADY
in DRESS & UNDRESS.

Robert Dighton, *A Fashionable Lady in Dress & Undress*, 1807, etching.

to think what a course I did take by lying to see whether my wife did wear drawers today as she used to do – and other things to raise my suspicion of her, but I found no true cause of doing it.'4 But five weeks later he was still observing her closely, alive with jealousy: 'I did so watch my wife put on drawers, which poor soul she did, and yet I could not get off my suspicions.'5 It has been said that English women, unlike the Italian and French, did not begin to wear drawers until the end of the eighteenth century, yet here is Pepys more than one hundred years before then discussing the garment, the item already denoting proper, modest behaviour in a good and faithful wife.6

Wearing drawers as a feature of high fashion, however, is a different matter. Buoyed by the Industrial Revolution, which made mass production possible, in the early 1800s drawers were initially advertised for young girls, designs coming to England and the United States from France. They were rapidly adopted by adult women as convenient and comfortable items of clothing, though many continued to rely on their petticoats alone, as they had always done. Drawers were confining and an additional expense, but even though they went unseen some began to feel incompletely dressed without them. What convinced many to purchase them was the glamorous depiction of underwear promoted in ladies' magazines and the shiny plate-glass windows of the many new department stores. Even a poorly paid housemaid might aspire to these new, and promoted as essential, items of clothing. It was not only drawers that were available to early nineteenth-century consumers, but camisoles, petticoats, corsets of various designs and all the ribbons and laces, the scents and pomades, the sweat shields, new washing powders, starches and scented rinses they required. Men of fashion needed a barrier between their tight-fitting pantaloon trousers and the emanations of the body, and so had adopted underwear even sooner than women. King George II of Great Britain (r. 1727–60) was a man keen on punctuality and the organization of small matters. Keen to ensure that the royal underpants received equal wear, he insisted upon them being numbered for each day of the week. As statesman and wit Lord Chesterfield remarked, though he was admittedly out of favour with the king at the time, 'little things . . . afflicted [the king] more than great ones.'[7]

Underclothing can be the seat of internecine dispute, as anyone who has watched the British ITV soap opera *Coronation Street* will know. The knicker factory Underworld is the seat of local gossip, secret affairs, petty theft, counterfeit schemes, arson and, on one occasion, murder. In this context ordinary people reveal their hidden resentments and passions against the backdrop of underwear production.

Underwear can be a talisman, as when trusty old underpants are worn for an important event, for comforting reassurance and perhaps luck. Underclothing is part of the contradictory, chaotic, occasionally exciting, often embarrassing and even at times tragic twists and turns of our lives. Once, maybe, men may have been less concerned with the look of their underpants, so long as they did the job and their quality was sufficient to match the wearer's standing in the world. In the years of darkening sartorial austerity from the late eighteenth century to the end of the nineteenth century, a man of substance in the West came to understand that he should be discreet about his clothing. In a study of dark male dress, John Harvey makes the crucial point that 'black served for gender-coding'; the act of drawing attention to one's manner of dress, for a man of means and status, implied a lack of essential masculine gravitas.[8] For women, the elaborations of not only what was seen on the surface of their dress but the sophistications of their underwear marked out their status.

The pleasures of male underwear were more discreet, with the finest knitted linen and polished silk jersey underpants, with tiny mother-of-pearl buttons and perhaps embroidered forget-me-not details, and it would rarely have been seen by others except for one's servants. Nonetheless, such particulars might still have eased a longing for the colourful clothing so long denied to men. There have been periods when some paid greater attention to their underpinnings, and both men and women have at times refined their body shape to suit the current fashions with the help of corsetry. Increasingly today many men aspire, or may feel under pressure, to consider items as 'more than functional' and hopefully 'as desirable and erotic'.[9]

The first material evidence of underwear is a Sumerian terracotta bas-relief dated to about 3000 BCE, now housed in the Louvre. Two women are shown, one wearing a loincloth and the other dressed in something resembling a pair of modern briefs; both items are made from what appears to be animal skin rather than manufactured cloth, and are fastened at the waist with a tie.[10] Gradually, over centuries, different designs emerged and types of underwear increased. Like a reverse striptease, these changes indicate shifts in attitude to the human body, from the classical ideal of naked perfection to shame and humiliation. Pilgrims in the late thirteenth and fourteenth century might travel barefoot, clad only in their undershirts, to signify their humility and gain thereby the greatest amount of indulgence to mitigate their sins. The dress historian Shaun Cole describes how this practice fed into the idea of prisoners being forced to strip down to their underwear as a public humiliation. Cole mentions that 'In 1347, the burghers of Calais were ordered by the English king, Edward III, to surrender wearing only their shirts.'[11] There is an important distinction between an individual choosing to humble themselves and having humility imposed upon them. This deliberate denial of an individual's dignity continues today in many repressive societies.

In the seventeenth century the poet John Donne delighted in the revelation of the female form: 'Full nakedness! All joys are due to thee. / As souls unbodied, bodies unclothed must be, / To taste whole joys.'[12] In his poem 'To His Mistress Going to Bed', a woman removes each article of clothing until reaching the last item, her 'white linen'. It is only when this final barrier has been removed that she is wholly available to the man, body and soul.

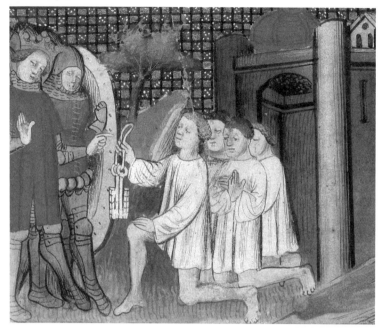

The burghers of Calais surrendering wearing only their shirts, miniature from a manuscript of Jean Froissart's *Chronicles*, 14th century.

Yet it is often not a fully naked body but a minimally covered one that induces desire. Arguably the nudist beach is less titillating than sunbathers wearing bikinis and budgie smugglers. In the nineteenth century, the focus is not so much on the naked body itself but on the underwear that enshrines it. Without the flimsy, layered barriers of cotton and linen that conceal the body from view, the flesh, it seems, may fail to excite. In Thomas Hardy's novel *The Well-Beloved*, serialized in the early 1890s, a man comes across a woman in a rainstorm, and together they seek shelter at an inn. She retires to a bedroom to remove her wet clothing, sending down each item, one at a time, to be dried before the hearth where he waits. As each piece arrives it becomes part of a ritual revealing, gradually increasing the tension as each item is hung before the fire. The steaming garments seem to the man to embody the essence of the woman who so recently inhabited them, like a striptease of the absent body. It is these items, the underclothing, that become the focus of his desire. Whereas Donne enumerated and named each discarded item, Hardy leaves them 'unnamed and undescribed', as if to do so would take away from their united symbolic power.[13]

The slaves of antiquity are often shown entirely naked on artefacts and wall paintings, but loincloths or skimpier cache-sexes are evident in paintings and vases showing wrestlers and those working in the fields. Such fabric coverings protected the wearers from injuries that might have resulted from their daily toils. Thongs, made from seal fur and leather, fringed and adorned with glass beads, were sometimes the only garment worn inside the home by Inuits into the nineteenth century. The National Museum of Denmark displays nappy-like garments that would have been tied to the body by a strip of fabric pulled between the legs and held in place with a belt or string, not unlike a Native American breechcloth and similar to the Indian dhoti, though made from reindeer skin and young seal hide rather than homespun cotton. Tribal costume in Cameroon and in the Democratic Republic of Congo, for example, has elaborately decorated penis covers, and sometimes also cache-fesses, like a small back-to-front apron covering the anus, the latter also worn by women.[14] Because they may be otherwise naked, the clothing seems unashamedly worn to draw attention to the wearer's body beneath.[15] In this symbolic tribal context, the covers act as a formal threat, with what is hidden from the onlooker remaining implicit. These are garments worn for ceremonial occasions, strung with beads and shells and coloured cords, whereas everyday protection is less elaborate.

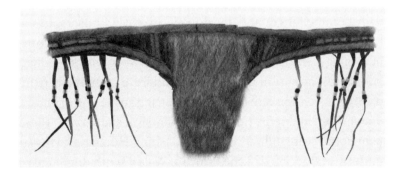

Inuit *naatsit* thong made from seal fur, East Greenland, 19th century.

In the medieval period there would have been little difference in design between the underclothing that children and adults wore. A European man of means might have worn open-crotch underwear that could be easily pulled aside to allow for convenient urination and defecation, and would also have served to protect the wearer's finer outer clothing. The evolution of Western male underpants began with rudimentary pieces of cloth held in place at the waist. Later, sewn garments like baggy shorts, known as braies, had wide legs that could be slid to one side for the purposes of relieving oneself. These gradually became longer and developed into early trousers. In the late eighteenth century, the fashion for close-fitting, front-buttoning doeskin breeches or pantaloons worn with knee-high boots drew attention to the crotch and were often made from pale fabric, reminiscent of flesh, 'producing an illusion of nudity, drawn from and reflecting a love of classical statuary'.[16] These pantaloons were influenced by the dashing Hungarian Hussar uniform and adopted by the Prince of Wales' Tenth Regiment of

Four recruits in white dhotis, page from the Fraser Album, c. 1815, pencil on paper.

Two women wearing cache-fesses, or *negbe*, Democratic Republic of Congo, photograph by Casimir Zagourski, 1929–37.

Light Dragoons, suggesting the classical, the martial and sheer foreign verve.[17]

One can imagine an enthusiastic interest in the finds of Herculaneum, for the beauty of polished marble, easily transferring to a fashion for the male form tightly encased to show off men's physique. In the eighteenth century shirt tails were drawn between the legs to protect the outer cloth of the new, tight knee-length breeches. Since the shirt fabric could easily become displaced and bunch up uncomfortably, a man who valued the line of his figure was often keen to sport the trimmer jersey underpants in cotton or silk. The new fashion for snugly fitting leg coverings required a lining to prevent chafing, and underpants extending to the mid-thigh or knee solved this problem. Fine woollen versions were to become the mainstay of a proper Victorian gentleman's apparel across the so-called respectable classes, and increasingly these were worn down to the ankle under fuller trousers.

Early braies were initially worn only by those of means across Europe. They would have been made of long and loose undyed cloth, sometimes falling to the calf and held in place with lacing. Eventually the convenience of an open flap was added, sometimes with buttons at the front. In our own time these openings are often retained, but are sometimes sewn closed in briefs and boxer shorts. The openings have become somewhat obsolete, since it is easier to avoid accidental wetting by pulling the underpants down instead of using the flap or leg hole. In Germany *Sitzpinkler*, men who sit down to urinate in order to avoid spraying, have become common. Some seats have been fitted with a device called a wc-Geist, which reproaches those men, in the voice of former German chancellor Angela Merkel, who attempt to urinate standing up. The Geist orders you, when you lift the seat, to sit down.[18]

As early as the twelfth century knights would have worn braies beneath their armour to prevent skin chafing against the sharp edges of chain-mail and heavy plate. Those of means also adopted the *chausses* or hose to cover the legs. The feet, because they tend to sweat most, were often left uncovered and wrapped with strips of cloth instead, making the need to launder the hose less frequent. Finer-quality hose were cut on the bias, at a 45° angle on woven material, which required a larger amount of cloth but allowed for stretch, again held in place with cords. In the early nineteenth century fashionable men took to wearing longer slim-fitting breeches or pantaloons, widely adopted after the French Revolution, often pleated into the waistband and so allowing more leeway around the crotch area and therefore greater comfort.

In the Middle Ages wool had been thought to harbour lice because of its lanolin content, so linen or fustian cloth, a blend with cotton, tended to be used for underclothing because it was more easily laundered, and usually more comfortable, when it could be afforded. Jewish law specifically rules against wool being mixed with linen – 'neither shall a garment mingled of linen and woollen come upon thee' (Leviticus 19:19) – though this does not refer to considerations of hygiene but is rather against the idea of blending, as in breeding together different species of animals or planting together different types of seed.

By the nineteenth century wool or cotton jersey combinations, or long johns, known as union suits in America, were popular, though for warmer weather separate underpants and undershirts soon became a more practical, flexible option. As sober dress took hold during the Industrial Revolution in the West, the design of men's underwear became increasingly uniform. For the foppish macaronis and later the more refined followers of George (Beau) Brummell, the idea of one's naked body coming into close contact with tailored outer clothing became an increasingly abhorrent idea.[19] What changes there were at the turn of the nineteenth century relate to fabric and the development of elasticated waistbands rather than any more obvious differences, though at first elastic was only possible to manufacture in shorter lengths suitable for shoulder strap insets in women's underwear.

Johnny Weissmuller, an Olympic gold-medal-winning swimmer of the 1920s, starred as Tarzan in Hollywood films of the 1930s and '40s and became famous for wearing the jungle dweller's signature animal skin loincloth, or sometimes the skimpier thong. Although raised by apes, Edgar Rice Burroughs's hero knows that he should keep his genitals to himself as a gentleman of the jungle. Maureen O'Sullivan was cast as Weissmuller's Jane, and she too appears to be wearing underpants beneath her brief dress or short skirt and abbreviated top, worn over the fashion-of-the-moment conical bra. Such bras, with their exaggerated angular shape, recall the uncompromising contours of earlier corsets, except the breasts are now held up

Johnny Weissmuller as Tarzan wearing an animal skin, and Maureen O'Sullivan as Jane, in *Tarzan the Ape Man* (1932, dir. W. S. Van Dyke).

soutien-gorge,
from Inès Gâches-
Sarraute, Le Corset
(1900).

by straps from the shoulder, known in French as the *soutien-gorge* or throat support. When Weissmuller was invited to play Tarzan in *Tarzan the Ape Man* (1932), he happened to be under contract as an underwear model to the American manufacturer BVD. The Olympian had been advertising their line of underwear and swimsuits with the slogan, 'Next to Myself I Like BVD Best!' In order to get the company to release him from the contract, Hollywood studio MGM was forced to agree to actresses Marie Dressler and Greta Garbo modelling BVD's underwear in return, which just goes to show the market value an underwear model can have, even at the outset of the 1930s. Weissmuller's potent image, of rippling meaty muscles and skimpy briefs, was made respectable given his sporting status, and influenced attitudes to the bodybuilder's posing pouch or skimpy thong and even perhaps male strippers' clothing. However, the latter's ultimate garment seems more often to be made from shiny, brittle, dark materials rather than pale cloth or animal skin, and is reminiscent of the Renaissance codpiece, couched in silk velvet and glittering with jewels, representing unyielding masculine power and potency.

The different words used for underpants denote their design and also sometimes our disparate and changing attitudes to them. For men, for whom the range has tended to be more limited until of late, there is a wide variety of minimal strings, thongs, banana hammocks or 'theatrical supports'. The latter term was preferred by Mrs Freed – of the store Freed of London, supplier of professional dance shoes since 1929 – to the expression 'jockstrap', and she was given to reprimanding customers who used the more graphic transatlantic term. Today 'jock-strap' has become widely accepted for both sports and dance. More everyday are the trunks and boxers and the more revealing boxer-briefs. Y-fronts were developed by the American firm Cooper's in 1935, after the company's vice-president, Arthur Kneibler, received a postcard of a man in French briefs with an integral fly front. This underwear feature, though it may not in practice be used as an opening, has layers of fabric that provide useful absorbency. The Y-front was advertised as offering 'masculine support' for the genitals, acting as a discreet suggestion, perhaps, that the clothing could disguise an inconvenient erection. Previously only sportswear jockstraps had offered the wearer the security of an elasticated waistband and leg holes. The new Y-fronts sold out fast.

Older men often stuck to their accustomed underwear preferences, and as is often the case, there were those of all ages who were slow to adopt such a new and fashionable feature of dress as the Y-front, after centuries of conservatism in male dress. It would be unusual, perhaps, for a man to collect and wear vintage men's underwear. In contrast, it might be deemed charming or sentimental for a woman to wear her grandmother's underclothing, evidenced in the prices antique cami-knickers and camisoles are sold for in vintage clothing shops. However, recently I saw a wool and silk mix male long-sleeved undervest on sale in an antique market off the King's Road in London, with silk lattice cords at the waist: highly wearable outer clothing for the young man-about-town.

Whatever changes have occurred in male clothing, in design and materials, the mainstream range of terms for women's underwear is greater, from wide-legged, two-part and open-crotched drawstring knickers all the way to G-strings, and from Brazilians that are cut away at the back so that the lower part of the bottom is left uncovered to tanga briefs that occupy a halfway house between the thong and regular briefs. There are high- and low-cuts, from minimal bikinis and back again to boyish

shorts. The most revealing of G-strings are about as uncomfortable as cheese wire, with little more than a cord or flex between the legs, which can irritate the skin and exacerbate infections such as cystitis, though they do have the advantage of drawing attention to what they pretend to conceal. They also avoid the VPL, or visible panty line, which appears when wearing clothing that clings tightly to the body. For the striptease artist or the porn actor, extra care is often taken to remove all traces of pubic hair from sight, including bleaching darker areas of skin, so that the body is homogenized for the final reveal when a G-string is discarded. Such means create an idealized, tidied-up image of female and male genitalia. The jockstrap or male dancer's theatrical belt usually, like a female sports bra, gathers together and disguises the parts it covers. This deception echoes how for many centuries female bottoms were presented in their layers of petticoats and skirts, appearing to be a single whole rather than two separate cheeks with a deep cleft between.

This is not the only example of the duplicitous potential of the petticoat. A nobler example lies in the reputed bravery of a cobbler's wife who led a group of women to capture and detain a party of twelve French soldiers in Llanwnda near Fishguard in Wales in 1797, during the last invasion of the British Isles. Armed only with a pitchfork, Jemima Nicholas, also known as Fawr, managed to trick the enemy into thinking they were being attacked by musket-wielding British soldiers. She ordered her troupe to throw their scarlet flannel petticoats over their heads to give the impression of redcoat uniforms. Apparently the French had been drinking, or they might not have been so easily fooled. Jemima gained both a lifetime pension and a place in history.

A fictional example of red petticoats serving the greater good occurs in Edith Nesbit's *The Railway Children* (1906), set in the idyllic Yorkshire countryside, where three children – Roberta (Bobbie), Peter and Phyllis – keep watch over a train line. A pivotal scene in the film version of 1970, directed by Lionel Jeffries, shows the children noticing a landslide that may imminently cause a train to crash. The two girls quickly shuck off their petticoats and all three children use them to flag down the train. An accident is averted. The children receive watches engraved with their names and become known as 'The Railway Children'. This incident is often remembered as involving red knickers being waved about rather than petticoats, underclothing having a distinct hierarchy, with knickers being potentially funnier than petticoats.

Children in the early twentieth century were still wearing clothing including underwear that was merely a smaller version of their parents', but matters were beginning to change. Underwear models as late as the Second World War still seem oddly homely and innocent today, with their sensible cellular long-legged underpants and vests, so used have we become in the modern day to sexy underwear advertisements. They are a far cry from the humour of the British television series *Are You Being Served?* (1972–85), which followed a long tradition of music hall double entendres. The BBC sitcom is set in a department store, specifically on a single floor where two departments, ladies' underwear and gents' outfitters, have been relocated. In the show's second episode, titled 'Dear Sexy Knickers', young assistant Miss Brahms and her senior, the older Mrs Slocombe, discuss what should be done about the problem of being able to see into the men's changing room:

> Miss Brahms: Well, it wouldn't make the centre page of *Cosmopolitan*.
> Mrs Slocombe: Now that's something I just can't understand: why anybody wants to buy a women's magazine with a picture of a nude man in it.
> Ooh, I think it's awful.
> Miss Brahms: I thought Burt Reynolds looked quite sexy.
> Mrs Slocombe: Well, you couldn't see anything: his arm was in the way.[20]

Embarrassment can serve as a halfway house between comedy and serious drama. In the twentieth century, Cecil Willett and Phillis Cunnington chronicled the editorials and advertisements of fashion magazines to study changes in our attitudes to dress, noting the reluctance of the buying public to entertain certain newly fashionable items. At the beginning of the twentieth century wide-legged 'skirt knickers' were increasingly deemed 'out' and tight-fitting pantalettes back 'in'. C. Willett Cunnington, in his *English Women's Clothing in the Present Century* (1952), quotes a contemporary magazine article which claims to be 'more amus[ed] than words can describe to observe how frequently the fashion is ignored'.[21] It is worth remembering this pervasive feature of dress: though many outwardly follow fashion, they lag behind when it comes to their underwear, keeping instead to tried and tested items. Many may prefer to stick to the underwear styles of their youth, or simply choose to avoid the additional expense. A reluctance to follow fashion is easier to conceal in matters of underwear.

The term 'knickers' is nowadays sometimes associated with fancy and possibly foreign, very possibly French, lingerie. Female underpants often retain features that celebrate the less streamlined past, such as the tiny satin ribbon bow that commonly adorns the centre front, representing the former, pre-elastic design that included a thin drawstring, but also, *in parvo*, suggesting long-lost frilly, fancy excess. Some snip this feature off in minimalist distaste, disliking the suggestion of dinky femininity, but it is not uncommon for many, while tugging on a grey utility sports bra, gender-neutral joggers and a baggy T-shirt, to enjoy this nod to a more fanciful era, an echo of the past.[22] It is also a feature of women's underwear appreciated by some cross-dressers. A practical function of the obsolescent bow is that it helps someone locate the front of their underpants when trying to get dressed in the dark.

White underpants often appear to symbolize purity and sometimes virginity. At the misbegotten trial of Anthony Broadwater for the rape of the novelist Alice Sebold in 1981, a key piece of evidence was her stained briefs, the dried blood making a telling impression on the jury, 'her white underwear, now wrapped in plastic . . . passed around as evidence', even though it did not in fact link the accused with the crime.[23] Broadwater served sixteen years in prison before being exonerated in 2021.

Shorts, on the other hand, a version of male trunks, seem more breezily transatlantic, and those marketed for women often retain a non-functioning fly front. At the height of the character's high-fashion, highly feminized popularity, Carrie Bradshaw, of *Sex and the City* fame, wore plain apparently male Y-fronts, matching those of her boyfriend at the time. These were not so much snug tighty-whities, for they were baggy and cutely too large for her, reminding us of her fragile and childlike rather than androgynous persona. This interplay between the masculine and feminine is often expressed in a woman's underwear drawer, which tends to contain widely differing styles to suit the mood of any occasion. For many, some underpants never get worn; the right opportunity never quite comes to pass.

The idea of knickers dancing in the wind on a washing line has often been the nub of risqué jokes, as with Donald McGill-style postcards. Many choose to hang their 'smalls' inside to dry, away from prying eyes, or at least in a discreet position where -front bra. they cannot easily be seen by neighbours, thinking them too

saucy or perhaps too dull and worn to want them on show. Contemporary Buddhist regulations in Burma insist that female postulants keep their drying underpants hidden from view. Modern-day washer-dryers and drying machines mean that for many an outside washing line is becoming something from the past, though for others hanging out the washing on a bright, breezy day is a cheerful activity.

For the washing line thief, whether playful or driven by a more serious compulsion, laundry hanging on a line remains an opportunity to acquire underwear. The ska band Madness's 'In the Middle of the Night' evokes a furtive newsagent, George, skulking about in the dark collecting underwear.[24]

Even cats can be driven to steal, and the rubbery texture or perhaps 'chew' of some underwear seems to be irresistible to them. Harry, a Derbyshire cat thief, regularly brings home not birds and mice but neighbours' clothing, including socks and sports bras, the latter being his favourite prey.[25]

Before the pervasiveness of trousers and joggers, small girls were taught that they should never sit with their legs apart for fear of their knickers being seen. The idea of someone seeing your underpants, even when not being worn, is often considered something worth avoiding. We might simply not want our worn and stained items to be on show, or perhaps worry that we might seem to be signalling a sad pass of sorts. Others might well have the confidence to enjoy washing line's potential to show off what is usually hidden and wish to conjure up an image of themselves so dressed. Much can be read from what hangs from a washing line, of private modesty, penury or on occasion of secret sexy lives. The outwardly elegant dresser may certainly harbour old and comfortable underpinnings beneath their polished exterior, but at the same time the modest, colourless dresser may be concealing the discreet pleasures of saucy scarlet lace.

The language of underwear can divide us, even among fellow English speakers. The British dancer Liz Pilley told me that as a student she and her classmates had been puzzled by an

American tutor telling them 'to get your fannies to face the ceiling'. Since they were already posed in the yoga downward-dog position, with their bottoms facing the ceiling, it seemed impossible to comply. The word 'fanny' means backside to an American English speaker, but refers to private parts, and the vagina in particular, to someone using British English.

Euphemism can be misleading or misunderstood. Language relies on shared understanding and in the field of underwear subtle distinctions are easily lost. A reference that may be alive for one person can be lost on another. Nouns like 'noodle', 'banana' and 'blancmange' and verbs such as 'wobble', 'poke' or 'quiver' easily elicit a smirk or snigger even when not used in a knowing way. Children learn to find certain words and a suggestive manner funny, long before the phrases' possible sexual connotations are at all understood. A small child picks up that the words are somehow naughty and delights in glimpsing such adult, light-hearted rule-breaking.

Our vocabulary develops over time, and a certain sentimentality lurks concerning underwear terms, as if embarrassment about the function of underwear is best avoided by adopting a cute attitude. In the 1660s the type of tight trousers that became fashionable in Paris were known as pantaloons, after an Italian comic character in *commedia dell'arte*, Pantalone: a foolish, greedy old man with skinny legs. These eventually became known as underpants, pants or panties. By the mid-nineteenth century a knee-length version was still being referred to as pantaloons. Baggy trousers for women gathered at the ankle came to be known as bloomers, popularized by the American journalist and rational dress activist Amelia Bloomer, and were initially worn under a mid-length skirt for sporting activities such as tennis, biking and hiking. Bloomers allowed women to take part in exercise which a skirt alone would have made impossible, although restrictive corsets did continue to limit ease of movement. 'Bloomers' became a term to denote women's white linen or loose cotton underpants, worn to the knee or ankle. Long-legged frilled drawers were known as pantalettes and were worn by young girls, in an idealized pastoral fashion. Thick, loose, baggy knickerbocker trousers, worn by Dutch settlers in New York, were named after the narrator in Washington Irving's *History of New York* (1809): Diedrich Knickerbocker. They became known as knickers or knicks, shortened in word and deed. As with pantaloons, they also closely resembled a much earlier fashion, a modified version of Renaissance padded trunk hose breeches.

Early in the twentieth century underwear began to be referred to as 'undies', as if a diminutive best befits this category of clothing, even when the items worn were sometimes substantial.[26] Indeed the euphemistic term 'smalls' continues to be used in Britain, and in American English the word is also used for smaller household linens such as pillowcases, further distancing underwear from its primal purposes.

To tackle a recent term, if a woman is 'upskirted', it means that her crotch has been photographed from below without her permission. If someone were to suggest to the woman that she should try wearing pants in future, she, if British, might take offence. 'But, I always wear underwear!' she might retort. An American English speaker would simply have been suggesting that she consider wearing trousers ('pants') rather than a skirt, and not that she had been going commando. 'Going commando' is an American term from the Second World War period, derived from the idea that commando troops would, after days without being able to change their clothes on an offensive, leave off their soiled underpants. However, the term has gained kudos, nowadays suggesting sexual availability rather than a necessary hygienic measure. The idea of men going commando can also suggest sexual licence, such that Lenny Kravitz's wardrobe malfunction at a concert in 2015 appeared to enhance his reputation as a raunchy rock star. A more playful impression was made by the 1970s Scottish band The Bay City Rollers, known as the 'tartan teen sensations', who rarely wore underpants beneath their close-fitting trews.

Not wearing underwear is often thought of as daring and even erotic, as if the person, in doing so, was more naturally and fearlessly sexually available. Others believe that wearing underwear in bed is better avoided on principle, because the clothing can make you feel grubby and constrained. In the novel *The Paper Palace* the protagonist explains, 'My mother believes that wearing underpants to bed is bad for your health. "You need to let yourself air out at night," she told us when we were little . . . The whole idea seemed embarrassing, dirty.'[27] Going commando can be merely a sensible measure for treating yeast infections and other intimate complaints, allowing fresh air to circulate more freely. It may also be a way of avoiding a VPL situation. When more women began to wear trousers in the 1970s, there was some disquiet at seeing more clearly the contours of the female bottom, accentuated by the edges of any underclothing. The acronym VPL has more recently been adopted to describe a visible penis line in men's briefs, drawing attention to that 'curious appendage – half-comic, half-dangerous and wholly indecent'.[28] Dancers rarely wear underpants in performance, since they can disrupt the unbroken line of their costumes. When fashions became sleeker in the 1920s in Europe and America, baggy drawers or knickers that bunched up were soon replaced by more streamlined versions for fashion-conscious men and women. The 'stiff, clinging underbodice known as a *cotte* defined this new skinny ideal. Large-busted women bound strips of cloth around their chests to acquire the small-breasted look then in favour. Women with floppy breasts sewed pouches into the top of their dresses to lift them as high as possible.'[29]

Embarrassment surrounds the language of underwear and of underpants in particular, and the distinctions can be small but important. The word 'knickers' for underpants, for example, has an old-fashioned, comforting, sometimes self-consciously cloying or knowingly cute association with children's clothing. It can also be associated with more risqué frilly drawers, as for a can-can dancer at the Folies Bergère. Thus it retains both its childish and its overtly feminine associations, as worn by a pantomime dame. For centuries knickers were worn by those who could afford them, but also by prostitutes, who needed to keep warm on the streets. When the term is used nowadays by adults it can connote a self-conscious sense of class, as if the user hopes to be associated with a long-standing, securely affluent sector of society, though it might also inadvertently echo a less salubrious association. The fashion historian Rosemary Hawthorne claims that up until the last decade of the eighteenth century, females who wore underpants would have been considered 'lewd, loose-moraled creatures of ill repute', though might there not have been women who opted to keep warm in cold weather, or who might have chosen some such garment to keep their period rags in place, whatever the more general fashions of the day?[30] Hawthorne further describes the reluctance among many to wear closed pantaloons, put off no doubt by the expense of acquiring yet another item of dress, and one that inevitably required more frequent laundering than other clothing, so that 'it would take a good dose of Victorian propriety to urge the disinclined masses into these newfangled articles.'[31]

Today there are concerns about how to clothe astronauts who might have to wear the same underwear beneath their life-sustaining spacesuits for days on end, often in extremes of temperature. Stinking garments may not kill us but they hardly aid concentration or keep the spirits up. Given the difficulties concerning urination and defecation while wearing a spacesuit, NASA designed a type of bag-like nappy with an adhesive edge that can be stuck securely to the skin. However, given the lack of gravity it can be tricky to keep faeces at the bottom of the bag. There is always a danger of them floating free. However, one astronaut reported that releasing 'a urine dump' into space at sunset was the most beautiful sight he had ever seen on a voyage.[32]

Concerning female astronauts, the question of whether or not bras are worn has recently been aired. When in space astronauts are hardly troubled with the pull of gravity, and thus one might think they could happily do without. However, daily rigorous exercise running on a treadmill, despite being in a state of inertia, does mean that 'their rib cage is constantly changing its direction of motion and other more delicate parts are resisting those changes.' Sports bras are worn, although it is left to the individual whether they wear them when not exercising, for as Robert Frost, a flight controller at NASA, admitted tactfully, 'it is not really our business.'[33]

Innuendo surrounds what is worn under the Scottish military kilt, and a view still survives that the true Scotsman would never be so unmanly as to countenance wearing underpants. It is likely that the belted plaids of the sixteenth century, pleated into a belt, would have been worn over a linen tunic common for centuries across Europe. What we would recognize as the modern tartan kilt, with sewn-down pleats and buckles, dates from the eighteenth century. It is claimed that during the First World War Scottish regiments were regularly inspected by an officer who passed a mirror under their kilts to check that

Oliver Hardy and Stan Laurel in the film *Putting Pants on Philip* (dir. Clyde Bruckman, 1927).

underpants were not being worn.[34] Stan Laurel in the 1927 silent film *Putting Pants on Philip* plays a young Scot arriving in America. When he crosses a ventilation grating his kilt blows up, anticipating a scene some thirty years later with Marilyn Monroe in *Some Like It Hot* (dir. Billy Wilder, 1959). Unfortunately Philip mislays his underpants, so he is accidentally exposed to several women, who immediately faint from the shock. In a similar vein, in the comic film *Carry On Up the Khyber* (dir. Gerald Thomas, 1968), a British outpost is threatened when one of its soldiers, Private Widdle (Charles Hawtrey) of the Third Foot and Mouth Regiment, is caught wearing underpants beneath his uniform kilt. Word spreads, inciting a rebellion at the news that one of the feared Devils in Skirts is in fact dressed so feebly. The uprising is quelled when the regiment is ordered to lift up their kilts towards the enemy . . . who are duly terrified and hastily retreat. As the old pun goes:

> Is anything worn under the kilt?
> No, everything is in fine working order, thank you.

The word 'underpants' can seem more neutral and thus less prurient for all genders. The American word 'panties' used for adult women's underwear can seem too coy to a British English speaker. Terms such as 'panties' or 'tighties' retain a sense of diminutive childishness, even so far as to make a man using such terminology about a woman seem insulting to some. 'Pantyhoe' is contemporary slang for someone who leaves their underpants behind after a one-night stand, or who allows a thong to show above low-slung jeans.[35] 'Panties' may be a standard term for women's underpants in American English, but 'hoe' remains a derogatory term suggesting a promiscuous woman.

Thongs that cover just the genitals and anus and leave the buttocks bare have been around since the ancient loincloth, though mostly worn by men for protection. Now they are worn by both sexes, associated with youth and considered by some as an offence against public morals. We can all be blind about how we look, and the desire to dress attractively can lead to serious sartorial errors, but a tight thong on soft buttocks remains a sad affair. North Myrtle Beach, South Carolina, has banned thongs and topless bikinis altogether for all ages on its beaches, prohibiting the exposure of specific anatomical parts:

> It shall be unlawful for any person to intentionally appear in public places in such a state of dress or undress so as to expose to the view of others the human male or female genitals, pubic area, pubic hair, buttocks, anus, vulva or any portion of the female breast at or below the areola thereof.[36]

The ban has been in place since the 1990s and perpetrators risk arrest, fines and even jail time for the most flagrant offences.

Our underclothing is capable of eliciting a lasting sense of shame. At the Goldenbridge Industrial School in Dublin (1831–1983), for instance, a school and laundry run by the Sisters of Mercy, the girls who were incarcerated there had to suffer the indignity of having their underpants turned inside out and examined regularly before being issued with fresh ones.[37] If they were judged to be dirty by the sister in charge, then the underpants were hoisted up on a pole so that everyone could witness the girl's disgrace.

A common enough piece of advice is that you should beware of going out in less than clean underwear, for fear of an accident and disgracing yourself in front of the medics who come to your aid. A poster campaign in 2016 for a children's charity showed a small child in a grubby white vest and underpants, without comment, effectively illustrating neglect and possible abuse. Underwear, exposed to public view, can suggest a potent image of malicious cruelty and disregard.

During the COVID-19 pandemic around 2020 the term 'face panties' was used by some for face masks. It led those opposed to mask-wearing and other lockdown safety measures – on the grounds that their civil liberties were under threat – to interpret the term literally and wear women's underpants over their faces. Images of this type of protest usually have men adopting grave, self-important expressions. The problem is that underpants, like bananas, nudge at the ridiculous, and it was difficult to take the protestors seriously with lacy underwear veiling their moral scorn. In Giovanni Boccaccio's fourteenth-century *The Decameron*, one tale involves an abbess who hopes to discover one of her nuns in flagrante with a lover, and who hurriedly gets out of bed in the dark to catch the accused in the act. In order to maintain her dignity, the abbess reaches for her coif to cover her head, but accidentally 'donneth instead thereof the breeches of a priest who is abed with her'.[38] Her error means that the novice nun 'is acquitted and hath leisure to be with her lover'. Years ago I recall a party on a narrowboat. It was a gusty day and the man at the tiller had pulled a pair of women's knickers over his head to stop his long hair from flying about in the breeze. This gave him something of the air of a Viking warrior, with hair escaping through the leg-holes and giving the effect of horns on either side of his head. It was a practical, impromptu solution, very different from a face-panty self-conscious act of defiance. If it appeared at all saucy to some, it was impressively of absolutely no concern to him.

If to a British English speaker the word 'panties' can seem arch, in American parlance to refer to a man's 'panties' might suggest a slur, a way of mocking and feminizing him. 'Getting your knickers in a twist' is a phrase that denotes unnecessary panic, but similarly when applied to a man further suggests unsuitably girlish behaviour, for a nervous state is traditionally found more forgivable in women, poor things.

Unlike other animals we wear clothes and we are concerned with the detail of what we wear. Even leading a solitary existence, we may feel the need to consider what we should be wearing, including those items that go unseen. Changing our underwear

Sister Isabetta in front of the abbess, who has confused her coif with her lover's underpants, detail of a miniature from a manuscript of Boccaccio's *Decameron*, 15th century.

and keeping it clean is an important element of self-respect, for those that have the means to do so. We might feel amusement, and on occasion distaste, when we see other animals in human clothing, in response to a lapdog in a nappy or a pet monkey in tiny velvet lederhosen, but many of us become warier the wilder and more human-sized the creature. Children's literature abounds with illustrations of clothed animals, such as some of Beatrix Potter's and Alison Uttley's creations, for example, but it is of note that until recently it is mainly outer clothing that is adopted by the animal and often it is only one item, such as a jacket or apron. Their true fur and feather nature is allowed to remain.

47

In the young children's picture book *A Fox Got My Socks* by Hilda Offen (1992), a gust of wind blows clothing off a washing line, to be picked up and worn by various animals, leaving a child happily in nothing but its nappy. It can be disturbing to see wild animals in human dress. Images of an old-fashioned circus come to mind, the majesty of a black bear or the magnificence of a tiger reduced. Contrarily, the lack of clothing on a human being who is not on the beach or in the sauna can read as deranged. Clothing distances us from our primal functions, creating the impression that we are not merely creatures that need to drink, eat and fornicate to survive. Clothing disguises signs of arousal, incontinence and menstruation, and muffles flatulence, for example. From early childhood some may recall the interesting experience of relieving oneself at will, then the relief of having your nappies or diapers changed or maybe the misery of being left to stew in soggy ones. You grow older and still the small joys of getting clean and putting on fresh briefs can retain some of these comforting associations. When delayed in a foreign airport, a toothbrush and a spare pair of underpants can make all the difference.

Clothing offers the possibility of warmth and protection, but in many creeds this is only after a fall from grace. There was a time, it is claimed, when we might never have had to resort to covering up our bodies. Original sin made us ashamed of our God-given but potentially and perhaps in-built sinful flesh. Without this sinfulness, would the natural naked form have then seemed normal and acceptable even for the less conventionally formed, the damaged and the withered with age? Indigenous traditional custom seems to bear this out. Such beliefs are arguably held by romantics, and possibly by those who crave the imagined uncomplicated luxury of a tropical naked beach existence. Sadly, the less delectable might feel rather less welcome in such an Eden. When nakedness is seen as somehow more honest, this must imply that clothing is somehow more dishonest, a used to cover up the truth. In this light, underwear might be interpreted as particularly heinous, misrepresenting what lies beneath the outer layer of clothing, without having the decency to declare itself, by misrepresenting our true natural form.[39]

Early humans appear to have covered their genitalia. In 1991 the remains of a Neolithic man who lived 5,300 years ago was found in the Tyrolean Alps and given the name Ötzi. He was wearing a hide coat, fur hat and hay-stuffed shoes, and also a stitched loincloth fashioned from strips of leather. Genetic analysis revealed that he was in his forties when he died and that the skins were taken from animals closely related to modern domestic European sheep, suggesting that he was a farmer and herder.[40] His leggings were made of goat leather sewn together with sinew, similar to a 6,500-year-old pair found in Switzerland, and fashioned much as Native Americans were wearing at the end of the nineteenth century.

In societies prior to evidence of sewn clothing, a loincloth seems to have amounted to little more than an animal skin tied around the loins, as seen in cave paintings, akin to those still worn by some remaining Indigenous peoples. It was not only ancient Egyptian field workers who wore loincloths to guard themselves against accident, for they were also worn as fashion items by the upper classes and known as *schenti*. Tutankhamen took with him into his tomb 145 fine white linen *schenti* cloths in preparation for the afterlife.[41] Roman gladiators and wrestlers also wore a form of loincloth, known as the *subligaculum*, and the higher classes wore the *femoralia*, a form of breeches. In the eighth century Charlemagne wore *femoralia* made of linen beneath his *tibiales*, or gaiters.[42] However, for those able to indulge in the game of fine fashion, it is the impression of cut and fabric that is often most valued, and its changing form is largely associated with Western civilization.

The origin of underpants and drawers can also be traced back to Chinese wrapped cloth and Japanese *fundoshi*, the latter of which were important to the self-respect of samurai warriors as their power began to decline.[43] To be seen in anything but

Aboriginal man wearing a loincloth, near Borroloola, Northern Territory, 1911, photograph by Gerald F. Hill.

spotless underwear, despite their outer disrepair, would have been shameful to a samurai. Baggy cut and sewn medieval braies gradually developed into outerwear trousers. For women, the advent of the crinoline meant that two-piece open-crotch drawers held together by a waistband alone became too exposing, with closed underwear granting greater modesty. Women had adopted drawers in Germany and Holland from the sixteenth century, but, it is argued, generally much later in France and England. Gradually these drawers became shorter and tighter fitting and known as knickers, or bloomers, suitable for sports and for less forgiving tailored clothing.

There is a small museum that would never have come into being were it not for two pairs of such drawers that were found in a jumble sale. As examples of more streamlined underwear, they seem generous to a modern eye. An enthusiast for the ephemera of the past, one Peggy Gye had not been able to resist buying them. Her husband, exasperated perhaps by her growing stash of antique clothing and artefacts, suggested that she might like to start a museum to house them. Thus the Market Lavington Museum in Wiltshire was born, opened in the mid-1980s. Both the 'free-trader' pair, consisting of separate legs held together by lacings, and the other, known as a falling trap or trapdoor pair with a buttoned hatch,, became the inspiration for a collection now housed in what was once a gardener's cottage. Inspired by Gye's hands-on approach, the museum offers a rare opportunity for visitors to handle the museum's collection.

Cotton and wool long-john combinations have much in common with contemporary thermal and other high-tech fabric underwear. The fabric of thermal underwear is customarily combined with polyester to wick moisture away from the skin, which would otherwise create clammy, uncomfortable conditions for the wearer. The first long johns were named after the American prizefighter John L. Sullivan (1858–1918), who wore a combination jersey suit in the ring. They are more often termed 'union suits' in America, covering the body from neck to wrist and ankle. In the eighteenth century they were worn under outer clothing in cold weather and were often, as with much underwear through the ages, kept on as nightwear. Such underwear might be worn for long periods when washing facilities were limited, and brings to mind Lee Marvin in the film version of *Paint Your Wagon* (dir. Joshua Logan, 1969) in his worn red all-in-ones. In design they resemble an ancient Chinese form of underwear.

Underwear styles tend to be sold in gendered terms, but in practice basic underclothing is often remarkably similar for both sexes. However, it is misleading to see underwear, and underpants in particular, as exemplars of historical progress towards gender-neutral clothing. So much of what seems to represent change in underwear refers back and reinforces past gendered distinctions.

There was a lack of Western-style underwear produced in Japan in the first half of the twentieth century as women in traditional dress had not required it and there was therefore no experience of its design and manufacture. Western clothing required underwear.[44] What was not provided to the military or garnered from abroad by those of means had to be cobbled together from remnants of old cotton *yukata* kimonos, stitched together in multiple layers when extra strength or absorbency was required. Traditionally, nappy-like lower garments, *omutsu*, were often provided by a bride's mother-in-law 'as a celebratory gift for her first baby', in sets of five rather than the European half-dozen.[45] Even when in the midst of hard physical labour, it was considered vulgar to be seen scratching one's bottom, particularly if it was uncovered. Female miners, from the beginning of the Meiji period (1868–1912) to before the Second World War, wore nothing below the waist: 'private parts [were] exposed as they squatted and crawled.'[46] Influenced by post-war advertising of American underwear, Japanese women later began to sew bloomer-like underpants, often using the linings of old futon covers. However, older female miners tended to prefer to work naked, finding it cooler and less cumbersome for the gruelling work. *Momohiki*, or long-legged underpants, were worn by young women working in the paddy fields, but these were often discreetly removed in the sweltering, stagnant water, many preferring to work naked like the men:

Men may be said to wear nothing. Few of the women wear anything but a short petticoat wound tightly round them, or blue cotton trousers very tight in the

legs and baggy at the top . . . From the dress no notion
of the sex of the wearer could be gained.[47]

The *momohiki* were quickly put back on as soon as the women
left the water.

The gusset sewn or glued into the crotch of most women's
underpants is usually made of cotton, even in otherwise synthetic briefs, since the material helps to keep the area well aired
and thus prevents infection. Cheaper underwear, made from
unsmart, non-wicking synthetic fibre and lacking a layer of
natural cotton cloth, encourages bacteria to grow. In this gusset
one seam is customarily left open, at least in cheaper and mod-
erately priced underwear.[48] Since the economist Adam Smith's
pioneering ideas on economics came to influence industrial production in the late eighteenth century, each separate task in a
manufacturing setting is now taken into account in order to
achieve the fastest, most economic process. Given that such a
seam is not necessary for the structure of underpants, the few
seconds and amount of thread it would otherwise take to sew it
in place means that the seam is left undone. It has been argued
that the resulting pocket was once intended as a form of repository, for small-scale shoplifted or smuggled items, perhaps.
Whereas an open-seam gusset is a hardly noticeable but long-
established industrial cost-cutting measure, the little bow to the
centre front is a piece of ongoing nostalgia. An added advantage
of the lined gusset is that when needs must a pair of underpants
can be worn inside out in order to last another day.

Recently, with the mounting concern surrounding climate
change and global food production, a number of projects in the
United States, Australia and across Europe have been monitoring soil health, with campaigns including Soiled Pants (in the
uk) and Soil Your Undies! (in Australia).[49] Since cotton is bio-
degradable, and perhaps because underwear tends to appeal to
the public imagination, it is white cotton underpants rather than
other cotton items that are buried in soil, for periods of up to

eight weeks. They are then analysed and comparisons made in relation to the clothing's speed of decomposition. As a cellulose, cotton attracts microbes and other organisms as food. The earth, or rather the living constituents of that earth, gradually eat away at the cloth, but where the surrounding soil is less appealing to these decomposers – or worse, where there is a complete lack of decomposers – the underpants remain more or less undamaged.[50] When in an Australian version of the project the underpants' elastic waistbands were kept above the soil surface in order to mark their positions, the underwear mysteriously disappeared altogether. The culprit was subsequently found to be an inquisitive kangaroo. Even the long-running BBC radio soap opera *The Archers* included such a storyline in 2022, with the loveable rogue Eddie Grundy adding holes to the underpants he had buried in order to win a competition for the most fertile, wormy soil.

It is uncommon for people not to cover their genitals, if only in part, and if only during the daytime – and we are the only animals that do this. The Italian philosopher Mario Perniola investigated the theory of the intrinsic humanity of clothing, suggesting that if dressing ourselves is a human virtue then this might lead us to conclude that 'nudity is a negative state, a privation, loss, dispossession.'[51] Yet for many, since the ancient Egyptians and Greeks, and from remaining Indigenous peoples to nudists today, clothing hardly seems a necessary condition of being human. The concept of *aletheia* in Greek thought is translated by Martin Heidegger as *Unverborgenheit*, a state of unconcealment he uses to express the idea of truth.[52] In this respect, underwear could be seen as a way of concealing our bodies and thus of being dishonest.

Sometimes underpants are deliberately worn tight enough to accentuate, even stimulate, what they hide. The camel-toed effect of tight-fitting clothing on women draws attention to the vulva. If this effect is considered to be a problem then the resultant cleft can be disguised by wearing contemporary padded period underpants. For those who wish to disguise male genitals, there are items on the market that hide the penis and intentionally create the effect of the vulval divide. There has been a seismic change in the way advertising openly expresses male underpants' ability to enhance the genitals, without embarrassment. The Australian Wonderjock, for example, declares that it can make the penis look larger, 'just like women using the Wonderbra'. Seams and padding are claimed to enhance both length and breadth.[53]

Extra tight underwear is not necessarily a choice stemming from vanity. For instance, competitive swimmers who wear swimwear a size or two too small can travel smoothly at higher speed through the water with reduced frictional drag. Similarly, serious distance cyclists and triathletes wear tight shorts in order to achieve the best aerodynamic performances, apparently enabling them to feel like their bodies are travelling unimpeded through the water or air.

There are many stages in life where underwear plays its part. An infant wears what it is given and the schoolchild puts up with underclothing that is perhaps too big or too small, to make it last as long as possible. The young lover has not got enough money to buy what would suit them best; the reputable grown-up wears the underwear that suits their career and status. Once middle-aged, they find they no longer have a trim enough figure to look good in close-fitting underwear. Old age has underclothing hanging upon their withered frame; and finally, in their dotage, they come full circle and revert to the disposable nappy. The seven ages of man through our underpants.

Minoan snake
goddess figurine
from the palace of
Knossos, Crete,
with exposed
breasts and
a corset-like belt,
c. 1600 BCE.

2

Codpiece and Corset

*Happiness is the sublime moment when you get out
of your corsets at night.*

JOYCE GRENFELL

Christian Dior famously claimed that 'without foundations there can be no fashion.'[1] In contrast, T. S. Eliot, in his poem 'Whispers of Immortality', speaks of the erotic promise of an 'uncorseted' bust. A woman's corseting or lack of it can suggest someone dissolute or promiscuous and unconstrained; 'strait-laced' implies high moral scrupulousness. The corset, worn since ancient times – a one-piece that covers both the breasts and stomach – unlike other items of underwear seems to fulfil no function apart from satisfying the demands of fickle fashion. The tightest, most deforming design could, from the sixteenth century to the late Victorian era, prove your wealth and status. By squeezing the breasts together it created a new erogenous zone in the cleavage. More recently, it seemed that a fashion for the natural, gym-honed body would finally bring an end to its life, but the corset, with the aid of modern elastic materials, has survived stronger than ever.

The private nature of underwear has meant that it has often gone unmentioned and this has fed its association with the suggestive and sometimes forbidden. There are examples of corset-like clothing dating back to Minoan culture, from around 1600 BCE. A snake goddess has her waist bound tightly, her breasts supported from below but the flesh left uncovered. A manner of the corset was worn by women in ancient societies, under tunics and chitons, often consisting of leather strapping that supported the breasts and smoothed out the hips. Fashionable females since the first medieval reinforced camisoles increasingly relied on a rigid framework that could impede a person's ability to move freely. The *moxiong* corset is a late Imperial period feature of traditional Chinese dress, binding women's breasts and belly with a simple, tightly tied piece of cloth, intended to make women seem 'slimmer and weaker'.[2] Versions of the *moxiong* have recently come back into fashion in China. While corset combinations had gone out of fashion by the beginning of the twentieth century, old habits of dress die hard. Constance Larymore, a colonial wife in Nigeria in 1908, is amused when a friend insists on wearing her heavy old-fashioned corsets, yet recommends wearing some form of stays despite the heat.

> At least six pairs of corsets are necessary, the coolest kind obtainable, but I can assure you that to leave off wearing them at any time for the sake of coolness is a huge mistake: there is nothing so fatiguing as to lose one's ordinary support even with a view to being comfy. Always wear corsets, even for a tête-à-tête home dinner on the warmest evenings; there is something about their absence almost as demoralizing as hair in curling-pins.[3]

The corset had become an integral part of what it was to be a woman of status, supporting her husband in a foreign land.

The term 'corset', a diminutive form of the French word for the body, *corps*, was in use in the fourteenth century to describe a form of laced-up bodice. Many would have worn less constricting versions, referred to as jumps and made with less uncomfortable, expensive boning, more restrictive garments being kept for formal occasions. Many working-class women 'bought, were

Staybusk, inserted into the front of stays to keep the torso upright, English, 1789, wood. Often given as a love token from a suitor, here it is marked with initials, a flower vase and a heart symbol.

given, or made corsets, believing, as their middle-class sisters did, that corsetry supported the body and made the figure trim'.4 Made from strong linen and sometimes padded, corsets were also known as stays or as a pair of bodies. In the 1810s a version was briefly known as the divorces, or the divorce corset, a term that refers not to a marriage break-up but the separating of one breast from the other by means of a triangular-shaped piece of metal, padded for comfort. The point faced upwards, very much like the division of cups in a modern bra. Corsets often had a channel down the front to house a paddle-shaped busk intended to even out the pressure on the abdomen. They were made in strong but flexible whalebone, taken from the upper jaws of the baleen whale, or alternatively from metal or wood. The busk, or staybusk, could be seen as a romantic object, acting as a love token, perhaps carved with flowers and symbols and combining the names of the betrothed, sometimes including the date of a betrothal or marriage. Although the shape of corsets varied – in the sixteenth century they tended to flatten out and diminish the breasts, unlike those fashions that tended to accentuate both breast and hips – the structure remained fundamentally unchanged until the vulcanization of rubber, a process patented in 1844. The process meant that rubber suffered less from temperature change, and the resultant elastic could be incorporated in longer lengths into garments into the early twentieth century.

There is little extant material fabric evidence of the medieval age, but illuminated manuscripts of the twelfth and thirteenth centuries appear to show bodices that narrow at the waist with lacing and which usually come to just beneath the bust. They are fashioned without boning, their only function being to narrow the waist. The artist and illustrator John Leighton, in 1870, referred to the garment's possible history:

> Certainly the practice of lacing the body is not of
> classic date, but my friend, the late Mr Fauhott, in his

'Costume in England' speaks of the practice in the time
of Henry and Stephen, citing a most amusing authority
from a Norman illumination in the Cotton collection,
British Museum, where Our Saviour is being tempted
by his Satanic Majesty, in the full costume of a girl
of the period, whose ample bust and slender waist
are encased in a bodice, from the last hole of which
depends the ornamental tag or lace – the deep satire
of the Monkish artist being admirably displayed.[5]

Medieval corset-like garments must have offered some support but pretty much left the smock chemise worn beneath the
bodice to keep the breasts in place. Linen material tough enough
to withstand lacing would have been used, but bandaging was
also employed, particularly for fuller figures, to restrict the waist
and torso and to support the bust.

Tribal women from Georgia and the Caucasus region in the
medieval period wore tightly laced corsets from childhood until
their nuptials. The corset was believed to act as a guarantee of a
girl's virtue. On the wedding night the new husband's duty
would be to prove his self-control and reliability by unlacing his
bride with slow and steady decorum, somewhat at variance with
our modern romantic notions of sensual abandon.[6]

From the late fourteenth century both women and men of
fashion, influenced by the Burgundian court, wore a simple
form of corset that underwent many changes in its design, sometimes as narrow as a belt or wide enough to cover most of the
breasts and hips, either flattening out or accentuating the
figure. The Spanish court introduced stays of rigid wood,
whalebone and metal into the corset and it was worn even by
children, as in a painting by Diego Velázquez, *Las Meninas*
(1656), which depicts the five-year-old daughter of Philip IV of
Spain, the Infanta Margarita Teresa, rigidly corseted. A contemporary, observing the fashion for such corsets in the Spanish
Habsburg court, described the waist as being shut up in a 'prison',

which reduced 'Breasts into such streights, that they soone purchase a stinking breath'.[7] The corset was widely believed to be a cause of consumption.

In the High Renaissance of the sixteenth century the form of the body and in particular the female bosom was accentuated and revealed, often lightly veiled in transparent gauzy fabrics or sometimes wholly laid bare. Following the lead of the European courts and particularly Italian fashion, in the courts of Henry VIII and Elizabeth I nipples became fashionable. Thomas Nashe in 1594 mentions in some shock, 'Theyr breasts they embuske [place in ambush] . . . and their round Roseate buds immodestly lay foorth.' Their exposure became associated with cancer: 'A Flemish cleric, in a very nasty pamphlet entitled *Cancer of the Female Breast-Covering* (1635), tried to make a connection between breast cancer and breast exposure.'[8] As soon as a particular feature is in fashion, someone will often suggest that it is in some way harmful and possibly sinful.

Elizabeth I of England is depicted in many of her portraits standing tall in her rigid corseted splendour. The farthingale, a padded roll worn under a hooped petticoat, broadened the hips to an increasingly exaggerated degree, further restricting a women's ease of movement, but its exaggerated impracticality meant that it was increasingly associated with those of the highest status.

The sixteenth-century male codpiece is the forerunner of the modern-day jockstrap. A fine male figure in the Middle Ages would have been decked out with hugely padded shoulders, known as *hoîtres*, in the Burgundian mode and worn with a padded *braguette*, or codpiece. It is these two features that balance each other out, achieving a telling dramatic contrast with an otherwise close-fitted male torso. A form of the codpiece was worn by men and women in ancient Crete, answering the primary need not only to protect but to enhance so significant an area of the body. Both the ancient Olympian athlete and the medieval knight in armour required the padding of a codpiece to prevent chafing, but it was also an essential feature for protection against assault – and perhaps to add a certain swagger. By the fifteenth century the codpiece, buttoned or strung to the top of hose, and still functioning as a layer of protection for male genitalia, seems not to have been considered an indecent fashion. Indeed in the Burgundian court the flag-bearer had customarily supported his flag-pole by balancing it upon his protruding *braguette*. The fashion historian Shaun Cole suggests that the codpiece was intended to be threatening rather than sexually alluring.[9] It was to become a sublime feature of conspicuous consumption in the courts of the Renaissance, in glittering black and studded with sequins and pearls in Spain, and emblazoned with jewels and gold thread-work on scarlet and purple velvet in the English court, but each style relied on an underlying padded structure. For those who could afford it, a codpiece could subtly or sometimes brazenly declare a man's economic status.

From a modern viewpoint it is easy to associate the codpiece with engorged sexuality alone, though given its etymology – 'cod' deriving from the Middle English for 'scrotum' rather than the penis – in the past it would more likely have suggested the power of procreation, and in a king his ability to extend his lineage. What had provided protection in armour had become a feature of high status. Soon the men of the Tudor court were all similarly decked out. As well as flattering an important part of the physique, they were convenient for urination and provided a useful repository for small essentials. It has been argued that in a time of widespread venereal disease, the codpiece was also a means of holding poultices in place, 'a variety of herbs, minerals, syrups, and decoctions' held close to the genitals to protect and treat sufferers.[10] It became a feature of fashion that represented masculinity to such an extent that the codpiece was worn even by small boys.

The notorious chastity belt appears to be something of a hoax. There is little evidence of its existence before the sixteenth century, despite the popular belief that knights going off to the

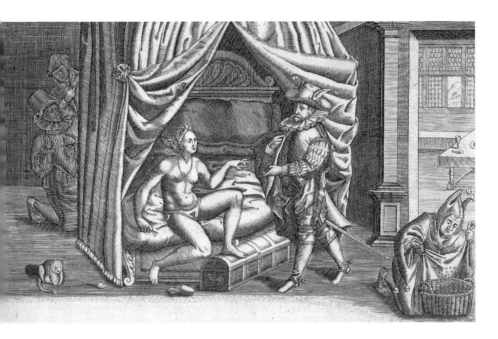

crusades placed their wives in such devices to ensure their fidelity.
The idea was that the knights would have felt reassured in the
Holy Land by possessing the key to that belt. Examples of chastity belts in museums are usually made of metal with leather and
linen padding, but they have been shown to be later forgeries.[11]
The British Museum accompanies their own fake artefact with
a terse caution: 'It is probable that the great majority of examples now existing were made in the eighteenth and nineteenth
centuries, as curiosities for the prurient, or as jokes for the taste-
less.' A print in the British Museum dating from around the late
1500s shows a woman, naked but for her chastity belt, handing
the key to her husband, who is wearing the donkey ears of a cuck-
old. Behind the bed-curtains crouches another man, grinning
wickedly and clutching a duplicate key.

Thorstein Veblen, in his *The Theory of the Leisure Class* (1899),
examined corsetry from an economic and sociological viewpoint,
accounting in particular for fashionable women's elaborate, constrained clothing in the nineteenth century.[12] In the context of
underwear, he suggested that its deliberate impracticality was

a means by which men could express their wealth without being directly implicated themselves. Women were fettered to express men's contrasting autonomy. They could afford elegantly dressed but useless women. Men's sombre dress, albeit of fine and expensively tailored cloth, did not suffer the indignity of the obvious display of women's and servants' outfits, a distinction that has rather disappeared.

Corsets of various description had been worn by affluent men for centuries. Towards the end of the eighteenth century and across the nineteenth men began to leave off more extreme restraints, at least for everyday use, but for leisure and sporting activities, such as riding, male corsetry garments continued to be thought necessary. Moreover, the older generation would have continued wearing their corsets, come what may in fashion. What account would Veblen have given of earlier male corsetry and extravagant, expensive male clothing in general before the Industrial Revolution? He describes the corset only in relation to female apparel, as:

> in economic theory, substantially a mutilation, undergone for the purpose of lowering the subject's vitality and rendering her permanently and obviously unfit for work. It is true, the corset impairs the personal attractions of the wearer, but the loss suffered on that score is offset by the gain in reputability which comes of her visibly increased expensiveness and infirmity.[13]

What impairs or detracts from a person's attractions must remain a highly subjective judgement, and questioning the corset on the grounds of its attractiveness or otherwise informs us only of Veblen's personal taste. We might hold the view that women's metal neck rings, for instance, worn across Asia and Africa, are dangerous from a physiological point of view, but to decry them as being unattractive is merely one culture unable to take on another's idea of beauty. Corsets, like neck rings, are a way in which wealth can be displayed – they are expensive to produce and suggest that the wearer is not involved in manual labour. For both genders they are worn to enhance the fashion-relevant characteristics of grace and beauty, which are values that are constantly changing. The new tight-fitting pantaloons of the Renaissance dandified male drew attention to a fine pair of legs, augmented with shin padding when required. Veblen's theory of dress might lead us to consider whether those finely dressed men, achieving the trimmest waist or, by way of padding, the broadest chest and lean but muscular legs, are somehow less evolved than the post-Industrial Revolution's soberly dressed man. They might be said to have taken it upon their own person to express their status and refinement rather than via their dependents. In the context of today's male shapewear, and bearing in mind Veblen's view, it appears that male fashion may have somehow reverted in this respect, and men are once again at the forefront of fashion. Such a turn of the tide serves as a major instance of the cyclical nature of fashion.

Veblen's theory suggests that corsets play a part in demonstrating male power and control, without showing the whip hand. But is this sartorial reticence or does it suggest a puritanical attitude to fine dress, in men who valued their status but found it vulgar to be seen to do so? Certainly during the nineteenth century female corsets grew longer and ever more restrictive. Some suggested that this lengthening was a useful moral restraint: 'It is an ever-present monitor indirectly bidding its wearer to exercise self-restraint; it is evidence of a well-disciplined mind and well-regulated feelings.'[14]

A wealthy man of the sixteenth century might well have looked more sombre than in the previous, generally more exuberantly dressed century, but the great courts of Europe continued to be finely and expensively kitted out. Fashion may have become more modest in terms of how much flesh was revealed, at least in reference to décolleté for both sexes, but along with the jewelled and figured velvet, the padded codpiece and the peasecod belly

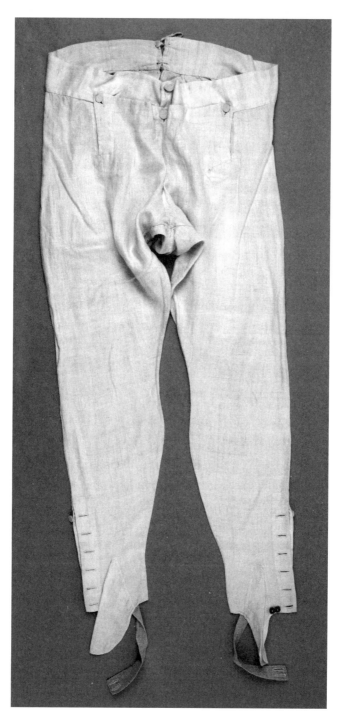

Pantaloons,
American,
1830–40, linen.

(an elaborate padding out of the stomach), continual attempts to transfigure the body occurred.[15] That waspish satirist Philip Stubbes held a particular dislike for the swollen peasecod doublet: 'What handsomeness can there be in these dubblettes which stand on their bellies like, or muche bigger than, a man's codpiece.'[16]

The cavalier of the seventeenth century, festooned in elaborate lace collar, frilled shirt front and cuff and richly coloured silks to emphasize the neck and male chest, was laced into restrictive clothing often more extreme than that of females and servants. When an aristocrat adopted such exaggerated fashionable dress, as in Baroness Orczy's *The Scarlet Pimpernel* (1905), what seems effete and weak turns out to be a disguise.[17] The corseted carapace of Sir Percy Blakeney's mincing manner and fancy clothing conceals his daredevil mission to rescue aristocrats from the guillotine.

The fop of the early eighteenth century is often associated with the social climber, a monied bourgeois attempting in part via his restrictive, expensive clothing to represent himself as an aristocrat. The army officer had long worn stays in order to perfect the elegant line of his uniformed silhouette on horseback. It was Beau Brummell whose sobriety and apparently simple style linked the excesses of foppery with true nineteenth-century mercantile gravitas. Brummell was a significant influence in the early 1800s on the dress of the Prince Regent (crowned King George IV in 1820), even if the latter was unable to match the former's elegance. Thomas Creevey, a politician and social commentator and a contemporary of Brummell, described the fashion for the corset with some distaste, complaining, 'A man is to be pinched in and laced up until he resembles an earwig.'[18] For the man of fashion, though, slender waistlines necessitated tight lacing, and the head had to be held high, fixed in place, looking neither to back nor side, by a stiff collar and copious cravat. The true dandy was dressed 'in the ultra pitch of fashion, collared like the leader of a four-horse team, and pinched in the middle like an hourglass, with a neck as long as a goose, and a cravat as ample as a tablecloth'.[19] Nonetheless when the prince left off his corset, Creevey again became disparaging: 'Prinny has let loose his belly, which now hangs over his knees.'[20]

Brummell's immaculate image influenced both the nineteenth-century aesthetic and twentieth-century male dress movements. The emerging middle classes of the nineteenth century, in their uniform dark frock coats, ostensibly removed obvious dress divisions between clerk and manager and over-lord. However, the Mods of the 1960s did not emerge from an aspiring middle class. They wore tailored suits and were interested in the finer details of dress, including neat, fitted underwear that would not spoil the line of their outer wear. Their stylish Continental fashions were more rebellious compared to the Teddy Boys of the 1950s, who despite stealing 'the clothes off the back of their superiors . . . were content to wear them only in their own dilapidated back alleys'.[21] While the British Teddy Boy youth subculture was influenced by American fashions, Mods challenged the existing class system by turning to Europe.

Dress reform movements from the mid-nineteenth century argued for a change in attitude to restrictive clothing, particularly targeting the corset, protesting against 'the introduction of any fashion in dress that either deforms the figure, impedes the movements of the body, or in any way tends to injure the health'.[22] Whatever the physiological truth of the damage done by such contrivances to bone formation and the inner organs, claims that such restrictive wear subjugated women were often expressed as undermining what was natural and good, London's Rational Dress Society specifically linking the corset with moral depravity.

Followers of the dress reform movements set out to limit the extremes of fashion in clothing, particularly women's corseting, aiming to combine 'beauty and utility' – in line with William Morris's declared views on interior design to a Birmingham audience in 1880, to 'Have nothing in your houses that you do not know to be beautiful or believe to be useful.' However,

Lovis Corinth,
Girl in a Corset,
1895, lithograph.

Aesthetic dress of the late 1800s to very early 1900s seems to have amounted to an approximation of medieval fashion cobbled together from manuscripts of the period combined with romantic guesswork. Fashion reform societies across Europe and Japan did have a major effect on styles of underwear, which could be more discreetly modified than outer clothing. There were those who adopted the flowing robes of the Pre-Raphaelites, and others who attempted to find what was thought of as a new and more natural simplified form of dress, such as George

Bernard Shaw's all-woollen Dr Jaeger suits. G. K. Chesterton described Shaw's outfits of the 1880s as being of knitted wool, one brown and the other of silver-grey stockinette, an elasticated jersey fabric. Chesterton viewed Shaw's clothing as 'part of his personality: one can come to think of the reddish-brown Jaeger suit as if it were a sort of reddish-brown fur.'[23]

A problem for the clothing historian is that it tends to be only the least worn, most formal, sometimes least loved clothing that is preserved for the future. Mother Hubbard dresses, for example – high-necked, loose, comfortable everyday women's wear, worn in rural America of the nineteenth century and adopted by women in the reform movement – had a simple yoke and full, straight skirt. In prairie America they were likely to have been washed and worn many times, and then cut down into children's clothing and, of course, underwear, until they were good only for rags. The name alone, derived from a nursery rhyme, 'Old Mother Hubbard', suggests age and poverty, hardly an association that induced longing in its time, unlike a Marie Antoinette corset or Madonna cone bra. It is not that stays would never have been worn, but they would have been less restrictive. By mid-century cheaper mass-produced corsets had become available, though they were more often worn just to the waist to allow relative ease of movement for all but the most leisured, with only those in dire poverty wearing nothing but a basic chemise beneath. In the later nineteenth century the Mother Hubbard dress could indicate the wearer was required to do relentless manual work and therefore bestowed a sense of shame. In North Dakota and Oregon heavy fines were levied on women who wore such dresses away from home. Bills were posted warning women that 'they would be ticketed if they wore the dress in public, since it would "scare the horses and ruin businesses".' The *Dodge City Times* reported in July 1883 that two girls were arrested in Topeka 'under the idea that they were out in their night gowns'.[24]

Germany was a centre for dress reform, with local societies formed and scientists such as Heinrich Lahmann and Gustav

Jaeger promoting the cause through the Allgemeiner Verein zur Verbesserung der Frauenkleidung (General Association for the Improvement of Women's Clothing), instituted in 1896. The Nazi architect Paul Schultze-Naumburg wrote in the late 1890s 'an indictment of women's fashion (specifically the corset) rooted in its violation of hygienic, aesthetic and ethical qualities of the human body', and designed what he held to be more suitable and artistic clothes for them.[25]

Women in the suffrage movement had most success in questioning attitudes towards the more restrictive corsets, but although these new designs garnered enthusiastic support, many of the new fashions still relied on modified versions of the bustle and the S-bend corset, which pushed the bust and pelvis forward. This led to back problems, despite being promoted as healthy. Corsets were to remain a significant feature of women's underwear into the 1960s. Boning could in some cases cause lasting disfigurement, the theatre and couture designer Stella Mary Newton describing what was held to be the dangers of compressing the inner organs:

> There are many who escaped death, who to this day bear evidence of the sad custom of using aids to distend the dress, carrying terrible brands, in the form of scars, where the flesh has been seared, and contracted joints have been broken, derangement of the system by which chronic aches and pains are continued to the end of existence.[26]

This is likely to be an exaggeration of the risks involved and photographic evidence of the suffragists seems to suggest that despite their views against restricting female freedom they too continued to wear tight corsets. A new fashion trend today calls on this contradictory desire to reduce and draw attention to the waist but, in some oxymoronic balance with leisurewear, also to want clothing to suggest a laid-back lifestyle. The corset hoodie was first developed by the Mugler company for the rapper Bad Bunny – who wore one for his performance at the music festival Coachella in 2023. The garment combines the comfort of soft cotton jersey with tightly restrictive boning, 'formalizing the most informal' of garments, a hybrid of lingerie and loungewear. When zipped up tight it is described as being like 'a back brace at the gym' but when left open it has all the qualities of relaxed streetwear, only 'a little more fierce, and also a little more comical'.[27] Some have lacing and low-cut necklines with the hood taking on the guise of a medieval peasant; the boned, zipped-up waist projects something of sci-fi futurism. When corset hoodies are made of cashmere and silk they are an

'Loosen me as much as possible . . Ah! I understand . . . you're going to have supper!,' from *Le Charivari*, 17 February 1865, lithograph.

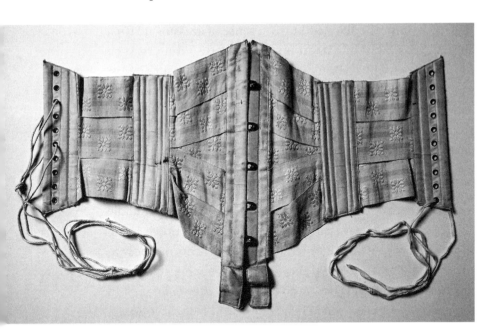

Ribbon corset
backed with
linen; steel bones,
back lacing and
suspenders
attached at the
front, Aberystwyth,
Wales, c. 1900–
910.

attempt to combine very different connotations: urban street
cool with high-end designer-branded affluence.

The Men's Dress Reform Party was formed in 1929 in Britain
and advocated less formality. They specifically objected to the
discomfort of collars and ties, as well as promoting the wearing of sandals.[28] There is little mention in their campaign for
reforms regarding underwear, suggesting that jersey, initially
woollen, combinations were already an acceptable option, and
readily available without the need for corsetry.

Female reformists were accustomed to wearing support
garments, and even today some actors find such items worn for
stage and screen dramatizations acceptable, even reassuring.
The actor Cate Blanchett, for example, is widely quoted as saying that she is 'one of those strange beasts who really like a
corset'. Blanchett does not have to wear them at all times, of
course, but then neither is it likely that Victorian women laced
themselves at the tightest gauge, except when they wanted their
figures to appear particularly fetching. Some modern-day
women also adopt uncomfortable boned items of underwear,

their discomfort perhaps adding to a sense of dressing up for a special occasion. While traditional underwear outfitters, such as London's Rigby & Peller, provide made-to-measure items, many have branched out into more exotic designs to meet the growing demand. Companies have been successful in building the market for special-occasion lingerie, which is to say underwear that is designed to be seen by others, either publicly or privately.

The British psychologist and psychoanalyst J. C. Flügel, in a development of Veblen's ideas, suggested that the new middle classes of the nineteenth century followed the example of the more affluent, putting their wives and dependents on show in order for them to look as if they enjoyed the same amount of leisure as the upper classes, even if in reality they did not.[29] In *Fashion and Fetishism*, social historian David Kunzle counters Veblen, suggesting on the contrary that such brutal underpinnings as the corset were in fact taken up eagerly as an opportunity for women to express themselves and flout the social order, behaving independently of their traditional roles as dependent women and mothers.[30] Fashion is thus mooted as a form of feminism, but the fact that corsets might have felt daring and taken a little courage to wear is not enough. It is a playful notion but women's lack of economic and legal power must throw doubt on such an optimistic view.

The idea that such restrictive underwear is a fetish derives from the term used by medieval slave traders in West Africa to describe objects of seeming magical value. Even today, the wearing of a corset – or codpiece – at least in the West, is driven by the fashion of the hour, and has come to suggest the erotic. Whatever the heady claims, it hardly seems to function as an engine of social revolution. It may be seen as expressing the mood of an era, where the idea of greater freedom for the individual is sometimes deliberately countered in its fashions. Dress historian Edwina Ehrman makes a cogent point about the corset's theatrical effect on the catwalk, arguing that it is 'seductive for designers interested in performance and display' and supporting the idea of restrictive clothing's close association with fetish and pornography.[31] It cannot of itself bring about change, or one might have to say that a sudden about-turn in fashion was grounds for, rather than evidence of, political revolution. It is a tempting idea, as if the clothing of the women serving the commander class in Margaret Atwood's novel *The Handmaid's Tale* (1985), in their uniform of long, modest Mother Hubbard-ish dress and bonnet, stands for or somehow explains the objectives of the dystopian regime in Gilead. Their clothing mimics, like the contemporary corset hoodie, the clothing of early modern peasantry. But such similarities can be misleading. When the protagonist Offred is required to have sex with the commander, it is only superficially comparable to historic situations when a couple's first copulation had to be witnessed.[32] In the French courts of the seventeenth century, a newly married couple would be formally undressed and duly provided with their nightclothes while surrounded by observers, but it would not have been considered as an injury to either party.

The importance of youthfulness in fashion became more important from the late eighteenth century, in an era of women in white linen shifts and minimal underpinnings and men in slim-fitting proto-trousers that were hard for anyone but the young to carry off successfully. However, it was not until the nineteenth century that underwear gathered force as 'a focus of sexual interest'.[33]

The suspender belt and corset, and the male codpiece, along with certain sadomasochistic restraints such as breast and penis traps and the apocryphal chastity belt, tend to be associated with distinct sexual roles and exaggerated mythologies have grown up around such items. While male constraints centre mainly on the genitals, female contraptions and mutilating features often tend to impact the breasts. Marilyn Yalom discusses the reasons for this attack on 'the locus of what is perceived to be women's greatest power' in their association with child-bearing. She suggests that 'It takes a lot of hate to mutilate a woman's most seductive and most maternal flesh.'[34] This view is persuasive but might be said to disregard the fact that so much of what people tend to find arousing is not necessarily to do with nurturing affection. Indeed what we find erotic often occupies a quite separate category of response.

The corset, training and torturing the body in its 'thirst for perfection',[35] remains a pivotal item in the range of fetish underwear, in part because it has also managed to remain an item of mainstream underclothing. Butt plugs and dildos may have their place, but corsets remain a mainstay of today's sexy underwear market. Their familiar presence in women's clothing has made them acceptable in a way that other fetishistic features are not. Men wearing corsets may do so for medical reasons, but otherwise they read as solely sexualized items rather than the uncertain middle-ground they occupy for women. They cannot, for example, be so easily aired by men on an evening out without risking opprobrium. Yves Saint Laurent's designs for women's 'African' restraint-wear, along with designs by Jean-Paul Gaultier, Christian Lacroix, Dolce & Gabbana and others, create a more socially acceptable face of fetish wear. Vivienne Westwood's punk designs of the 1980s are studded and zipped and buckled, but the question remains whether this is clothing of dominance or submission, rather like the idea of sexual congress being one of entry or engulfment. The dress historian Valerie Steele examines these inherently mixed messages, questioning corsets' association with 'femininity and [the] feminine'.[36] However, the more leather and vinyl-laced corsets and studded codpieces that appear on the catwalk, the less obviously sexual they appear to be, and the more ordinary they are likely to become. Gaultier's male black leather and fettered corsets of 1996 have lost much of their power to shock through sheer familiarity.

François-Timoléon, abbé de Choisy, pondered on his life as a cross-dresser in his diaries. The seventeenth-century writer and diplomat enjoyed the feeling of leather and silk 'close to [his]

body'. He used female disguise to seduce young women, preferring that they in turn wear male clothing. A favourite of the
abbé, Mademoiselle Charlotte, delighted in his apparel:

> I am not constrained . . . as I would be with a man
> . . . What an advantage women's clothes give you!
> The heart of the man is there, which has its effect on
> us, and on the other hand the charms of femininity
> transport us and quite disarm us.[37]

Charlotte undergoes a form of marriage with him, *en garçon*, with
her hair shorn and wearing trousers, and Choisy himself attends
en femme. He refers to her as 'him' and as 'my dear husband'. When
he sprains his ankle, he describes himself as wearing a Marseilles
corset, a full and proper matronly corset, sitting up in bed and
surrounded by his neighbours. At the same time, he is not averse
to the charms of Mademoiselle Dany, his Little Babet, whom he
kits out in: 'a shift embroidered with lace, cut extremely low so
that one saw the whole of her bosom, which was by no means
pendulous; they were two little apples, quite white, whose shape
could be seen, with a little rosebud on each.'[38]

The Poppicock brochure of 2002 housed in the Wellcome
collection abounds in rubber, latex and leather, with zip-front
briefs and bare-arse tights. Thongs have elephant trunk snoods
to the fore, but for all that, it seems curiously anodyne. The 'Love
is . . . Divine' pamphlet in the same collection promises more
affordable and comfortable leather-look bits and bobs that can
be tried on in 'closed stores'. A 2003 catalogue for Clonezone, the
UK's first 'queer superstore', promises male restrictive gear and
various cover-alls with strategically placed apertures, expand-
ers and probes, reminiscent of a scene in Quentin Tarantino's
Pulp Fiction (1994), yet somehow fails to shock. These more contemporary examples are illustrated with echoes of past baroque
Choisy-like details, in the feather boas, garters, see-through,
lacy fabrics and semi-transparent nylon tulle.

The s&m resonance of black leather: woman's corset, c. 1900, leather and metal (back and front).

Ann Summers, a British underwear retailer, advertises as a business run by and for women. In the 1980s women-only Ann Summers parties took place in people's homes to make buying sexy underwear a more homely activity, perhaps reminiscent of Tupperware Parties in the 1950s and '60s. Despite its success the company has met with frequent criticism. Buckingham Palace objected to an image of Elizabeth II appearing in one of its advertisements. The American lingerie firm Victoria's Secret, founded in 1977, similarly set out to make the sale of sexy underwear more mainstream, with its high-end annual catwalk fashion show and use of supermodels, known as its Angels. Just as Ann Summers sought acceptance by association with the domestic, it was a risqué but cosy idea of the Victorian period in England that provided the inspiration for naming Victoria's Secret, although perhaps not of Queen Victoria herself in her voluminous open-crotch drawers.

The tagline of a new underwear retailer in London's Covent Garden, Honey Birdette, also states that their business has been 'created by women for women'. The atmosphere inside the shop is quiet, even refined, like an expensive clothing boutique. The company's underwear is often purchased as glamorous night-out clothing. Veiled customers come to purchase their playful 'bondage' corsets and furry manacles for special night-in wear. The shop assistant reckons that the pricey merchandise is rarely bought to please males, but to make women 'feel like women', though this feeling must surely be premised on a possible response, imagined or otherwise. That such satin bondage bras and corsets with their pretty gilt locks attached should have this effect seems at odds with ideas about gender equality, but that is perhaps to miss the point. When the shop first opened, a lingerie model was employed to display the boutique's ensembles in the window. Apparently it was striking how it was men who stopped to gaze at the scantily dressed model while women seldom lingered. However, it was women who entered the shop and made purchases. When a woman is accompanied by a man, the assistant commented, once inside he will nearly always hang back even when asked for his opinion, rather as when buying outer clothing, perhaps.

But, of course, men differ. There is the narcissist, the fop or dandy, yesterday's metrosexual or those who adopt clothing to suggest sporting activity, and all are perhaps in the market for well-fitting, flattering underwear, with a suggestion of Lycra corseting, to show off a lean waistline or smooth out an incipient beer belly.

Antoine François Dennel, after Pierre Alexandre Wille, *The Test of the Corset*, 1788, engraving.

3

Modesty and the Immodest Torso

Female breasts are usually masked, veiled from too clear a view. They can be augmented with pads of wax or cotton and more recently various forms of smart-fibre padding to improve their visual impression. An 1800 ditty berates this duplicitous practice:

> My Delia's heart I find so hard,
> I would she were forgotten,
> For hearts be adamant
> When all the breast is cotton.[1]

In the interests of fair play male padding has been around since at least the thirteenth century, augmenting shoulder breadth in particular. An actor once told me that during a long theatre run someone she was working with would wrap his penis with toilet paper, to show himself to best advantage. Vests are now widely available that produce the effect of six-pack stomach muscles. From early Minoan metal chest belts worn by children as young as five, to the gradual emergence and development of the corset, the various reinforcements to alter the shape of the body, from padded bras to elasticated pull-on girdles and full-torso silhouette suits, have been around for a very long time. Ancient Egyptian women of status wore tightly fitted *kalasiris* sheath dresses that sometimes came to just below their breasts, the shoulder straps like modern bras offering some support;

belts and corsets of various designs support from below. In the early 1800s, Jane Austen looks back to a time of more highly restrictive corsets, writing to her sister Cassandra 'that the stays now are not made to force the Bosom up at all, *that* was a very unbecoming, unnatural fashion.' She was also relieved to learn that such a low, wide neckline was no longer a requirement of fashion: '[I] was really glad to hear that they are not to be so much off the shoulders as they were.' In one letter Austen describes a friend, Mrs Powlett, who was happy to bare her shoulders, as being 'at once expensively and nakedly dress'd'.[2]

In ancient societies the loincloth was worn to protect workers in the field, and primitive brassieres or breast cloths were adopted by Spartan female wrestlers, yet others, often of higher status, appear to have chosen to wear no underclothing at all. Younger women could use ribbons or cords to lift and draw attention to their breasts, rather than mask them, while others bound them tight as the flesh slackened to give the impression of youth. In ancient Greece women generally were not allowed to compete in the Olympic Games, where participants performed naked. Plato in *The Republic* alludes to a possible time when Greeks, like barbarians, might think 'that it was shocking and ridiculous for men to be seen naked . . . But when experience showed them that it was better to strip than wrap themselves up, what reason had proved best lost its absurdity to the eye.'[3] However, Plato admits that it might seem ridiculous to see 'women taking exercise naked with the men in the gymnasium? It won't only be the young women; there will be elderly women too, just as there are old men who go on with their exercises when they are wrinkled and ugly to look at.'[4] He suggests that nonetheless in time society would be likely to adapt to seeing women's – that is, non-enslaved women's – bodies. Certainly in the West today it is ordinary to see women minimally clothed both in sporting activities and on the street.

Whereas women, until recently at least, appear to invite sexual comment whether they like it or not, men perhaps feel

Corset with cords rather than boning, American, 1889–91.

less exposed when underdressed. A lesbian dominatrix, Chris Belcher, working in Los Angeles interrogated this disparity between male and female experiences in her memoir, detailing the lives of women who dress up in order to undress: 'I was envious of the absolute ease with which men, fat or thin, would undress in front of a stranger. My rare female clients bought new lingerie for the occasion.'5 To Belcher, men frequently seemed happier in their skin, less self-conscious, or perhaps it is just that their sense of self lies less in their bodily form. She found that women seemed more concerned to impress or at least avoid derision. Even in circumstances where punishment is on order, she noticed that male clients were more relaxed about being seen without their clothing compared to her female clients. Women and men have historically often had very different attitudes to their bodies, partly on account of their roles, concerning child-bearing and caring on one side and on the other that of aggressor or protector and economic provider. Even when these apparent opposites are far less clear cut, we tend to see our bodies as if these distinctions still exist. Women, for instance, continue to adopt a greater domestic role even when they are the major earner in a household.6 Is it perhaps such deeply held gendered attitudes that continue to support these disparities. In the light of greater freedoms in the West regarding non-heteronormative sexualities, underwear provides a telling indication of this contrary counter-revolution, in both the private and the more public sphere.

While one might think of modesty as a universal virtue, with particular reference here to the body and what we allow or are allowed to display, much depends upon context and culture. Human female breasts are permanently enlarged, unlike those of other mammals, and since breasts often sag, particularly after breastfeeding, losing their buoyancy over time, many women attempt to disguise this aspect of ageing. Advances in surgical practice allow lifts and implants for cosmetic reasons and the demand for procedures such as buttock

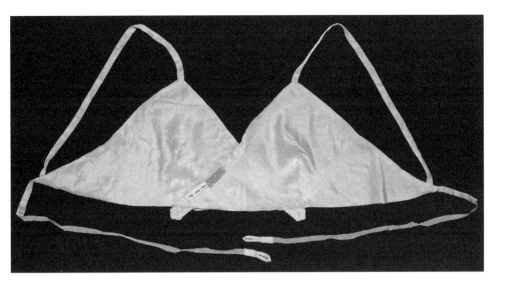

Linen brassiere with elastic cross straps across the back, which fasten with buttons at the front, manufactured by Kestos, 1930s.

enhancements have also increased rapidly in the 2020s, including surgeries for men.

In 1889 *Life* magazine included a corset catalogue containing a two-piece brassiere and girdle patented by Herminie Cadolle, and by the beginning of the new century the bra was being advertised separately as a garment in its own right, usually made of elastic material and fitted with adjustable shoulder straps. In contrast, in the 1960s elastic mesh bras offered only minimal support and were worn with matching briefs, mainly by younger women.

The dress historian Jessica Wright discusses the way modern-day shapewear often echoes Victorian attitudes, referring to a contemporary underwear company, Hourglass Angel, whose advertising relies on a nineteenth-century idea of the ideal woman as 'small-waisted and curvaceous', the 'angel' of the home:

> this ideal was completely deconstructed and rebuilt
> throughout the nineteenth century; the 'erotic zones'
> of the female body shifted from the belly towards the
> bosom and buttocks, and therefore '[t]he new female

objets du désir possessed exaggerated breasts, thighs, posteriors, and relatively diminutive waists and bellies'.[7]

We come in different shapes and sizes, and idealistic views decrying certain, usually exaggerated, fashionable proportions suggest that women, and presumably men, might do well to avoid trying to transform themselves into the fashionable shape of the moment. There is an implicit suggestion that we should perhaps avoid altering aspects of our bodies just because they are not currently in fashion. The constant flux of fashion design will always have its detractors, as well as its more determined adherents. Since fashion will surely change again and again, the body risks being in constant and painful reorganization. Just as you have achieved a plumped-up behind as pneumatic as a Kardashian in a bodycon dress, fashions change and we find ourselves longing for straight up-and-down adolescent contours, lean muscularity and a tiny waistline. Underwear, or rather the new shapewear, comes to the rescue with its modern 'future' fabrics that can constrain and enlarge with equal ease. Twenty-first-century underwear producers claim their state-of-the-art sustainable technologies and use of eco-friendly materials will take our bodies wherever fashion dictates while also 'saving the planet'.

Advances in surgery have helped those recovering from mastectomies. A range of enlargement and reduction possibilities serve transgender patients. Since ancient times breasts have been bound with bandages, but modern-day adhesive tape does the same job, though it can be hard to remove without discomfort. The selling point of such binding is that it makes someone look as if they have no need of a bra, and suggests 'the promise of recreating the appearance of one's younger, fuller bust – a bust full of youthful potential and hope, unravaged by the sands of time'.[8]

Most women in a position to enjoy fashion are likely to possess a range of bras, rifled through and selected depending on the day, or night, ahead: which is most comfortable, which looks best with whatever other clothes one is wearing and also whether it is likely to be seen and judged. At the gym you might prefer to bind yourself firmly in place for rigorous exercise, the sports bra making the breasts into one smoothly evened-out mound, avoiding painful jiggling. Perhaps you are challenged by a clinging dress that will expose evidence of droop and surrounding bulge, and so you need to search for the most accommodating, flattering item. There have been times when a softer, more mature bust was extolled, evidenced by the great screen sirens of the 1940s and '50s. Moreover, sometimes old film, perhaps less well defined or the colour faded, can allow a more forgiving gaze.

Given the different shapes and sizes of female breasts and how they lie in relation to the torso, the brassiere is a complicated item of clothing to construct. The cups, band and bridge between the two cups vary considerably, and yet many women assume they continue to be the same size for life, though this is far from true. The writer Alison Lurie describes how young girls' 'training bras' often have little practical function, but act as a sign for the child that she is on the way to becoming a woman.[9]

Bras provide different degrees of coverage: full, half or sometimes covering only the lower quarter of the breast. If the nipple beneath is not matched up with the point of a dart in the outer layer of clothing then it can spoil a smooth silhouette.[10] If a bra is to offer support and fit accurately, then careful individual measurements are required. Those experienced in selling underwear sometimes claim they can assess precisely what size a woman should be wearing at a glance. Few would attempt to manufacture their own bras today, and in any case even the finest sewers of the past might not have aspired to the sort of precise fit that a modern bra can in theory achieve. That said, a fitter at Marks & Spencer confided that most women are entirely ignorant of what size they should be wearing and may either insist on purchasing the size they have always worn or alternatively depend on the one-size-fits-all (OSFA) stretch of the sports bra. Too tight and the flesh will be squeezed and bulge; too loose and little support is given. Apparently many of us would do well to simply adjust the length of our bra straps to gain a better fit. Such knowledge – and tact – is gained from years of fitting women of all shapes and sizes. We can be embarrassed and defensive about such intimate matters, blinded by self-deception, or simply resistant to looking at our bodies with any degree of objectivity, particularly in the bleak, bright mirrors of many a fitting room.

Mildred Lathbury in Barbara Pym's *Excellent Women* (1952) is a modest-mannered, intelligent and ladylike single woman who is brought up sharp against the beautifully dressed Mrs Gray. She contemplates her washing with dismay: 'It was depressing the way the same old things turned up every week. Just the kind of underclothes a person like me might wear, I thought dejectedly, so there is no need to describe them.'[11] When she is visited by an old school friend, Dora, who duly washes some unlovely smalls and hangs them up to dry, 'within half an hour the kitchen [is] festooned with lines of depressing-looking underwear – fawn locknit knickers and petticoats of the same material.' Mildred declares that Dora's underwear is 'even drearier than mine'.[12] Mildred is appalled when the dashing Rocky Napier enters, 'threading his way through the lines of dripping garments'. However, later in the novel, she has begun to find him rather less attractive and cares less what he makes of her clothing:

> Rocky followed me into my kitchen and stood under
> the line of washing, which I noticed with irritation had
> become too dry to be ironed comfortably. He began
> pulling down the garments and making jokes about
> them, but I felt that this was not the time for coyness
> and embarrassment, so I took no notice of him.[13]

More sombre in mood is an example in T. S. Eliot's 'The Waste Land'. In Part III of the poem, 'The Fire Sermon', a typist returns from work and carries out her solitary domestic tasks; her combinations are hung up to dry, but here with the sun upon them there is a suggestion that they are communing with a heavenly body. It is rare for single women past their youth to be allowed sexy underwear in fiction, and when they are it is presented as a ridiculous vanity capable of evoking pity at best. Men, it seems, retain their sexual status for far longer, whatever their outward appearance.

In the confident youth culture of the 1960s couture fashion was increasingly directed towards the young, with even couturiers like Yves Saint Laurent, for example, producing sheer blouses that were intended to be worn without a bra. The period is sometimes referred to as the burn-the-bra era, a time when some feminists must have wanted to support female liberation but might have felt conflicted if they happened to have larger or less-than-firm breasts or simply found the idea of going without a bra immodest. At the 1968 Miss America pageant, held in Atlantic City, New Jersey, on 7 September, a demonstration led by the feminist group New York Radical Women (NYRW) was widely reported to have burned 'female torture' items, notably the bra. It appears that no actual bra-burning took place and the story was merely a media ruse to trivialize the women's objectives.[14] On the one hand, women might have wanted to be fashionable and show their allegiance to the hippie counterculture, but on the other it could be uncomfortable, even painful, for them to leave their breasts unsupported. Wearing a bra, and particularly a supportive bra rather than a more minimal fashionable design, risked seeming prim and perhaps politically conservative. The business of breast-feeding made for further practical difficulties, as lactating breasts are often particularly sensitive and in need of extra support.

In the history of women's fashion the cleavage has hardly ever been entirely out of sight, yet when a corseted evening dress was depicted with one strap astray, it created quite a furore. The portrait of Virginie Gautreau (1883–4), the young American wife of a French banker, shows her wearing a dark satin dress, her body facing but her head twisting away from the viewer. One

THE VIRTUES OF UNDERWEAR

jewelled strap appears to have fallen negligently onto her bare white shoulder. The sense of sexy disregard stirred up considerable moral disapproval. The American artist, John Singer Sargent, was forced to withdraw the painting from the Paris Salon in 1884, and repainted the strap firmly in place, where it should in all decency have been all along. He also changed the painting's title to *Madame X*, ostensibly to protect the subject's privacy, but ironically endowing it with an added sense of dangerous suggestiveness.

As recently as 1984 the American athlete Joan Benoit Samuelson caused a stir in the media simply because she was pictured, after winning the marathon at the Olympic Games, with a plain white bra strap exposed, albeit safely on the shoulder.[15] It is only recently that showing a bra strap has not been seen as sluttish. Footballer Brandi Chastain received press coverage not so much for scoring the deciding penalty in the finals of the 1999 World Cup, but because in her jubilation she copied what men often do in such circumstances: she ripped off her shirt and swung it in the air. She exposed an impeccably modest black sports bra, and yet it set off 'a firestorm of debate'.[16] It was as if she had flaunted her breasts, even though the actual flesh was completely hidden from view. In comparison, when a male rugby player accidentally loses his shorts on the pitch and exposes his jockstrapped buttocks, he is unlikely to face disapproval. Such reproof remains directed towards the female.

For many younger women today the sports bra has become everyday wear. An experienced seamstress working for a couture bridal shop explained to me that she regularly has to remind her customers to wear a proper tailored bra for their fittings rather than their customary pull-on affair, or it would never be possible to achieve a good, close fit for their wedding dress toile. The finished garment would have firm, shaped bra cups as part of its inbuilt structure, so that no additional bra would need to be worn.

The concept of attractive dishabille is a decreasing asset: exposed underwear gains distaste or pity rather than positive attention as the years pass, as if an older person can no longer follow the same sartorial rules of femininity. With the disappearance of the corset, which had not required support from the shoulder, bra straps could slip out of place, a solution being to hold them in place on the underside of outer clothing with small poppered devices, either permanently sewn into a garment or safety-pinned in place. Significantly, more expensive and couturier garments continue to have such devices sewn in. It is an example of a small and unseen high-status feature of fashion, fast on the way to becoming obsolete, and for that reason its presence bears extra kudos. However, although it can be irritating to have a bra strap that is frequently falling down, the necessary hitching movement, accompanied by a small shrug of the shoulders, can be a highly suggestive gesture of apparently absent-minded seduction. What is replaced can also slip down again.

In 2022 there was a marked couturier fashion for lingerie being worn as evening wear, just as had been popular in the 1990s. At the Cannes Film Festival in 2023 see-through dresses over negligible underwear were splashed across the fashion pages. On London's streets in the same year young women wore stockings held up by suspenders under micro-mini skirts or shorts. The stockings were usually black fishnet, with tears for added grunge, and worn with chunky boots. It is a more manicured look than punk, but still, when I asked if the torn areas of the fishnets were deliberate, I was told that they were not, but that when they occur, as tears will on fishnets, then they are quite ok. Less successful was a fragile-looking girl in Holborn in similar suspenders and torn stockings, but whose skirt was so short that as she walked she had to keep tugging it down or risk exposing her knickers. A bolder person might have carried it off without bothering to check, and to hell with what the rest of us might see! If underwear can be worn as outerwear, then why should it matter if the crotch or underpants are in sight? The shock value of glimpsing usually private underwear is often the point of such fashion.

Underwear's private character when it is either accidentally or deliberately exposed takes on a range of possible meanings. British prime minister John Major was rumoured to expose the waistband of his underpants when he leant forward, having tucked his shirt under the elastic to keep matters neat, and was mocked by the British press as demonstrating prissy unmanly caution. The practice is common in Italy, though somehow the waistbands of men's underpants there are rarely exposed to view. In 2007 a similar idea was put about by the *New Statesman*, suggesting that the politician Menzies ('Ming') Campbell should be judged by a small feature of underwear he had on show: 'Does Ming the Merciless wear sock garters? I ask only because a colleague swears he saw a clip hanging out of the bottom of the Edwardian gentleman's trouser leg?'[17]

The trend for wearing low-cut jeans exposes the so-called 'whale tail' effect of thong underwear, often embellished with lace and rhinestone and suggesting the unseen private parts beneath. The association with the heft of such a mammal captures something of the problem. On all but the slimmest, a whale tail also has the tendency to accentuate so-called 'love handles' or 'muffin tops' of flesh pressed between the waistband of trousers and that of the underwear. If underwear should not be seen, then when underpants show through tight clothing many attempts are made to avoid the VPL. Various ways to camouflage these effects, such as avoiding too fine an outer clothing layer, vie with recommendations to wear boy-shorts or to go commando – and, to come full circle, to wear a thong.[18]

In the actor Jane Russell's first film role, as Rio McDonald in *The Outlaw* (dir. Howard Hughes, 1943), the sight of her impressive cleavage so shocked the censors that the film's release was blocked for five years. The Production Code Administration complained that 'the girl's breasts are shockingly emphasized.' A Maryland judge was moved to describe Russell's breasts as 'hung like a thunderstorm over a summer landscape'.[19] Howard Hughes had been determined that his own seamless bra design would show off her breasts to best advantage by giving the impression that she was not wearing a bra at all. Although Russell secretly wore her own bra, lining it with tissues to hide any seams, the notoriety the censorship had caused and the publicity posters showing her lying on a haystack apparently braless meant that when the film finally appeared it was a huge financial success. Nevertheless, film companies subsequently preferred their stars to wear close-fitting garments that did not show too much embonpoint so as to avoid such costly delays, opting instead for accentuating the shape and size of the breasts but keeping them well covered beneath outer garments. Bras were padded and hitched up high.

The Hollywood of the 1940s had introduced the conical bra, which became more defined in the 1950s and was often termed the bullet or torpedo bra. Yet what people might find acceptable in a film could be found shocking and unacceptable when worn off-screen. A Pittsburgh police superintendent, Harvey J. Scott, feared national chaos over the new attention-grabbing pointed missile, and psychiatrist Edward E. Mayer, supervising director of that city's Behaviour Clinic at the Criminal Court, was also firmly against what he saw as the provocative bras, because 'They tempt and entice the male drinker who can't control his inflamed passions and likely rape results.'[20]

With nineteenth-century morality still influencing mainstream publishing even into the second half of the twentieth century, before the Internet age, many experienced their first images of undressed adult bodies from between the yellow covers of *National Geographic*. The evidence the magazine provided suggested not only that some societies did not see breasts as private parts of the body, but that some form of brassiere was advisable for women in the long run. In the 1960s models like Twiggy made the braless, breastless torso seem appealing, but soon designers such as Janet Reger were heralding a return to nostalgic items like the fancy padded bra. British designer Reger also promoted suspender belts and stockings as well as matching sets of bras

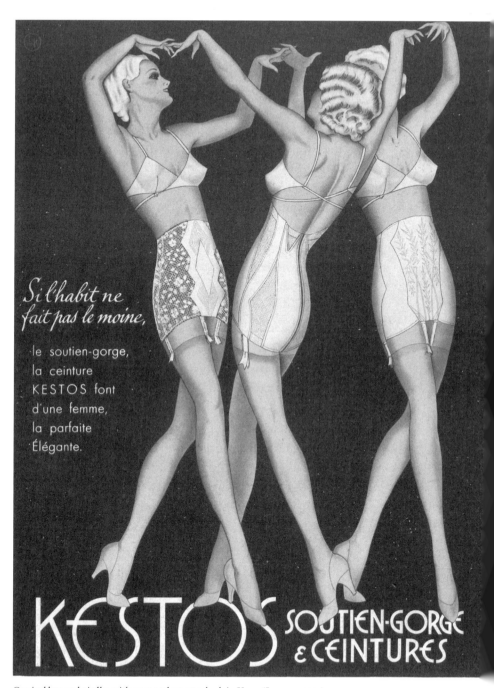

Si l'habit ne fait pas le moine,

le soutien-gorge,
la ceinture
KESTOS font
d'une femme,
la parfaite
Élégante.

KESTOS SOUTIEN-GORGE & CEINTURES

Conical bra and girdle, with suspenders attached, in *Vogue* (January 1937).

and knickers, emphasizing their sexual appeal. The journalist Lucy Mangan in *The Stylist* was surprised in 2016 to realize that she had never possessed a single matching set herself, and upbraided her husband for never having given her lingerie. He replied: 'I did! . . . Once. I bought you a matching set and you gave me a speech on the corrosive effect of lace on labia, your unswerving commitment to the cotton gusset and how your boobs were too small to deserve nice things.'[21]

Mary Quant, famed for her clean 1960s architectural designs, admitted to being drawn to fancy underwear, even though she understood how it could easily spoil the line of her outer clothing: 'I know I am always seduced myself by the prettiest, frilliest, laciest bras that look so good when you're undressed. But under a dress, they are nothing but unsightly lumps and bumps.'[22]

The market for elaborate lingerie-type bras and other items of fancy underwear is alive and well, from constricting mini wasp-waisted corsets to thongs that bruise the tenderest flesh and suspender belts, rather than tights, that ping undone and are chilly in cold weather. The question here is why this longing persists, at a time when many women appear to have gained a far greater level of autonomy. Do they dress to please themselves, delighting in the texture of fine silks and satins and the feeling of luxurious self-generated extravagance? In a scene from *Annie Hall* (dir. Woody Allen, 1977), Alvy Singer (played by Allen) gives Diane Keaton's Annie a sexy negligee as a present: 'Are you kidding? This is more like a present for you,' Annie retorts. News website *HuffPost* remarks that, 'not all undies-as-gifts are created equal. A vintage-inspired La Perla nightie is one thing, but what about a crotchless onesie? Or nipple tassels?'[23] Some hope that underwear may transform their bodies and bring about the desirability they surely possess, that has hitherto somehow been overlooked.

Similar distinctions can apply to male dress. Today there is pressure put on younger men, both gay and straight, to satisfy the idealized advertising images of models and film and sport stars. The post-Second World War desirable man, rugged from his experience saving the free world, has been overtaken by a tweezered and honed, gym-fit, moisturized ideal. He must not have love handles or a paunch, and certainly never be seen wearing sweaty, ill-fitting underwear.

Some buy sexy underthings because it makes them feel more attractive, or possibly as a strategy to attract and keep a partner interested and stop them from looking elsewhere. A series of essays concerning women's underwear in Syria describes the pressure to be seductive and keep husbands keen, with the threat of a replacement younger wife a realistic concern. Because of the constraints put on women in the Middle East, who must be seen to be modestly dressed on the street, the market for what is only seen in the home is far greater than in the West. During the 1960s, political unrest afflicting Syria meant that its residents were faced with border closures and a lack of suitable materials for their clothing industry, but the country still carried on producing cotton underwear, much of which was exported to Russia and Eastern Europe. Bras, which require more intricate engineering, were a different matter, and not manufactured in Syria until the 1970s. Women were forced to rely on what could be cobbled together using strips of jersey and elastic. Now, women in full dark veiling visit the fantastical underwear stalls of the souk, confronted by a sea of colourful, fanciful lingerie:

> Styles zig zag from prim virginal floral arrangements
> crowning a thong like a wedding corsage, to nippleless
> leotards reminiscent of Frederick's of Hollywood.
> There are colourful plastic butterflies and flowers
> sewn onto underwire bras and zippered breasts
> and crotches verging on a crudely innocent version
> of s&m. Some of the bra-and-panty sets sing and
> light up. Others can be eaten.[24]

While sex is used to sell more or less everything in the West, in Syria, despite *sha'abi* – which translates as popular verging on the vulgar – there seems to be a more innocent air about these stalls, with the lingerie industry claiming to represent 'an important rite of passage from virginity to respectable, married womanhood'.[25] There are apparently few raunchy or sadomasochistic styles, but strategically placed slits over breast and genitals and prettied-up bondage suggest the industry is perhaps at an earlier stage of development than in the West. Egyptian scholars issue fatwas against unclothed marital intercourse. In 2006 Rashad Khalil, former dean of *shari'a* law at Al-Azhar University, issued a fatwa suggesting that a state of undress somehow negates the properly modest state of marriage. One suggestion, by the chairman of the university's fatwa committee, Abdullah Megawar, was that married couples might at least avoid looking at each other's genitals.[26] Quite so.

While the backroom factories in Damascus and Aleppo house the female machinists hard at work, the vendors who suggest suitable items to customers are male, proffering the itsy-bitsy fripperies – chocolate hearts that break open to reveal a silk G-string, for example, or selling pairs of lingerie knickers embellished with images of President Hafez al-Assad, to prove one's political orthodoxy, perhaps. Bras have half-cups in the form of birds' nests from which fledglings emerge with tinsel wings and jewelled eyes. The emphasis though is on cheerful colours and children's cartoon humour, but in the plate-glass windows of the souk it is not Arab women who are modelling these fripperies. It is Eastern European women who display the underwear 'not in a sexualized manner as seen in the advertising of Victoria's Secret or Calvin Klein, but in photos by local photographers that featured nipples, crotches and big friendly smiles'.[27] Until recently Syrian women were not allowed to work in public places, which meant that female customers had no choice but to buy their underclothing from men, a difficulty that was widely commented upon when the liberalization of religious laws was under discussion.

The crisp, itchy nylon lace, the bows and the rumpled satin ruffles often turn out to be less than flattering, but these aspects of such underwear are hardly confined to the Syrian market. Such elaborate garments offer a welcome respite from the ultra-modest street dress, albeit they are only to be worn in the home and with your husband. In the West there may be more choice but often clothing in practice is practically unisex and its primary principle is comfort. When getting dressed in the morning, you might consider that taking care over what you are wearing, even over your choice of underpants, is simply a practical and fleeting aesthetic consideration. The fact that such choices are unlikely to be noticed by others does not necessarily stop our imaginations from its many dalliances. Fancy underwear seems to provide a light-hearted escape from the everyday, even so minor a feature as that obsolete miniature bow at the centre of a bra.

Victoria's Secret thong, 1993–7, cotton, elastic.

Man dressing a
mannequin in
lingerie, 1958.

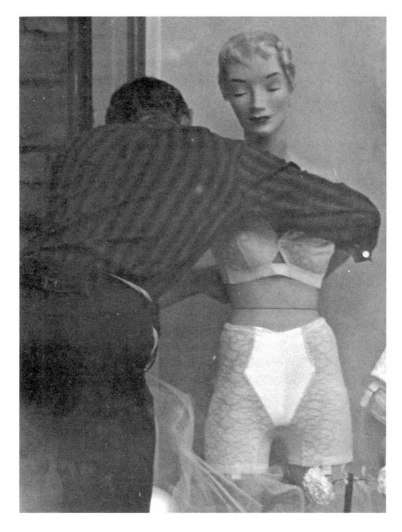

In the summer of 2023 lacy, fanciful bras have been on show
on the boulevards of elegant European capitals and the most
upmarket streets of New York. Unsurprisingly, it is a fashion
largely adopted by younger women and only during the summer
months – although on the streets of some British cities on a
Saturday night it has long been common to see women sporting
minimal items of lingerie, even in the dead of winter. A lingerie
bra can be part of evening dress, as with American singer-
songwriter Camila Cabello's see-through bra for the 2023

Grammys made by the designer Patʙᴏ, made from strings of pearls. The actor and model Julia Fox has been photographed in barely-there clothing, with bandeaux that are sometimes no more than a strip of fabric or tape in line with the nipples. One of her outfits consisted of a network of narrow white bandages over a surprisingly substantial pair of white knickers, working the look of a sparklingly clean zombie.

These choices may seem a long way from Victorian prudery, which had fostered its own more discreet erotic charge. There is a risk that so much exposure might mean that even beautiful bodies cease to be a novelty, when there is so little left to the imagination. Fox creates interest because her outfits seem daring, but when the duct tape is eased away then arguably there is nothing much left to see.

Recently, a friend working as an examinations assistant at the London School of Economics had a hard time explaining to a student that it was not acceptable to wear a bikini to her finals, even though it was a particularly hot day. He eventually managed to persuade her that her clothing might distract others. Modesty is of course dependent on culture and context – beach and changing room versus the formalities of a funeral and perhaps the majority of job interviews – but today matters seem to be moving fast.

The sports bra prototype came about in 1977 with the sewing together of two jockstraps. It was marketed at first as the Jockbra but later as the Jogbra, as apparently an association with male jockstraps was not deemed a positive sales feature. What was intended for athletes, and particularly for larger-breasted women, was taken up by many non-athletes, including nursing mothers. Nowadays the sports bra is worn by the majority of women: young and old, the gym-fit, the occasional jogger and by those who simply find them comfortable. Possibly women enjoy wearing an item that is by definition associated with fitness.

In the 1920s it was briefly fashionable for the sexes to dress similarly above the waist, and to some extent the same might be said of 1960s hippie culture. Of the 1920s it has been said that 'the heavy harnesses of old-fashioned underwear were exchanged for supple fluid jerseys and silks,' but this was true only for a tiny – and slender – minority.[28] The see-through hipster slip dresses and miniskirts in the 1960s, of Paris designers like Pierre Cardin and of Carnaby Street in London, favoured a boyishly slim figure. Such clothing made it easier by far for young women to eschew support. The bras that were worn were less cumbersome, using fine and mesh fabric that was often transparent, perhaps incorporating metallic thread for the space-age look, as if that time required underwear to seem hardly there and barely functional. The midriff in the 1960s was sometimes wholly bare or covered with see-through fabric, a look that made the support of the corset impossible; the stretch body stocking with poppered crotch came into vogue.

The exposure of women's breasts in the 1920s and '60s are exceptions in modern sartorial history in that they relied on a fashion for the boyish frame. In the West, breasts have consistently been a focus of attention, whether covered or semi-covered and with the cleavage accentuated by various means. Sigmund Lindauer was the first to put the bra into mass production, patenting his design in 1913 in Böblingen, Germany. With the First World War there was an increasing demand for steel for armaments, and the fate of the corset was sealed. The 'two-hankies bra' invented by American Mary Phelps Jacob in 1914 was first intended to support and separate the breasts above the corset, avoiding the mono-bosom effect, but crucially it required no metalwork. Without the attending corset these bras were only really suitable for those with smaller chests, and older women simply went on wearing the corsets they already possessed. Jacob must have been aware of the potential sexual connotations of her design: she adopted the name Caresse Crosby for her business after her marriage, and she was often accompanied by her dog, Clytoris.

If these fashions appeared to suggest dress was becoming somehow more natural, and certainly less restrictive and gender-defined, they failed. Post-war, Ida Rosenthal, a refugee from Belarus, opened a dress shop with Enid Bisset called Enid's Frocks in New York. Finding that their clothes were ill-served by the underwear available, Rosenthal designed a bra that accentuated and lifted the breasts rather than flattening them. The shop was renamed Maiden Form and Rosenthal's bra was duly patented in 1922. Cup sizes were standardized by her husband, William, and by 1942 maternity bras were added to the product line with an adjustable fastener incorporated into the design. The latter had the advantage that when their bra, the Maidenform, began to lose its close fit, the fastener could easily be hooked more tightly and ensure a longer life. Most innovative were Rosenthal's ongoing advertising campaigns, including one that associated the bra with glamour which appeared for more than twenty years, 'I dreamed . . . / I walked a tightrope . . . / I had tea for two in my Maidenform Bra.' Most oddball among the company's products are the laced vests that Rosenthal produced for homing pigeons during the Second World War, which allowed paratroopers to carry the birds with them safely and securely when parachuting behind enemy lines.[29]

The minimal bras of the 1960s and '70s were usurped by the super-bra, the push-up Wonderbra, interlined and padded and yet lightweight. Moe Nadler had founded the Canadian Lady Corset Company in Montreal in 1939, which was later rebranded as Wonderbra in the 1960s. The plunging, push-up style was given the nickname the *Pigeonnant* ('pigeon-breasted'), and was to become a best-seller across Europe and America during the 1980s and '90s, coinciding with the age of the supermodel. The familiar images of Naomi Campbell, Linda Evangelista, Claudia Schiffer and the like in advertisements and on the catwalk with their splendid hoisted-up breasts seem like figureheads on a galleon, like Neptune's angels in the age of so-called power-dressing, when the support of an accentuating bra was essential. In the film *Bridget Jones: The Edge of Reason* (dir. Beeban Kidron, 2004), when Bridget is released from a Thai prison where she has been incarcerated for smuggling cocaine, she gives her fellow inmates presents of what she knows will give them most pleasure and comfort: copies of John Gray's *Men Are from Mars, Women Are from Venus* (1992), bars of chocolate and a huge cache of 'Superbras'.

Now not only do a plethora of lace and underwired bras fill the shops, but new technologies have produced low-cost pre-formed, seamless, lightweight designs, which are more comfortable but still accentuate and exaggerate the breasts. There are also new bras that offer inexpensive solutions for post-mastectomy bodies and for chests pre-breast augmentation. Designers like Vivienne Westwood and Jean Paul Gaultier brought the adapted breast out into the erotic open; Madonna gained worldwide attention in her shell-pink satin conical bra, the colour and texture reminding us of the 1930s, but the attitude and desire for exposure distinctly of her own time.

A trend for wearing minimal underwear, and specifically micro-shorts and bras, on the hot airless streets of Manhattan in the summer of 2021 has been attributed to a response to COVID-19 restrictions. If you could not get to the swimming pool or beach, then the idea seemed to be to dress as if you were already there. Some find this sort of public exhibitionism unacceptable: on 8 July 2021 American Airlines took issue with a female bodybuilder, Deniz Saypinar, who attempted to board one of their flights wearing buttock-baring shorts and a minimal 'taut brown tank top'.[30] She was allowed to board a later plane, but only when she had agreed to dress, in the airline's terms, 'more appropriately'. Saypinar complained on social media that she was deeply offended by the experience and insulted at the indignity of being made to dress with more constraint, that is, enforced modesty. The journalist Guy Trebay reported his surprise at catching sight of a young woman on New York's Fifth Avenue, one of the most expensive shopping streets in the world, dressed in 'a pair of cutoffs, and sandals and – it is fully legal to do this – naked above the waist'.[31]

The u.s. Army has been working on a prototype bra for its female soldiers.[32] It is only since Operation Desert Storm in the 1990s that the function rather than the appearance of bras worn in combat has been addressed. A questionnaire sent out to 18,000 female soldiers discovered that keeping their breasts from jiggling about was a major concern and that many resorted to binding their breasts or wearing bras that were a size too small, or even wearing several at once, rather as the serious swimmer or cyclist does. In the main the women preferred black bras, because they would not show the dirt. Ashley Cushon, a clothing designer for the u.s. Army, has designed four types of sports bra, all of which had to be resilient enough to withstand many washes and have the security of the double closures of zip and Velcro. Apparently, the first American soldier ever to wear a bra-like garment was a certain Robert Shurtleff of the 4th Massachusetts Regiment in 1782. After seventeen months of good service during the American War of Independence Shurtleff fell ill, and was subsequently discovered to be a woman, Deborah Sampson, who had managed to disguise her breasts with linen bandages. She was summarily dismissed.

The underwired and padded bra, using new lightweight materials, now finds a place in many women's top drawer, as well as bras that are designed to reduce and constrain, or intended to appear altogether absent, like the next-to-invisible nipple-concealing T-shirt bra. New technology silicone gel 'padding' can create some of the flow and movement of a larger natural breast and can be in the form of separate pads, or 'chicken fillets' that are worn inside the bra. Modern shapewear bras are lightweight and uniform, and can even up the appearance of breasts that are of different sizes. In the past the means of padding was often improvised and was often more likely to become dislodged. In the time of the sweater-girl and her pointed bra, J. D. Salinger's Holden Caulfield in *Catcher in the Rye* (1951) complains about when such shaping goes astray, criticizing a young woman for wearing her 'damn falsies'.[33]

For both sexes in the West, plain, loose medieval wool or linen shifts that eventually came to be worn under a courtier's sixteenth-century doublet were effectively worn as underwear, glimpsed at the neck or billowing out from slashes cut into sleeves, or perhaps from beneath a sumptuous Eastern-style kaftan. Such clothing forms the foundations of modern underwear. Shirts for men had become a luxurious item of dress in the Renaissance, for those who could afford them, in finest gathered linen and tied with coloured silken strings, or with lace or ruffle-trim in the seventeenth and eighteenth centuries. In the 1830s, while outer clothing had become dark and uniform for men of business across the classes, it must have been a relief to introduce some colour and richer fabric in a sleeveless waistcoat, or vest, over one's undershirt and beneath jacket and coat. By the end of the nineteenth century shirts worn during the day were less elaborate and confining than evening wear. The dress historian Shaun Cole points out that in France at the time shirt fronts were often highly worked, to avoid too plain a design giving the impression that they were ready-made.[34] This was a new anxiety, given the availability of sewing machines in the home as well as increasingly affordable factory production. Contrariwise, the cotton sailor's vest, derived from the union suit, or long johns, cut off at the waist and arm, allowed for greater ease of movement. At the end of the nineteenth century the British Navy allowed such T-shirts to be worn for deck work. In 1913 the u.s. Navy formally adopted the plain white T-shirt as an undergarment, since it was more comfortable and quicker to dry off than the previous flannel undershirts.[35] By the 1960s the T-shirt had become the uniform of rebellious youth prompted by such screen idols as Marlon Brando in *The Wild One* (dir. László Benedek 1953) and James Dean in *Rebel Without a Cause* (dir. Nicholas Ray, 1955), and by the 1970s women too were wearing T-shirts. From its humble beginnings an adapted piece of underwear, the T-shirt, has gradually become an item worn by all, in high and low fashion. Cheap and easy to mass-produce, sometimes worn only once for a particular event, the T-shirt has become a significant element of clothing waste.

The outerwear peasant shift came to be worn as higher-status underwear in medieval Europe. Women's linen and cotton chemises in Europe and America included seams that went some way to offering support underneath the breasts, though for the heavier chest this role was far better supported by a corset. However, even from the latter years of the nineteenth century there are examples of flimsier, bandeau-like early brassieres likely to have been worn under a chemise. Just as in our own time, we are not so uniform in our clothing choices as portraits, fashion plates and contemporary dramatizations would seem to suggest.

Charities in the West have found that of all items of clothing, even when in second-hand condition, the bra is often the most desired article in poorer societies. Tangled bags of unsold clothing may be sent abroad, to more poverty-stricken regions. They are often intended for fabric recycling, but valuable items are picked out and worn again. The brassiere, that most sophisticated, architectural and useful form of underwear, plays its part in the movement between the modest covering-up of the body and its playful exposure – but for many women it remains an item of longed-for luxury.

4
Outer to Under
and Back Again

Fashion is in a constant state of flux. Canute is said to have commanded the incoming tide to retreat in order to demonstrate – in humility and piety – that even a great king cannot stand in the way of God-given nature. Fashions change, shuttling back and forth in a process that no individual or group of individuals can stop. The great historians of dress and chroniclers of human behaviour find various ways to account for the tendency of fashions to fall out of date and then a generation or so later return to the forefront of our desires, in a seemingly never-ending cycle of delight and repulsion and longing. Some find this off-putting and believe that fashion is something we should resist, while others accept it as an indication of our common human nature, unavoidable and often a telling metaphor for the drives and passions that make us what we are. Some believe that clothing, or rather taking an interest in one's clothing (here concerning its most hidden items), denotes a shallow trait and should be fought against in oneself, and despised and punished in others. This sort of view in part accounts for the many versions of sumptuary law, more often supporting the elite in maintaining their position. As one grows older it is difficult not to find oneself resisting fashions that seem too outrageous, forgetting what once moved us in our own heyday.

One can be trivially minded and yet have no interest in clothing at all. One might appreciate items of high fashion, perhaps once worn by a grandparent, say, yet consider our parents' fashions far less appealing. A generation too close for comfort. I recall my mother being surprised when I turned up in a faded 1930s crepe dress bought at a jumble sale; it was a style she associated with her own mother, and something she could not imagine my wanting to wear, so untailored, so floral, so horribly outdated. Fashion may be cyclical but matters do appear to have speeded up, so that anyone who lived as an adult through the 1980s must now come to terms with a younger generation keen for violently coloured, square-shouldered jackets and being informed that they are excitingly retro and vintage.

Charles II of England attempted in 1666 to draw a halt to fashion altogether, at least for the less impressionable sex. He hoped to persuade manly men to a permanent, elegant and truly English style of clothing. The doublet and hose had strong links to French fashion, and the English court was criticized for slavishly following France's every trend. Charles advocated what he considered a less effeminate design of tailored coat and vest, which amounted to leaving out the padding and whalebone shaping. A sleeveless layer worn under the doublet now became visible, as the vest, later waistcoat. The writer and English courtier John Evelyn was one of those who decried the tendency to follow the French: 'would the great Persons of England but owne their nation and assert themselves as they ought to do, by making choice of some Virile and comely fashion.'[1] He championed Charles's new designs, which were meant to embrace an individual's 'natural form' and do away with foreign influences for good. The king extolled the virtues of good, honest English wool, procured from English sheep, and without the silks and fancy elaborations that were forever infecting French fashion. And yet there is little evidence that this new permanent fashion was taken up, and Charles himself continues to appear in portraits in his fine gilded velvets and lacy jabots, no doubt still wearing the impeccable white, silky undervests and drawers advocated by the French.

When Charles I was to be executed in 1649, he asked his gentleman of the bedchamber Thomas Herbert for an extra undershirt, or under-vest as it was then known, for fear that he might shiver in the cold and the crowd take him for a coward. It must be hard for a monarch, used to the best quality as his ordinary and everyday, to dress down, even when it might have been better to make an impression of modest acquiescence. The shirt he wore, acquired by his physician Dr Hobbes from the scaffold, now housed at the Museum of London Docklands and stained with Charles's blood, is not a simple linen affair. It is made of an intricately woven, patterned French silk, fit for a king.

The Dutch States General formed a company of whalers in 1722 to satisfy the growing demand for basket-shaped panier skirts and their supporting framework, made from whalebone. When hooped skirts first appeared in the 1800s in England and America for those of means they were initially of moderate size and stiffened with whalebone, which was both strong and

Queen Elizabeth I's simple linen nightshirt (top section).

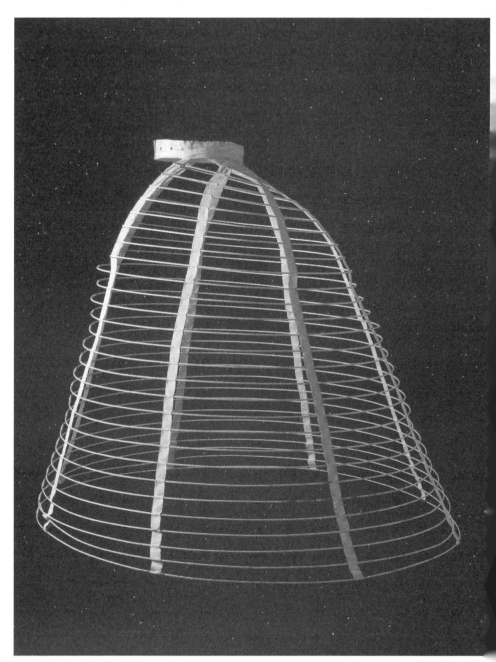

Woman's cage crinoline, England, c. 1865, cotton-braid-covered steel.

flexible. An underskirt of linen, cotton or silk held in place five hoops, which gradually became smaller the nearer they got to the waist. Arthur Grimble's novel *A Pattern of Islands* (1952), set in the Pacific Isles, concerns a trainee administrator and his new wife, Olivia. Accompanying her husband for the first time, the new bride is proud to show off her fashionable horsehair fabric crinoline, as worn by Queen Victoria and the beautiful Empress Eugénie of France, wife to Napoleon III. But boarding their ship, Olivia has not yet found her sea legs. The ship rolls suddenly towards the shore and as suddenly swings back out again, just as she is attempting to come on board, resulting in a moment of wildly embarrassing comeuppance:

> The accompanying downward plunge caused an uprush of air beneath her skirts which lifted them over her head. Skirts were worn voluminous in those days . . . she was left dangling in the void by her hands only . . . [The captain] grabbed at one of her wild legs as they swung out at him, and gave a good strong jerk. She came apart from the ladder like plucked fruit, and hurtled down upon him . . . His only remark when I got into the boat was that women ought to be careful to wear bloomers for occasions of that sort in the Pacific.[2]

The lack of modest underwear, or of wearing anything at all beneath, threatens Olivia's grace and dignity. The crinoline made wearing underpants essential. Previously the layering and sheer weight of an underskirt had meant they could be optional items and their function was to protect the body and outer clothing rather than to prevent the legs and private parts from being exposed. In the V&A Museum in London are examples of steel-framed crinolines with the hoops sewn into channels in the fabric, and sometimes padded with a wide hem of horsehair or wool to a width of 30–45 centimetres (12–18 in.), to give the framework greater ballast and so ensure that they are less likely to tip up and frighten the horses.

Before the crinoline craze a fashion for thicker, heavier satins and brocades had meant that layers of underskirt were required, frilled and sometimes embroidered, in order for the outerwear to stand out to advantage. In the eighteenth century, for the most affluent, underskirts were covered with a petticoat that matched or certainly matched in grandeur the robe and stomacher above. Multiple layers put a wearisome strain on the waist, and the crinoline can be said to have solved this problem. It was comparatively lightweight and it must have felt thrilling for a woman to feel such an airy sense of freedom about her nether regions. The ability of the frame to swoop and dance was a zestful selling point, so many opted to wear the cage frame without weighting it down. Ethnologist Marianne Thesander makes the point that the volume of the crinoline had the effect of drawing attention to what lay beneath, positing that 'The crinoline seemed, because of its size, to be an impregnable fortress, designed to keep the opposite sex at bay.'[3] Yet few would not have witnessed a crinoline being upturned. Combined with the formidable barrier of a tight corset, it created a sartorial oxymoron, a mixed message of restriction and availability that is often at the core of erotic desire.

A pertinent small feature of underdress in the 1700s and 1800s was the female hidden pocket, often worn as a pair of pockets, tied around the waist and worn under the skirt and over the petticoat. The pockets were accessed via slits in the skirt, and used rather as the Renaissance male codpiece was, to provide safe or secret storage. A nursery rhyme reminds us of its function to house money and other small essentials:

Lucy Locket lost her pocket
Kitty Fisher found it;
Not a penny was there in it,
Only ribbon round it.

Chamois leather pocket, patched and mended, worn by Ann Benyon (1803–1885), who sold eggs and butter at a market in Pembrokeshire, Wales.

Some were exquisitely embroidered on silk with flowers, trees, birds and abstract designs, others in plain utilitarian linen, and some of the most touching have paid long service. A farmer's wife, Ann Benyon of Flimstone farm in Pembrokeshire, made her own pocket from a single piece of chamois leather. In the mid-nineteenth century she used the pocket to hold money from her eggs and butter sales at market. It survives today, darned and mended, with the mouth of the purse evidently reinforced to prolong its working life.[4]

When fashions changed and scanty Empire-line dresses came into vogue, a pocket would have created an unsightly interruption of line if worn beneath, and thus it became worn on top of the outer clothing. These little bags or reticules were often made at home from netting and crochet, embroidered and quilted satin, wool-worked for everyday use perhaps, and sometimes made out of leftover fabric to match a dress. They were also became known as 'ridicules'. When previously hidden items of dress change their position and become visible to all; they are often satirized, as if the act of what once was underwear becoming outerwear is intrinsically comical. The reticule, often fastened with a drawstring, is the forerunner of the handbag and further conjures Freudian associations as a symbolic representation of the vagina. This may explain why charity shops abound in second-hand bags, perhaps few wishing to associate themselves with old bags. There was an echo of that once secret hiding place in the small pockets in gym knickers in the 1950s and '60s, which have in turn transformed into fashionable modern day exercise gear, with their running belts built to house a mobile phone and Lycra sweatpants fitted with zippered pockets for keys and credit cards.

The crinoline's size also acted as a useful contrivance for thieves and smugglers, by way of hidden hooks and pockets sewn into the framework, which must at least have helped to stabilize the wearer.[5] Thesander makes the point that from the

Honoré-Victorin Daumier, 'The usefulness of a crinoline when cheating the customs', from *Actualités*, in *Le Charivari*, 1857, lithograph.

mid-nineteenth century, 'Women from all levels of society wore crinoline dresses.'[6] Crinoline frames were being mass-produced, but even if they were too expensive for some, the poorest could still bone their skirts with stiff rope. Petticoats and camisoles were more often made at home, some women adapting worn-out outer skirts or acquiring second-hand those discarded by the better off. A working-class woman could now aspire to own her own high-fashion form of altered silhouette and the cage crinoline was an impressive feature that was potentially available to all. In a time of open fires crinolines were not only impractical but could easily be set alight, creating a fireball that was difficult to extinguish, with pitiful results to the wearer and thousands dying from such accidents. Fanny Longfellow, wife of the poet Henry Wadsworth Longfellow, died in this way from severe burns in 1861. Even so, an element of risk has never inhibited the dedicated follower of fashion.

Despite the dangers of the crinoline and its unwieldy form, many a modern-day bride seems to crave a tightly laced corset and voluminous skirt to make her feel special. Coming into fashion on the heels of the Regency muslin shift dress, the crinoline, when given a ballasted hem and layers of petticoats, was more substantial. Victorian women's clothing weighed in at as much as 16–17 kilograms (35–7 lb).[7] Modern versions of the crinoline are now made with lighter-weight plastic hoops and fire-resistant fabric.

In the nineteenth century there were many who warned about the dangers of the crinoline, such as Friedrich Theodor Vischer, a German poet and professor of aesthetics in Zurich and Tübingen, who railed against the fashion for 'distorting' the natural form of the 'feminine' body. He attempted a scientific justification for his fury:

> When the contours from the hip downwards increase to an impossible size, the eye no longer seeks to compare the huge bulk with the small diameter of

the waist; it is all the same, it does not matter whether
one is slim or not, there are no longer any laws in this
fantastic lie. And that is surely ugly, very ugly! The
crinoline is impertinent. Impertinent because of
the large amount of room taken up by its wearer . . .
impertinent because of its conspicuousness, because
of its monstrous challenge to the man.

Vischer seems to relish imagining the coquette in crinoline, who
he imagines wantonly addressing his sex:

Would you like to step down from the pavement, or
do you dare to brush past me, to press against me?
When you sit next to me in the stalls would you like to
take my dress in your lap or to sit on it? Can you feel
the iron hoops? Can you feel the impregnable castle,
the Malakoff wreath, the terrible chastity belt which
presses into your calves?[8]

Before this female fashion, men had often worn restrictive
underclothing, and often continued to do so on the sly, in corsets whose form depended upon the tastes of a particular era.
Male corsets held more shame, associated with a vanity that is
often considered more shameful in men. With the Industrial
Revolution, men's figure-improving underwear became more
hidden, increasingly seen as effeminate and better kept secret.

The *tournure* or bustle is a recurring feature of female dress
in the West. In the 1860s it came back into vogue in response
to the prodigious crinoline, as a rejigged development of
eighteenth-century padded underwear. The silhouette of the
1770s–80s had moved away from the wider pannier shape, with
robes drawn up into pleats and gathered up and bunched over
the hips. A dress of 1780 in the collection of Japan's Kyoto
Costume Institute appears neatly tailored in wide red and
cream striped silk faille, which is then scooped up towards the

back in a mass of pleats over the matching petticoat.[9] It would probably have been worn with a roll of padding at the back, sometimes called the *Cul de Paris* or the Paris Arse. When in the early 1800s this form of bustle fell out of use, a sausage of covered padding became popular, and in France a version called the frisk was worn on the outside, making what was recognizable as underwear saucily on show. Bustles of the later nineteenth century took the pleats and padded-out fabric further back still, leaving the figure looking elegantly streamlined from the front but elaborately exaggerated at the back. The cushioned bustle accentuates the tilt of the bottom and was at first embellished with vividly contrasting linings, lace and large satin and velvet bows before styles became more tailored. Thesander mentions that the rustle the silken skirts made in motion led to the onomatopoeic term 'frou-frou'.[10] In the 1850s and '60s the bustle was carried low, and fanned out to form a train.

Bustles required a longer and therefore more restrictive boned corset, sometimes referred to as the S-bend, whose shape could be most easily appreciated from the side. Its more extreme high-fashion examples relied on a steel frame, patented by an American, Alexander Douglas, in 1857. It was held in place by strapping that reached down below the knee, creating an effect for the wearer similar to the modern pencil skirt. Attention is drawn to the buttocks, with the wearer unable to move about freely except in small geisha-like steps. Sitting down could create severe difficulties. A contributor to the *Boston Medical and Surgical Journal* in 1888 expressed his contempt for the bustle:

> The woman in a bustle can never sit down in a natural position. It is absolutely impossible for her to rest her back against the back of any seat of ordinary construction. I have no doubt some of the severe backaches in women whose duties keep them seated all day are, due to, or at least aggravated by, this disability.[11]

A woman so dressed found it easier to remain standing in public, or risked a most inelegant descent, rather in the manner of how a fish might try to sit.

The 1950s pencil skirt was streamlined without the bustling swags. It allowed for the now-familiar gesture of sliding a hand under the buttocks to smooth the cloth before sitting down. On the one hand this merely stops a skirt from creasing and riding up, but on the other it can be an understated gesture of refined seduction. In the Benjamin Black novel *A Death in Summer* (2011), the pathologist Quirke muses on this apparently unconscious female habit: 'Francoise came back and took her place opposite him again – he always found stirring that way women had of sweeping a hand under their bottoms to smooth their skirts when they sat down.'[12] The novel is set in mid-1950s Dublin, and this elegant habit is now far less common, associated with a time when it was more important to avoid wrinkling one's clothing. Today's padded shapewear knickers might be described as a modern-day version of the bustle, but are accompanied by less risk to health and comfort. Men's silhouettes can similarly be firmed with Lycra undervests, whole body suits that reduce the waist and broaden the shoulder, and underpants that enhance the genitals can provide a more rounded muscular rump. The latter are more often discreetly advertised, though with names such as the Rear Riser and the Butt Booster their purpose seems clear.

Although the crinolette bustle – with a similar framework to a crinoline but worn at the back – inhibited an easy gait, necessitating a trembling motion of the hips, the most limiting skirt style of all is perhaps the narrow-hemmed hobble skirt, which came into fashion for a few years prior to the outbreak of the First World War. Just as women seemed to be gaining more independence, easy physical movement was made practically impossible. It was claimed that French couturier Paul Poiret was the source of this new shape. One story suggests that the design had been first thought up to flatter an actor's stationary pose beside a pillar on stage, to accentuate the curve of female hip and rump. Another notion is that after the first trip by a female passenger in an aeroplane, American Edith Ogilby Berg had tied her skirts together at the ankle to keep them from blowing up in the wind, and that her resulting gait had inspired the trend. In order to achieve the hobbled effect, a woman had either to bind her knees together or wear a form of shackles at her ankles, as otherwise the narrow skirt would have torn apart at the seams. Both designers Jeanne Paquin and Lucile attempted to make the skirt less restrictive by inserting hidden pleats, though even so it remained a fleeting high-fashion fad and the impression it made of frivolity was out of keeping with the war. However, the distinctive impression it made was not forgotten and became more practically achievable with the advent of stretch Lycra-based fabrics that allow sufficient movement while providing their own form of corseting. The designer Vivienne Westwood, renowned for her mini-crini hooped miniskirt (1985), also produced variants of the bustle and hobble skirt. Worn over bottom-contouring shapewear, the silhouettes of the past were recreated.

The exquisite miniature 'Pandora' fashion dolls of the eighteenth century were not children's toys but made to allow the rich to see the newest fashions up close, in detail. Marie Antoinette could sample Rose Bertin's revolutionary shepherdess styles and see how little petticoat was required compared to the previous cumbersome court gowns. Her dresses were found shocking because to a contemporary eye the wearer appeared to be wearing nothing but her underwear. Following the Reign of Terror, during the French Directory (1759–99) some fashionable women of means in Paris adopted a decadent style of dress so flimsy and transparent that undergarments were not worn at all. These Merveilleuses, or marvellous women, left off their stays and underskirts altogether, to show off transparent muslin shift dresses to even more shockingly naked effect. Many wore a chemise beneath their low-cut dresses, but Empress Josephine is said to have preferred not to wear any underclothing at all, and only admitted to owning three pairs of drawers, for exceptional circumstances. Underskirts were reintroduced, but whereas before they had been attached to a corseted bodice, by the mid-1830s a corset was more often separate, with cotton or linen covering its structure. It was only later that the petticoat as we know it came into existence, worn completely hidden under the outer skirt.

Paul Poiret, in the first decades of the twentieth century, is sometimes said to have banished the corset, but here in his best modest manner he claims that his job was merely to anticipate the need for change demanded by his customers:

> I know that you think me a king of fashion. It is
> what your newspapers call me, and it is thus that
> I am received, honoured and fêted everywhere by
> great multitudes of people . . . We are not capricious
> despots such as wake up one fine day, decide upon
> a change in habits, abolish a neckline, or puff out a
> sleeve. We are neither arbiters nor dictators. Rather
> we are to be thought of as the blindly obedient servants
> of woman, who, for her part, is always enamoured of
> change and athirst for novelty. It is our role, and our
> duty, to be on the watch for the moment at which she
> becomes bored with what she is wearing, that we may
> suggest at the right instant (*à point nommé*) something
> else which will meet her tastes and needs. It is therefore
> with a pair of antennae and not with a rod of iron that
> I come before you, and it is not as a master that I speak,
> but as a slave, a slave, though, who must divine your
> innermost thoughts.[13]

Poiret may be flattering his audience, but the art historian Quentin Bell is right to remind us that no single individual can ever be responsible for seismic changes in politics or, for that matter, clothing fashion. Bell asks whether someone of wealth and power can ordain a new fashion, and gives us as an example Elizaveta Petrovna, empress of Russia (r. 1741–62). She happened to have an uncommonly fine pair of legs in a period when it was the fashion to keep legs hidden. Despite despotic political power she still felt the need to follow the fashions dictates of Paris or risk seeming provincial. Her solution was to concoct circumstances that would give her the opportunity to show off her attributes without seeming unfashionable: she decided to make her courtiers cross-dress at her regular soirées:

> The *metamorphose* was an occasion when the sexes
> exchanged clothes, as in the Saturnalia of the
> Romans . . . Evening after evening the dowagers
> of the Imperial Court (most of whom of course
> had legs which had better have remained hid) had
> to expose their deficiencies to the public. Evening
> after evening elderly ambassadors and sedate
> administrators had to struggle with hoops and
> panniers, stays and petticoats.[14]

Quentin Bell insists that as an autocrat of Russia she would have had the power to enforce a change in what people wore in order to display her legs as a woman, but, since covered legs were 'in' for women at that time, she knew this would not be possible without seeming maladroit, even ugly, in the eyes of the wider fashionable world.

Underwear may go largely unseen, but it travels in and out of fashion and sometimes more so than outer clothing in its supporting role. However, in museums original historic underwear is rarely on display since if it survives at all it tends to be in a fragile condition. When outer clothing is shown it is usually worn over replica corsets and petticoats.

You might argue that 7,000 years ago underwear was the only form of clothing, in the form of loincloths worn for protection. Even then there might have been those who had more of an eye for selecting the most suitable leather, choosing a softer, better cured and more becoming pelt and perhaps learning to line it with fur for added warmth or with moss to make it more absorbent for menstruation. Such items rarely grace our museums today, having rotted away millennia ago, but there is evidence to be found in remaining Indigenous customs of the inherent aesthetic sensibility of human beings. Thus the distant past demonstrates not only the wonder of cave drawings and tool making, but clothing too, chosen, manufactured and worn sometimes with self-conscious pride.

Underwear may seem to play a merely supporting role to the prevailing fashions, sometimes at the expense of great discomfort and even pain for both sexes; the sixteenth-century philosopher Michel de Montaigne, for instance, appeared puzzled by what he saw as the foolish desire for a fashionable silhouette over practical comfort: 'To get a slim body, Spanish style, what torture do they not endure, tight-laced and braced, until they suffer great gashes in their sides, right to the live flesh – yes sometimes even until they die of it?'[15]

The fundamental bodily form of a species alters very little, but the structure of our underwear has come to emphasize and at other times downplay particular physical characteristics. There have been times when a large bottom and breasts combined with a small waist were de rigueur, and others when for women in particular a prepubescent figure would have seemed the most beautiful form.

Men's need to express strength has, historically speaking, limited the range of options open to them, certainly after the French Revolutionary period when men uniformly began to wear predominantly dark and similarly sober clothing. Exceptions are scarce and tend to be short-lived, such as the much-lampooned Incroyables – corseted, drenched in scent, peering through their monocles at the post-French Revolutionary world – or perhaps the golf-playing boyish young men who, after the First World War, appeared slight and cute in pastel-hued exaggerated plus

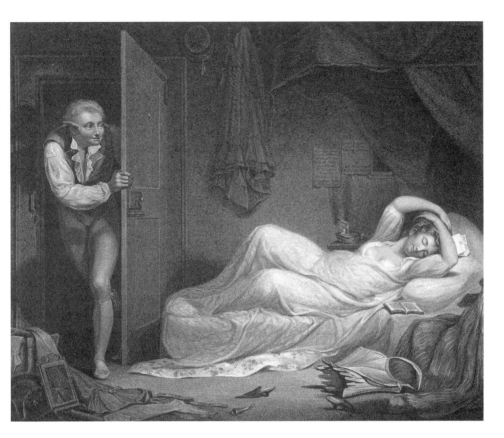

Thomas Gaugain, after James Northcote, *The Wanton in Her Bed Chamber*, from the series 'Diligence and Dissipation', 1796–7, engraving. In the bottom right corner a corset has been discarded.

fours and oversized golfing caps, looking as though they must once have belonged to a far larger man, possibly to their fathers. Such anomalies are associated at times with immorality and also with unmanly feebleness, their equally skittish female counterparts received with less disapproval. When fashion goes to extremes, such as with the Merveilleuses in their transparent knickerless muslin dresses, they are found amusingly feminine or arguably vulgar, whereas a man is more often seen as eccentric and possibly deviant.

Extremes of silhouette have been achieved by the increasing efficacy of corsets, girdles and modern foundation and shapewear. The popularity of the film *Bridget Jones's Diary* (dir. Sharon Maguire, 2001), in which the heroine wears oversized bottom-firming support knickers for her date with publisher Daniel

Cleaver, played by Hugh Grant, made it seem witty rather than sad to wear such items, causing sales to rocket. Since the 1960s, restrictive underwear had been considered out of the question for the younger woman, but then outer clothing got tighter and more revealing, while people got fatter. Bridget's chutzpah wins the day. The corset was an essential feature of a Victorian woman's life from puberty and sometimes earlier still. Not to wear one was to risk appearing lax and immoral. The average Victorian corset is calculated to have exerted a force of 9.5 kilograms (21 lb) on the internal organs, and fashionable tight-lacing cranked that up to as much as 40 kilograms (88 lb).[16]

The call for modesty tends to lead to subtler and more underhand ways of allowing particular zones of the body to attract attention, albeit undercover. The farthingale-hooped petticoat with its increasingly restrictive stomacher, for example, as the dress historian Alison Carter points out, resulted in references to fertility moving from the belly to the hips.[17] This took attention away from the potential damage wrought by restrictive corseting to the inner organs and focused on the concept of child-bearing hips: 'Her mydle braced in, as small as a wande . . . A bumbe lyke a barrell, with whoops at the skyrte.'[18]

There are regional preferences and differences in clothing fashion between town and rural life. In sheep-farming Wales, for example, a belief grew up in the intrinsic goodness of wool, for keeping a baby warm in a flannel binder or for protecting a miner working hundreds of metres below the ground in long-legged flannel drawers. Flannel has been described as the original personal protective equipment (PPE), because of its ability to offer protection from germs and to absorb moisture.[19] In a memoir of the 1930s and '40s, the everyday importance of wool flannel underwear is recorded:

> You'd come home on a wash day and see lines and
> lines of Welsh Flannel undershirts and long johns
> and drawers all flapping in the wind. The copperworks

wasn't dirty like the collieries were but it was sweaty work and you needed the Welsh Flannel to absorb the perspiration.[20]

Many of the most exaggerated and uncomfortable foundation garments were only worn by those who could afford to live a relatively leisurely life, the eighteenth-century panier underskirt that was largely confined to court life a case in point. There are also perhaps national preferences, with the historian Marilyn Yalom suggesting that France, the centre of high fashion, has long maintained a partiality for greater slimness in women, whereas Germanic countries tend to prefer the fuller figure, 'propped up by heavy corsetry'.[21] Their relative cuisines would seem to bear this out.

Every generation has attempted to accommodate particular body shapes to the prevailing fashion, and this can apply even to those who consider themselves to have very little interest in such sartorial adjustments. Fashion can influence our choices by stealth. Moreover, trends that seem to imply greater modesty, for instance, may be merely a nuance that works against any such tendency. Such was the function of the late eighteenth-century fine muslin *fichu* shawl, worn crossed in front and purporting to mask the breasts, but in practice often allowing a dress to be cut so low that the nipples could show through the fine cloth, as if by accident. Apart from rare exceptions such as with the Incroyables, it was women who tended to take the blame for such vanities. An eighteenth-century pamphlet, with the splendidly lengthy title 'The Degradation of the Human Race through the Use of the Whalebone Corset. A Work in which One Demonstrates That It Is to Go against the Laws of Nature, to Increase Depopulation and Bastardize Man [that is, women], So to Speak, When One Submits Him [that is, her] to Torture from the First Moments of His [her] Existence, under the Pretext of Forming Him [her]', by French Cavalry officer Jacques Bonnaud, lambasted both the corset and crinoline.[22]

John Leighton, writing as Luke Limner, describes the crinoline corset combination as 'a more summary and terrible manner than any perversion of clothing yet devised', and further describes its victims as 'destroyed by hoops and crinoline . . . [with] scars from burns, and pains from broken limbs, [which] to this day bear testimony'.[23] Leighton criticizes both the particular fashion as exhibiting 'not only an egregious absurdity of conception and of figure, but an alternate depravity of taste and purpose', and also attacks fashion in general as 'a gross imposition upon mankind'.[24] Such vituperative language can be seductive, but the extremes of fashion involving some discomfort and even longer-term disfigurement is hardly unusual when there are individuals with sufficient money and leisure wishing to entertain themselves with novelty. You only have to consider some modern-day women's shoes with cripplingly pointed toes, toppling stilettos and high-wedge heels. The crinoline was a craze that like all such exaggerations was temporary, and yet the splendid impracticality of its form has ensured it sufficient influence to crop up again from time to time. The corset has been blamed for more than 97 'diseases', including consumption, epilepsy and even the birth of ugly children, though there is little evidence that not wearing corsets ensures the production of pretty ones.[25]

The attention given to women's love of fashion inevitably seeks to place men in a more respect-worthy position, looking on wisely with indulgent wry affection and possibly hidden contempt. As the Industrial Revolution created vast wealth among a small but growing sector of society in the West, it was not that men eschewed all interest in the detail of clothing, including their underwear. After all, if you eat well and do little physical exercise, there may be a need for corsets and restraining vests to flatter the flab of economic success. The greater extremes of women's corsetry tended to be worn only for special, social occasions; male constraints were generally designed to be more comfortable, and were more hidden away. One notion is that because men have been more restrained in their attempts to fashion their body shape, therefore this kept 'men's underwear plain and functional [and which] could secure male bodies as a bulwark against unrestrained sexuality'.[26] Certainly there has been less effort until recently to make such male corsets attractive rather than merely functional.

Men's underwear has become less of a private matter, with more attention given to whether or not it is flattering and allowing for more individual choice. This was less common in the nineteenth century with the pressure on men to express their dominance in part through a disinterest in fashion, though one should not forget the elaborate male fashions of the sixteenth century, say, when the exquisitely corseted, ostentatiously presented torso was no less important than it was for women of high status. Men's underwear has, for the majority, been chosen for its practical merits and worn until it falls apart. Handkerchiefs, socks and sensible underwear are still customarily considered the most acceptable presents for brothers, fathers, husbands and sons, though it would be unusual for a male friend to give another such items.

With gender roles in a state of flux in the West, changing attitudes are reflected in our underwear, so that flimsier, more 'feminine' fabrics are available for men's underpants, and women can find more masculine styles such as boxers and Y-fronts in thicker fabrics. When Patrick Mauriès describes there being a direct line 'from Beau Brummell and the original dandies of the Regency era, who had also been a major influence on the Bright Young Things', to the style of Mr Fish in the 1960s and Vivienne Westwood in the '80s, we find a common use of luxury fabrics and range of designs and colours appearing on the catwalk.[27]

Today the greater availability of surgical alterations means that underwear also has to accommodate the flux of bodily fashion, one might say from beneath, for the liposuctioned, silicone gel-implanted, potentially perfected body. It has become big business to surgically augment or reduce the body, the commercial viability of cosmetic plastic surgery working rather like the tide of interior design fashions, with builders being paid to double-glaze a house and then in due course to alleviate the problem of condensation it has brought about. Undergarments are designed to fit the prevailing bodily ideal and when you do not possess that ideal then remedial measures must be sought.

Like Superman in his red over-underpants, underclothing is sometimes deliberately on show. In the children's novels by Dav Pilkey following the adventures of Captain Underpants (1997–), a nasty school principal transforms into his jolly alter ego Captain Underpants, in white Y-front briefs and a red cape with polka dots, at the sound of snapping fingers. As a superhero he possesses 'wedgie power', the ability to generate an unlimited amount of underwear from out of his waistband.

When underpants are worn on their own they can function as suggestive items, perhaps echo a boxer's or weight-lifter's posing pouch, but in an increasingly sexually aware age, snug, high-cut, low hipster briefs tend to be advertised coyly, obliquely referencing what is veiled but unseen. The codpiece of the Renaissance period appears to demand greater attention but had more to do with power and status among men than the more blatant sexual suggestiveness of the 1990s and 2000s. An unspoken function of men's underpants is to constrain an erection, an involuntary bodily response that might otherwise be embarrassing.

In a well-known advertising campaign from the early 1990s, underwear is used to promote outer clothing. The model Nick Kamen, in the television advert, presents as a clean-cut young man who strips off his Levi 501 jeans and T-shirt in a 1950s-style launderette to Marvin Gaye's 'I Heard It Through the Grapevine'.[28] He is left in nothing but his white cotton boxers. The campaign might be said to appeal to both sexes by reversing the traditional focus of the male gaze. The launderette seems alive with tension and curiosity. We witness that he is aware of the attention of the various women and an older, overweight man, who are all closely observing him. In contrast, a year later

Jakob Seisenegger, *Emperor Charles V*, 1532, oil on canvas.

in an advert for Calvin Klein underpants, Marky Mark (Mark Wahlberg) has a far more menacing rapper-style presence. Both adverts might be described as erotic or homoerotic, in that both men demand our appreciation, and what we recall is the focus on their underwear.

Is the sometime impression of the past as a more sexually innocent time true when it comes to underwear? It hardly seems likely that there was less awareness of another's beauty and desirability in previous eras. To career back into the ancient past, when a vast Persian army sent scouts to spy on Spartan soldiers guarding the pass of Thermopylae in 480 BCE, they reported that the enemy had almost no armour or protective clothing of any kind. The Spartans would have been wearing a loincloth or a short scarlet chiton tunic, and possibly a himation cloak. There they sat oiling and combing each other's long hair. Did their manner seem reassuringly effeminate or far too relaxed not to seem suspicious to the scouts? Plutarch warned with terrifying understatement that 'they were the only men in the world for whom war brought a respite in the training for war.'[29] Their long hair was the sign of being a free man and to comb their hair was to assert their autonomy. Despite being vastly outnumbered, the Spartans managed to hold the enemy off for many days; minimal loincloth clothing to resist a magnificently kitted-out Persian force. My schoolgirl imagination gloried in the spectacle they conjured: beauty against brute force.

The Japanese kimono derives from the upper-class *kosode*, which was originally worn unseen, as an undergarment. As the samurai warriors lost power they nonetheless continued to value the cleanliness of their underwear as a point of pride. Ernest Satow, who worked as a British diplomat in Japan in various roles between 1861 and 1900, was astonished to witness a travel-weary samurai undressing to wash himself by the roadside. When he removed his dusty outerwear, his impeccable white underclothing was revealed.[30] This was at a time when the status of the samurai was waning, but pride remained in what could not be seen, as for instance, in the unseen mechanism of a watch, which no one usually bothers to examine, but that should be kept clean and well-maintained. It is akin to the finest, most delicate lingerie, where for the best lacemakers their skill was confirmed by the underside of their work, which had to be just as perfect as its outside, even though few would ever have noticed if it wasn't.

Clothing conceals us but how we wear it can also reveal us more profoundly. Alison Lurie wonders whether, for example, male cross-dressers, in their clothing choices, 'seem to imitate the most vulgar and unattractive sort of female dress, as if in a spirit of deliberate and hostile parody'.[31] Does the exaggerated style of some female impersonators suggest hostility, even if this tendency has become less pronounced in societies where gender freedoms are greater? It is notable that when women appear in drag the connotations are rather different. Female comics finger their groins and belch and fart – the comics Dawn French and Jennifer Saunders dressed in sweaty fat suits and string vests to

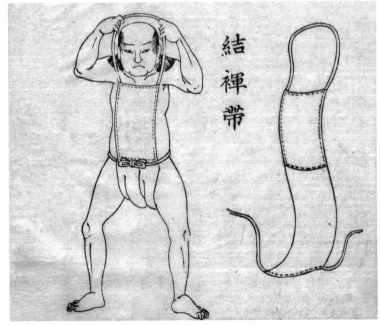

Samurai putting on a *fundoshi* (loincloth), woodblock print from Murai Masahiro, *Banki Yoriaku: Hi Ko Ken* (The Illustrated Essential Horseman: How to Put on Armour Unassisted), 1735; this edn 1837.

portray old blokes in their sketch show *French and Saunders*. It is notable that men exaggerate female sexiness when portraying women, whereas females playing men have to be gross before it seems they can amuse us. Currently greater openness about bisexuality has exposed just how much historic male power has affected our attitudes to clothing. Gender diversity issues around fashion – such as the need for non-binary underwear by brands such as Urbody that cater for a wide range of gender identities – are currently widely under discussion.

Long johns, or combinations, absented men for a long period from any consideration of underwear, just as their dark outer clothing avoided that of outerwear fashion. For women in the West underwear as outerwear continued to make an appearance, though often by stealth. The number and variety of petticoats was one such liminal area of dress, concerning what might or might not be glimpsed, for example along the hem. After Elizabeth Bennet tramps through the wet fields to visit her sister Jane in *Pride and Prejudice*, the edges of her petticoats become soaked in mud. She is met with disdain by the two Bingley sisters, who complain to Darcy about her 'most country-town indifference to decorum'. He, on the other hand, notices again Elizabeth's 'fine eyes', a case of dirty linen confirming an attraction.[32]

Whether lace was hand- or machine-made could single a woman out for admiration or derision. Once bras were widely available, a separate straight-cut or more fitted slip, from shoulder to hem, helped make clothing hang as it should. As modern textiles became available, slips could also help avoid static cling. Some women continued to wear their corsets, which at least could be made more comfortable with the addition of elasticated panels, though more flexible nylon boning continued. Indeed, the post-Second World War New Look silhouette introduced by Dior relied on feather boning and elastic to create its distinctive hourglass shape. Between 1948 and 1958 corset sales doubled.

It was once considered coarse for your underclothing to be on show, and the slip petticoat helped avoid aspects of this problem. However, the widely circulated photograph in 1980 of Diana Spencer, prior to her engagement to Prince Charles, where the outline of her legs is seen through an unlined summer skirt, received a generally positive response. It might have made quite a different impression had she not been nineteen years old when the photograph was taken, and had less attractive legs.

Swim- or sportswear is now often worn as underwear, much of which has become indistinguishable from outer clothing. The two-piece close-fitting jersey body adopted by the French acrobat Jules Léotard in the nineteenth century eventually transmogrified into the fitted swimming costume and one-piece body stocking of the twentieth.[33] Léotard had worn the *maillot*, which subsequently became worn by circus strongmen and gymnasts.

Early swimming costumes, baggy and frilled and made from fabrics that soaked up the water, were nonetheless the beginnings of women's sportswear. One might argue that the fact that they were often worn with stockings and corsets looks forward

ules Léotard,
. 1865.

to modern times, when clothing initially designed as under- or swimwear has been adapted into outer clothing. Post-Second World War, in the rush to re-establish family life, mothers were encouraged to produce homemade swimsuits for their children. Hand-knitted, often in mercerized cotton or even left-over woollen yarn, the clothing stretched considerably when wet. Moreover the outfits were extremely slow to dry out and as itchy and flabby as a wet nappy. This proof of maternal affection was not always welcome.

The jersey material that a young Coco Chanel introduced into women's fashion in the 1910s and '20s had previously been used only for male sportswear. Employed for high fashion clothing, and when made into swimming costumes, it freed women from the cumbersome frocks and bloomers that had previously been all that was available. The 1912 Olympics was the first major public event in which women wore swimwear similar to men's, with briefs worn beneath fine jersey costumes for both genders, and with no corsetry at all. The women's breasts became only too evident once the costumes were wet. The Olympic suits were intended to help the swimmers move easily through the water, but though the effect of transparency was noticed, the nature of elite sport meant they were protected to an extent from disapproval.

Rudi Gernreich, an Austrian designer of the 1960s, must have been aware of those brave female Olympians of forty years before. He was the first to produce swimsuits for the general public without a built-in bra-shelf, ripping out the boning and wiring that had made American swimsuits in the 1950s effectively seagoing corsets.[34] His monokini, a garment that wholly exposed the chest with straps running between the breasts to around the neck, is blatantly provocative, reminiscent of an ancient Egyptian upper-class fashion. Unsurprisingly there was a limited take-up. It was easier perhaps to wear a bikini and remove the top when stationary. Gernreich also designed some of the first male thong briefs.

Men had continued to wear combination garments as underwear, with relatively minor adjustments such as a summer option that had shorter sleeves and legs. Younger men often preferred the greater flexibility of wearing two-piece garments and advertisements for 'improvements' to male and female underwear became widespread in national newspapers rather than tucked away on the back pages of women's magazines. We all may be prey at times to the temptation of a small fashion pick-me-up, but a man is even today perhaps less likely than a woman to search for a nice new pair of underpants. Lingerie is designed to draw women in, offering a sense of decadent frippery in a perhaps sensible, utilitarian life, whereas for many men choosing the right underpants remains a largely practical business.

Bernice Kopple, photograph used in article 'Bonny Scot Beach Girl', Australia, 1950s.

The string vest was invented by Norwegian Henrik Brun in 1933, derived from a fishing net, with the Brynje brand promoting it as keeping you 'warm, dry and strong'. It became popular in Britain, worn by builders and miners, and the cartoon character Andy Capp (1950s–). The BBC's comedy character Rab C. Nesbitt (played by Gregor Fisher, late 1980s) wore a grubby string vest with his signature threadbare pinstripe suit.[35] In the twentieth century, when in some countries homosexuality was no longer illegal, what had been solely sports or work wear for manual labour was appropriated by the gay community. In Australia in the mid-1980s Chesty Bond sleeveless singlets became an ironic – and body revealing – fashion statement for gay men. In the club scene well-developed 'Muscle Mary' men started wearing boxer shorts and exercise Lycra as outerwear, a mode of dress rapidly taken up by heterosexual men too.[36] String vests call to mind Madonna's clothing in *Desperately Seeking Susan* (dir. Susan Seidelman, 1985) and archetypal punk figures such as Siouxsie Sioux in a Vivienne Westwood string vest and masculine army-style boots. The string vest is an example of underwear becoming outerwear that served to blur distinctions between male and female fashion.

A delicate, embroidered Elizabethan undershift, with only the edges visible, was capable of being as suggestive and resonant of a state of undress as, say, a Westwood bra worn over rather than under a sweatshirt in 1982. It compared in shock value with the 1990s trend for underpants showing above low-slung 'sagging' trousers, a street fashion among younger men of colour dating from the late 1980s and popularized by American hip-hop and specifically rap artists. Some claim it was derived from a prison-style get-up, as if the guards had taken away your belt. Others suggest the practice is intended to signify sexual preference, but whatever the case, it was not a look that favoured any but a young, lean body. Initially it was important to display the up-market brand of your underpants, though it soon extended to any makes, all intended to reveal what was more usually considered private. In a study of attitudes to sagging in Zambia, which was instigated to investigate why the fashion had become so popular there, the authors asserted that underwear should be 'washed in private, put out to dry in private, worn in private and kept as private clothing'.[37] One of their findings was that the practice seemed only to occur among unmarried men; there is a suggestion not only that they might not be looking to attract women and further that such men might not always launder their underpants sufficiently, implying that the exposed fabric might show signs of excrement. Although some of the females interviewed had only minor criticisms to make, and some positively enjoyed the carefree attitude that accompanied the style, the study nonetheless recommended that country-wide measures should be taken against a heinous and corrupting habit.

It has always been difficult to legislate against fashion, trends tending to run their course whatever law is passed. Objecting to a particular feature usually has the effect of making it stay in fashion all the longer. Perhaps one of the reasons for widespread disapproval of sagging is because it is young male urban fashion, and therefore seen as dangerous. As in the Zambian study, those of a certain age have made attempts to enforce modern sumptuary prohibitions. An example of this prejudice involved the mayor of Pikeville, Tennessee, who argued in 2014 that '8 out of 10 saggers' suffered from premature ejaculation. Perhaps the mayor should have been slow to rely on the evidence of a Dr Mansbach of the National American Medical Association (NAMA), particularly on April Fool's Day. Neither Mansbach nor NAMA exist.[38] It has moreover been suggested that sagging creates an improper gait. Concerns about others' gait is often given as a reason for disapproving of new fashions, as with corsets, crinolines, bustles and hobble skirts. Mary Sue Rich of Ocala, Florida, claimed that she was 'tired of looking at young men's underwear' and managed to lobby her council into passing a law against the practice in July 2014, with fines of up to $500 or prison time. She revealed what fuelled her disquiet: 'I would wager 9 out of 10 of them don't have jobs.'[39] It seems that it is not so much the display of underwear or bottom cleft, but that the fashion is enjoyed by the young, unemployed and often those of colour. Part of the point of youthful street style is to create such unease. Exposing one's underwear functions as a form of private membership.[40]

In contrast, rather than exposing her underwear, Jennifer Beals in *Flashdance* (dir. Adrian Lyne, 1983) manages to remove her bra from underneath a sweatshirt without taking the sweatshirt off first. This modest form of striptease is seductive because the item remains unseen until it has discreetly left the body. When a skirt is unwittingly caught up in a pair of underpants, or male flies are left undone, the embarrassment may reverberate in one's memory. We relive the times when we suddenly become aware of a state of undress that others have seen. If yesterday's underpants happen to fall from the bottom of a trouser leg while in company, it can also be embarrassing, particularly as it might suggest a less than wholly fragrant domestic life. Somehow women seem to feel these minor disgraces more than men, and in the history of underwear and clothing in general, women continue to be more easily ashamed about how they are seen.

In post-Second World War Japan, young women were beginning to imitate the way American women dressed, in particular by wearing bras. In the mines, for example, where men had often worn nothing at all, women had customarily had their breasts uncovered in the humid heat below ground, their lower half either naked or protected by an apron-like cloth or *makubeko* tied around the waist.[41] Wearing Western-style underwear became a symbol of adapting to a changing society.

When Western-style female outer clothing is worn covered up and unseen in public places, such as under the burka in Saudi Arabia, it becomes in one sense a form of underwear, and when revealed indoors represents a privileged view that is private and perhaps intimate. In contrast, when the slip, onesie or pyjamas are worn as casual outerwear, it can look wrong, misplaced, even grubby, and the more public the place it is seen the more incongruous.

Second-hand utilitarian underwear, particularly underpants, are difficult to sell in charity shops, but some previously worn underclothing with a designer label or made from more luxurious fabrics remains sought after. Perhaps found in a vintage store and priced high, such items are often purchased as outerwear. Lingerie is associated with luxury and private sensuality. The fashion for wearing silky shorts over tights was initially derived from practical athletic wear and thereby potentially attaches to the wearer the idea of a fit body but also allows private luxury clothing to be seen in public. Male rock stars have underwear thrown at them on stage or sent in the post to express their fans' devotion. Johnny Flynn, in his role as a folk musician, mentions that he once had a pair of underpants thrown at him on stage, only for the woman to return later, a little sheepishly, to ask for them back, 'because she hadn't packed anything else for the weekend'.[42]

It seems that this form of expressing admiration is mainly female, offering up their most intimate clothing as a ritual sacrifice as if in hope of at least their underpants coming into contact with musician they admire.

One might think it would make more sense if female rock stars sometimes had Y-fronts thrown at them. Do male performers, in a climate of changing gender roles, have high-end briefs and boxer shorts tossed onto the stage from admirers of whatever identity? In a period of non-binary sensitivity perhaps there needs to be a wider range of underwear considered for such offerings.

In couture fashion as in ballet dancers' stage costumes, sometimes models are sewn into their clothing in order to achieve the best rumple-free effect. When it is important for a skirt to move with the wearer then loose pantaloons may be sewn into a dress and attached at the hem. A liquid Yves St Laurent evening dress, named Scheherazade to suggest the veils of an imaginary harem, has a skirt 'sewn to knickers so it would move attractively when worn'.[43] Similarly, though many may prefer to avoid wearing corsetry today, to achieve an impeccable fit boning can be sewn into a garment instead, extending from bust to waist or further to encase the hips. A good tailor understands the careful use of padding and corsetry restraints in order to achieve a smooth silhouette that is designed to avoid unsightly bulges.

The slip, sometimes made with an inbuilt bra, became the modern-day slim-cut petticoat, and when it came to be made in nylon jersey it had the advantage of being stretchy and thus able to fit closely without feeling overly restrictive. It should not be confused with its false friend in French, where *le slip* refers to underpants alone, and moreover can be a euphemism for incontinence pads. The slip and half-slip help the way outer clothing looks. Lately such slips have become less widely available, and in cheaper clothing linings are left out altogether, as a cost-cutting measure.[44] Consequently too much is revealed as outer fabric sticks to the clammy flesh beneath. The slip remains an echo of more elaborate lingerie, in its lace trimmings, satin shoulder straps and tiny bows. Examples from past generations are valued for their pretty elaborations as much as any practicality. On their own they have been worn as daring minimal evening wear. We may strive to make connections in the design and use of clothing through history, but one has to be wary. Vivienne Westwood is sometimes said to have been the originator of underwear as outerwear but would herself have recognized the existence of a punk movement that pre-dated and was independent of her designs, not to mention the audacities of the Merveilleuses.

Underwear becoming outerwear affects how clothing feels on our bodies, and it follows that it alters the way we behave. It can make people move differently and affects how they are perceived. We are accustomed to underwear being unseen, so to put it centre stage can give a sense of greater freedom or daring. It might make a person feel enjoyably shocking, observed by those who simply cannot grasp that it is fashion at work and look on in consternation. It is possible to see fashion as a never-ending series of similarities and dissimilarities that dress us up and down perpetually, like a series of cut-out paper dolls through history. The fashion writer Patrick Mauriès rightly questions this notion of the clothes we wear, implying that dress alone cannot define us. He asks us to question if it is 'legitimate to wonder whether the "modesty" or "reserve" that were thought to be "natural" in women . . . [was] not so much the cause as the effect of the tightly corseted garments imposed by fashion, of the gestures they made necessary'.[45]

Corset shop, Boulevard de Strasbourg, Paris, 1912.

5
Fabric and Fit

D esign may help draw attention to the body, but our early childhood impression of clothing is grounded in the materials used, whether they are soft or warm enough or perhaps cool enough and whether we are held fast or able to stretch and move about. It is only later that we come to consider whether fabric is fine enough to accentuate or flatter or disguise the body beneath. It may be comfortably worn from many washes or elegantly tailored and deliberately restrictive, heightening a sense of our presence in the world.

There is an intimate connection between cloth and clothing. There are times when to dress alike, uniformly, for a corps de ballet or to demonstrate for a cause perhaps, means that we choose to be part of a greater whole. Do we have such feelings about our underwear? For many, even the poorest of the poor, clothing tends to be the most significant and personal aspect of our possessions, and this is true even when it goes unseen. Small accommodations of dress can make our clothing seem more personal, such as a name embroidered on the hem of linen drawers, a darn neatly made, a stain or tear or missing button whose story we recall – even the imposed name tags on items of school uniform, perhaps sewn in place by a mother before a child is sent off to school.

In an age of cheap clothing for all in the affluent West, it is difficult to imagine what it might be like to have a much more limited wardrobe, when every item of a person's possessions must be acutely known to them. Imagine if you possessed only one change of underclothing, say. Or that you were a newly recruited member of the women's Russian Battalion of Death in the Second World War, and were given underwear for the first time in your life. Many can recall the prospect of school holidays after weeks of wearing uniform, and the sense of freedom in setting aside heavy, fleece-lined over-knickers – sometimes referred to as 'navy blue stinkers' – for a pair of pastel-coloured or patterned briefs. Like the relation between vibrantly coloured cotton saris and the individual itinerant tribal women in India who wear them, how we feel about what we wear is peculiar to each and every one of us.[1] In some respects this seems particularly true in relation to our underwear, and all the more so when resources are limited. How we feel may be influenced by what we know or think we know about what others are wearing, but because of the largely private aspect of underwear our judgements remain tentative. We rarely discuss and compare views on our underclothing, unlike our attitudes to outer clothing. Generally speaking, underwear is something we seldom chat about. Interrogating preferences for this or that design or choice of fabric, even among the serious-minded, can easily provoke responses of the nudge nudge (wink wink) variety. It is hard to speak about such an aspect of dress without it seeming silly or too irritatingly subjective.

Yet underwear can feel important, even if it is generally kept private, or if we have to pretend to find it all a jolly but foolish business. When shops began to adopt communal fitting rooms in the 1960s, for example, it meant that many found themselves donning their best matching underwear before facing the ordeal, just in case. Women might not wish to be seen by others in their more capacious period underpants, although recent advertisements for both menstrual and incontinence underwear are attempting to change this, suggesting that both can be flattering and fashionable and not something we should be at all embarrassed about. Anecdotally, men appear to experience less anxiety about being seen stripped down, although now that there is more variety in what is available to them, this may become less true.

The prospect of non-segregated facilities in gym, pool and retail outlets has some preferring to order clothing from the Internet in order to avoid the challenges of shared fitting rooms. Underpants arrive in the post, in several possible sizes perhaps, each with its uninviting, crackly hygiene tape to protect the gusset. One solution might be, for such intimate shopping at least, the possibility of virtual trying-on. Microsoft's Kinect sensor has the potential to not only show us on-screen clothing on a virtual human of our approximate size, but to read and incorporate the particular 3D contours of every individual, non-standard lumps, bumps and all. Presumably then underwear could not only conform to our measurements but include all the minutiae of design preferences. In the past, before the Industrial Revolution, handmade underwear for those of sufficient means would have been made to fit, but with the increasing speed of computerized machinery, clothing, in theory at least, can now be available to suit precise individual requirements with little delay. Yet this effort might still fail to satisfy a customer, who even if they have received samples of the cloth to be used will still not have had the chance to feel the perfectly sized garment on their person, prior to purchase. They might find it difficult to articulate their preferences for tightness, looseness or preferred texture, so that despite all algorithmic efforts the item just might not seem right, somehow not at all what they had imagined. The clothes we are happiest in may be so because of factors that are hard to recognize. However unconsciously, an elderly pair of M&S leopard print underpants might make a woman feel she took on a little of the seductive confidence of Mrs Robinson in *The Graduate*. Might not a man enjoy a frisson of youth in a new pair of perfectly white Calvin Kleins? Fit and fabric is important, but they are definitely not all there is to favourite underwear.

Before the Middle Ages underclothing for most people was indistinguishable from outerwear, being largely one and the

same, consisting perhaps of a pelt tied at the waist to keep it in place, or later a length of woven cloth with a hole cut out for the head and again held in place around the waist. In other words, clothing tended to be uncomplicated, unsewn one-piece items. With the development of spinning and weaving greater sophistication became possible, and along with the arts of sewing and knitting, cloth cut on the bias could allow enough stretch to make a tighter fit possible.

Women and men's bodies are remarkably similar, and increasingly today it seems feasible to imagine travelling back and forth between what have been thought of previously as unchanging polarities. Yet wherever we might stand on questions of gender and dress, to enter any department store is to experience a marked disparity between male and female underclothing. In Primark, the global cut-price fashion store, the female underwear section is usually spacious, colourful and

Interior of Joy, a corset shop, Littleton, Colorado, c. 1921.

offers a large amount of choice. In contrast the male department tends to be tucked away, much smaller and with only a limited range of styles in neutral colours. Male underwear is sometimes jokey, whereas what is on sale for females, when not attempting to be sexually appealing, is more often cute, designed in childlike pastels, neutral flesh tones or fail-safe virginal white or practical black.

In the 1960s and '70s for many it would have been considered laughable to try and impress others with a maker's label. But by the 1980s trademarks had become high status, increasingly worn on the outside of clothing for all to see. For example, the firm Calvin Klein writ large their name on the elastic waistbands of their male underwear. In the film *Back to the Future* (dir. Robert Zemeckis, 1985), the young Marty McFly travels back in time to when his parents were young, and meets his own mother, Lorraine, who refers to him as Calvin:

> Lorraine: I've never seen purple underwear before, Calvin.
> Marty: Calvin? Why do you keep calling me Calvin?
> Lorraine: Well. That is your name, isn't it? Calvin Klein? It's written all over your underwear.

In the 1960s, making one's bra from a knotted bandana or tie-dying a T-shirt was an expression of fashion, but fashion that deliberately avoided expense and therefore Veblen's 'conspicuous consumption'. Homespun and 'ethnic' fabrics were often preferred and clothing was meant to look as if it had not cost much; fabric and clothing were garnered from thrift shops and army-surplus stores and from family hand-me-downs, and importantly were not at the mercy of arbitrary changes from one season to the next. In Marxist terms, for those who saw themselves as part of the new counterculture, what they wore did not follow the 'murderous, meaningless caprices of fashion'.[2] The beliefs that burgeoned in the 1960s, standing out as a non-fashion fashion era, bear some resemblance to the Rational Dress movements of the 1880s, though in practice rational dress was meant to look simple but could often involve considerable expense. Moreover what we understand to be non-fashion-orientated dress may simply betray our ignorance of a given period and its social structures, much as in the depiction of Native American clothing in Hollywood films.

The first fabrics ever produced, tribal wood bark and leaves aside, were made from wool, linen and cotton, the first constituents of woven and knitted clothing and thus of underwear. Wool has been processed and worn since the first records of cloth and clothing, and there is evidence that it was used for underwear as far back as 4,000 BCE. It was Christopher Columbus who introduced sheep to America, with the Spanish taking them to Mexico.[3] The finest wool, with the greatest flexibility and least stiffness, and thus the pleasantest to wear, has filaments that have the narrowest inner core, or medulla. Coarser wools such as that from Scottish island sheep were less suitable to wear next to the skin. Wool was considered for centuries to act as protection, the fatty lanolin of wool-bearing mammals' sebaceous glands acting as a defensive barrier against disease. The domestication of such animals as sheep and goats created a symbiotic relationship with humanity: we nurture and protect them from predators and in return they provide us with clothing and sustenance. Not only did woollen fabric protect us against the cold, but sheep and goats are able to survive on leaner grazing than cattle, making them easier to farm. Unfortunately the lanolin-rich fleece could harbour disease and parasites such as fleas and lice, and could cause allergic reactions, particularly when damp and in close contact with our tenderest, most vulnerable parts. Wool could smell strongly, since washing was avoided in case it removed its believed protective function. For the ancient Greek and Roman citizen, the well-dressed wore woollen fabric that was kept clean-looking with the use of stinking sulphur and stale urine. Thus one might say that those who were able to afford to keep their clothing clean reeked of affluence.

Wool comes in many degrees of fineness and coarseness, of fibre and weave and knit, and also for millennia provided the warmest clothing available, worn in those regions where sheep, goats, alpacas and so forth could be raised. However, wool is slow to dry, particularly when the lanolin has either been deliberately removed or has leached away over time. In medieval Europe an open crotch was a sensible measure to limit soiling, but for all classes, the wearing of wool must have been extremely odorous.

In the second half of the nineteenth century in both Europe and America the role of perspiration in cooling the blood was held in such respect that people were encouraged to wear wool next to the skin even in the warmest weather.[4] This belief continued into the twentieth century, and woollen jersey cloth was produced in great quantities in the British Midlands for standard army issue underwear in the First World War, whether for the freezing, sodden trenches or the very different hot and dry conditions of the Middle East. Small children who suffered from respiratory problems, and indeed all children, were advised to wear wool next to the skin in all weathers as a precautionary measure. Arguably the modern notion of avoiding overheating would have been thought to miss the point: wool was healthy in whatever climate you found yourself. The Liberty bodice was introduced as children's wear and was still being worn into the 1970s, advertised as providing support without harmful restraint, but with its fleecy underside and reinforced taped seams, could get uncomfortably warm. Older girls had bodices with suspenders attached.

During the First World War many of the woollen uniforms gathered up from the trenches proved too damaged to be worth mending in the repair and laundry tents that followed the troop movements behind the lines. However, war limited the easy import of new textiles so that irretrievably worn and filthy clothing was shipped home by both sides during the conflict, hot washed and recycled into blankets and other rough cloth. Because of this material's association with human suffering and death, in England woollen fabric that was not garnered in this way adopted the label 'Pure New Wool'.[5] For many who may not now make this connection, the label still affects our feelings about wool as being a pure and natural material, conjuring perhaps the idealized snowy fleece of a newborn lamb.

By the Second World War memories of the trenches were fading and unrecycled woollen yarn now began to be known as virgin wool, more properly referring to what is produced from the first shearing of a lamb. As part of the country's war reparations, Germany supplied sewing and knitting machines to the Soviet Union. Women's underwear had been scarce during the war, the bulk of textile supplies going to clothe combatants, but now women in Eastern Europe and Russia, many of whom were employed in the underwear industry, often in straightened circumstances, were able to purchase the goods they were making for themselves, including non-utility underwear.[6] They were drawn to the new rayon garments that were in such contrast to the itchy woollen underthings that had been all that was available.

In England, the Leicester firm of Chilprufe had produced woollen underwear throughout the First World War, but by 1941, because of the lack of wool available for civilian use, the company opted to concentrate its efforts on making warm and hygienic underwear for children alone. However, post-1945 many firms turned their focus back towards women's lingerie, and as in the factories of Russia they drew on newly available artificial materials. The emphasis on practicality had shifted in order to satisfy the desire for new and luxurious goods. Clothes rationing may have continued until 1949, but many people were eschewing sensible wool for the delights of peach rayon georgette and lemon nylon tulle. American servicemen still posted to East Asia sent home so-called sweetheart underwear sets in colourful silk satins, embroidered with saucy messages and jokey warnings, such as 'off limits' and 'private property', not unlike a more individual version of the Calvin Klein-type trademark and registering the giver's right of ownership.

Manchester-based Aertex has produced a cellular cotton fabric since the 1880s, loosely woven and lightweight, advertised as providing both warmth and aeration and therefore ideal for underwear and sportswear. Since the 1920s the polo shirt, for example, has been worn even by those who have little

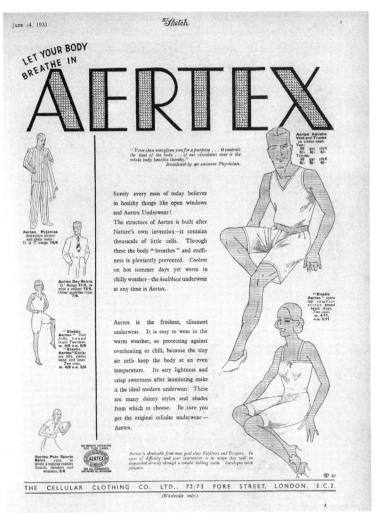

Aertex advertisement, in *The Sketch*, 14 June 1933.

interest in playing sport of any kind. After the two world wars underwear-producing companies had to refocus their designs in order to attract women and also men with more luxurious, leisure-orientated products. From this period a fashion house's sportswear collection would include smart casual clothing rather than only what was designed for the playing of sport.

Nylon was perceived as a 'wonder material', and when it first became available to the public in the late 1930s the Nylon Trade Fair the Nylon Trade Fair described it as bringing about 'miracles of colour, elegance and beauty'.[7] The new fabric was claimed to be softer and warmer than natural fibres, even more absorbent, and such was its initial glamorous image that it was experienced by many to have these characteristics, long before the blends and adjustments that in reality began to make nylon more acceptable to wear. New versions came onto the market fast, such as Ban-Lon, Tasian, Agiton and, appealingly, Fluflon. Recommendations, backed by medical science claims, sold

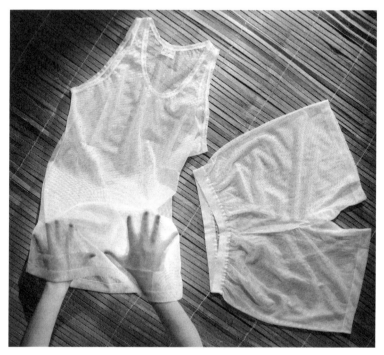

Nylon underwear,
c. 1953.

nylon as practically a cure-all, with such as the 'eminent painless birth specialist' Grantly Dick-Read promoting an all-nylon maternity belt that was in effect 'a nylon mesh maternity corset'. A film, shown regularly in the late 1950s at the Crown Theatre, London, described his natural childbirth methods and also promoted certain recommended and patented maternity and feeding bras made of nylon. On 12 June 1957 the *Daily Mirror* suggested that 'the lady in waiting' could enjoy a lightweight undergarment, sufficiently stretchy to fit all sizes, with suspenders that were 'detachable so that the belt may be worn without stockings during the summer', available in 'tea rose and white nylon mesh'. The emphasis on nylon as a stuff of luxury has *Reynolds News* suggesting that it was both pretty and dainty as well as having more sophisticated qualities, even for the prepubescent: 'Double nylon in two colours for undies to give an iridescent look . . . For instance, azalea over chartreuse . . . hyacinth blue over daffodil yellow . . . "Grown-up" nylon undies – frilly panties, half and full-length slips for ten and eleven year olds.'

Man Made Textiles magazine on 5 March 1957 declared that 'nylon has revolutionized women's taste in foundation garments.' The implicit suggestion was that a woman's femininity rested in part on her underwear, and that her willingness to adapt to new and luxurious fabrics was a way of expressing grace and good taste.

Recently images of the actor Katie Holmes attending a New York fashion show wearing jeans and a bra, not of a state-of-the-art material but made of wool alone, went viral. The bra was worn with a matching cardigan designed to fall negligently off the shoulder to expose the understated, but very expensive, item beneath, the combined twinset dubbed the 'bradigan'.[8] Wearing a bra that was impractically made of cashmere yarn further heightened its appeal, necessitating either ultra-careful hand-washing or sending it to a dry cleaner. The idea of wearing a woollen bra also implied the ultra-luxurious softness of cashmere, soft enough for underwear.

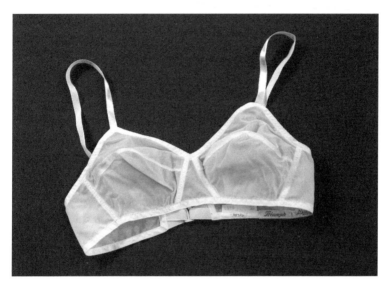

Nylon bra, 1953.

Nowadays it is cashmere that has taken over in the popular imagination as being the highest-quality, most luxurious material, though there are not enough cashmere goats in the world to provide the vast quantities that are marketed as such. Cashmere shawls, towards the end of the eighteenth century, had become the height of fashion. Empress Josephine is said to have owned more than a hundred such shawls imported from the Indian subcontinent.[9] Mixed with silk it was an option for only the most wealthy for fine, warm underwear. With today's most expensive boutiques awash with cashmere, there has been a move to again promote its use for underwear, but the sort that the wearer can openly display on the streets of a fashionable city.

The term 'cashmere' retains its association with quality and luxury, whatever its provenance. From fine, jazzy Fair Isle sweaters for the bright young things of both sexes in the 1920s to the more mature pastel womanly twinsets of the 1950s, and from 1970s clinging minidresses to today's high-end bras, cashmere still connotes conspicuous outlay. Close inspection of a garment's constituents label may reveal that only a small percentage of cashmere is contained in the 'cashmere' item. Terms such as 'silk cashmere' mean that a material is cashmere-like but the association still helps to sell it, in the same way that silk linen or rayon linen may have much the appearance or weight of linen, but lack either linen or silk. We are persuaded by the idea of cashmere, with or without its actual presence.

Shawls were brought over in large shipments from Kashmir in northern India to Europe during the nineteenth century, the word 'kashmir' being anglicized to 'cashmere'. It is not only goats that can provide this luxurious wool, as a particularly soft and lavish example comes from the belly fur of the chiru antelope. The animal has proved impossible to domesticate, and therefore a chiru must be killed for its wool to be harvested, resulting in the species' existence coming under serious threat. More sumptuous still is the wool of the vicuña, a graceful Andean cameloid with a fine, ultra-soft dense coat. Since it lives in the wild it can only be shorn every three years, and produces a particularly small amount of wool, the great difficulty and expense of attaining it assuring its high-fashion credentials, available only to those with the deepest pockets. Indian pashmina was originally sourced from the changthangi goat alone, but today, as cashmere begins to lose ground, charity shops are inundated with so-called pashminas that in fact contain few natural fibres of any kind.

Despite the enthusiasm for wool-based clothing since the fashions of ancient Greece, it is not uncommon to find detractors. For instance, James Boswell recalls his respected friend Samuel Johnson mentioning his distaste for wool during their tour of the Scottish Highlands in 1873. Johnson preferred to wear linen. This view he shared with the ancient Egyptians, who considered that wool was both unclean and foreign. Johnson attempted to justify his dislike of wool in rational terms by comparing the agreeableness of plant-derived sap on his fingers to the sticky residue and stink of animal-derived tallow. He declared, 'All animal substances are less cleanly than vegetables. Wool, of which wool flannel is made, is an animal substance; flannel is therefore not so cleanly as linen.' Johnson objected to silk, too.

What amused Boswell though was the way the 'majestick teacher of moral and religious wisdom', whom he so much admired, inadvertently admitted to harbouring fantasies very much like his own, of having a harem of women at his beck and call, though dressed in fabrics to his taste, of course:

> I have often thought, that, if I kept a seraglio, the ladies would all wear linen gowns, or cotton – I mean stuffs made of vegetable substances; I would have no silk; you cannot tell when it is clean; it will be very nasty before it is perceived to be so. Linen detects its own dirtiness.[10]

The way linen wears, quickly becoming crumpled and grubby looking, proves its value, for those who could and can afford to keep it clean and uncreased display their privilege in doing so. So far as the argument against animal-derived materials is concerned, Gustave Jaeger in 1882 took issue with Johnson's view, on health and hygiene grounds, recommending the wearing of wool next to the skin 'to help disperse bodily poisons', by allowing the skin to breathe and so regulate body temperature. He was also vehemently opposed to silk, and insisted that since wool alone had 'the ability to facilitate perspiration and maintain an even temperature', it should be worn whatever the weather.[11] No other fabric can be so beneficial: 'he regarded the wearing of vegetable fibres and of silk, too, as positively injurious to health . . . No animal other than man . . . wore linen and cotton for their covering and silk was, after all, not a natural covering but the excretion of a worm.'[12]

If we were to stand by Jaeger's notion to avoid the materials that animals avoid, we would, like Adam and Eve before the Fall, wear nothing at all, apart from our own sparse hair perhaps. Such objections aside, Jaeger was a proponent of practical comfort, and he favoured knitted over woven garments because their elasticity encouraged people to be more active. Writing in the mid-twentieth century, C. Willett Cunnington, quoting from a fashion magazine of 1904, suggested that despite the greater availability of linen and cotton blends at all levels of society, the wearing of wool was still considered a basic requirement, although other more feminine concerns are mentioned: 'Nearly every woman, I presume, wears combinations of wool or silk and wool. Knickers of fine flannel or alpaca with detachable nainsook linings are an economy, but to my mind lack daintiness.'[13]

Jaeger may have been a passionate supporter of woollen long johns as the perfect lining for our clothes, but he was hardly the first to recommend wool for underwear, even for animals in need, as in a scene from Elizabeth Gaskell's *Cranford* (1853) in which an exasperated Captain Brown attempts to allay a lady's concern for her ailing pet cow: 'Get her a flannel waistcoat and flannel drawers, ma'am, if you wish to keep her alive. But my advice is, kill the poor creature at once.'[14]

Wool was relatively cheap in the West. Flannel cloth could be produced using wool alone or blended with cotton and a flannel substitute or made from cotton alone, its most important feature being its texture, combining an unsmooth and thus absorbent, and yet forgivingly soft, surface. Wool flannel was considered the answer for both male and female underwear before the mid-nineteenth century because it was believed to allow the body to breathe, but only if it were worn sufficiently loose. It was argued by those concerned with the so-called irrational aspects of female dress in the nineteenth century – echoing what had been said in the sixteenth and seventeeth centuries – that women's clothing had become too close-fitting about the torso:

> not only is the insensible perspiration injudiciously
> and hurtfully confined, but that free play between
> the dress and the skin, which is so beneficial in gently
> stimulating the latter by friction at every movement
> of the body, is altogether prevented, so the action of

the cutaneous nerves and vessels, and consequently the heat generated are rendered less than what would result from the same dress more loosely worn.[15]

Linen and cotton could at least be boil washed and unlike wool were not considered to encourage parasites. Linen has the additional quality of being cool to the touch, but can be warmed by the heat of a fire in winter. It was believed by some that 'Conversely, on a sunny day, white linen reflected the heat from the sun and cooled the body, making heavy outdoor work more tolerable,' though there is little evidence that white clothing keeps you cooler. While white reflects most radiation from the body, dark clothing absorbs ultraviolet waves.[16] However, there are many grades of linen that have been thought to have greater cooling properties. For the ancient Egyptian, for example:

> The linen in the loincloth of an ordinary Egyptian had thirty seven to fifty threads per inch, while the linen in Tutankhamen's loincloths had two hundred per inch. The linen was hand-woven from threads of just three or four filaments of flax, a weave so fine it feels like silk.[17]

This reminds one perhaps of the one-upmanship of thread counts found on bedding today. Linen brought great wealth to the kingdom of Egypt, its value stable enough to be used as a form of currency.

The seventeenth-century poet Phineas Fletcher drew a parallel between linen and the fickleness of desire in Act III of his drama *Sicelides* – 'Love is like linen often chang'd, the sweeter,' arguing against constancy and perhaps age – while the playwright John Webster implies, in Act II of his play *Westward Ho* (1607), a contrary viewpoint, suggesting that 'old linen wash whitest.' It is worth adding here, in the context of underwear, that a softly crumpled pair of drawers or a worn vest redolent of an absent loved one's sweat may just hold an appeal that the newly clean and starched and ironed smooth cannot.

In nineteenth-century England the concept of underwear became synonymous with the word 'linen'. For both male and female the quantity and quality of linen on show was allied to a person's economic and social value. The Cunningtons make the elegant point that it is surprising how, rather than adopting warmer, thicker and therefore fewer underclothes, the affluent and fashionable of Europe from the sixteenth to the twentieth century continued to wear layer upon layer of linen, cotton and silk.[18] Pure, unadulterated, hard-to-manage linen continues to be worn as a more expensive shirting material, despite the availability of cheaper easy-care versions that are blended with artificial fibres. Similarly pure cotton and pure silk continue to enjoy high status compared with their increasingly hard-to-distinguish synthetic substitutes. The idea might be compared with views on racial purity, as if to mix fundamental genetic or fabric ingredients is to make something less morally acceptable.

The sleeved shirt is a development of the early shift and was worn as underwear, acting as a buffer zone between the emanations of the body and the outer jacket or coat. Since today men have largely stopped wearing undervests, this role, of shirt serving as undershirt, might be said to continue. Whereas the tunics of the ancients had to serve as both inner and outer garment, in colder weather an additional shift was worn beneath the top clothing, an additional sleeveless layer, or undervest. This layer in turn developed for women into the bodice, and reinforced with seams and boning became the corset, which was to a more limited extent adopted by men. Early linen and cotton shirts are square cut, much like simple traditional Indian subcontinent and East Asian designs, but gradually inserts and gussets, yokes and cuffs were added to better accommodate the body. While a fine homespun lawn kurta or kameez were unlikely to create uncomfortable bunching when worn under a close-fitting tunic, a simple insert under the arm was sufficient to allow ease of movement. A heavier linen shirt worn in colder climates could be bulky without more intricate shaping.

Eighteenth-century male undershirts not only had to be impressively clean and white, but they needed to flatter the line of a fine figure or come to the aid of the less trim, necessitating a more complex cut. The impact of a cut-away frock-coat could be spoilt by shirt-tails tucked between the legs which could easily get out of place and raise an eyebrow: the fashionable man about town was quick to adopt the new silk knitted drawers. George (Beau) Brummell was influential in promoting the idea of under-stated male elegance, where the cleanliness of a linen undershirt, 'which was in his palmy days changed three times a day', was all-important.[19] A neckcloth cravat was felt to be essential for the unimpeded grace of the silhouette. To support the lavish fullness of a cravat the undershirt had to be cut more narrowly at the side seams in contrasting simplicity. Brummell's collars, or winkers, were cut so high that their points, or ears, entirely covered the face before being turned down. They were so hard to maintain that it was said poor washerwomen miscarried at the thought of dealing with them.[20] Brummell was assiduous in his goal of the perfectly turned down collar:

> Then came the all-majestic white neck-tie, a foot in breadth. It was not to be supposed that Brummell had the neck of a swan or a camel – far from it. The worthy fool had now to undergo, with admirable patience, the mysterious process known to our papas as 'creasing down' . . . When all was done, we can imagine that comfort was sacrificed to elegance, as it was then considered, and that the sudden appearance of Venus herself could not have induced the deluded individual to turn his head in a hurry.[21]

Women wearing a bikini-like combination of a *subligaculum* (thong) and a *strophium* (breast-cloth), *c.* 300 CE, mosaic from the Villa Romana del Casale, Sicily.

rena combat between pairs of gladiators wearing thongs (*subligaculum*), 3rd–4th century CE, osaic discovered on the Borghese estate at Torrenova.

Early braies, detail of miniature from the *Trinity Apocalypse*, c. 1250.

Kneeling knight wearing *chausses* (hose), illumination from the *Westminster Psalter*, c. 1200–1250.

Anonymous artist, *Fountain of Youth* (detail), 1411–16, fresco. In the rejuvenating waters couples, stripped down to their underclothing, indulge in erotic play.

The Renaissance codpiece: Pieter Bruegel the Elder, *The Wedding Dance* (detail), 1566, oil on wood.

Jacopo da Sellaio, *St John the Baptist*, *c.* 1485, tempera on canvas.
He is depicted wearing the hair shirt of an ascetic.

Follower of Lucas Cranach the Elder, *The Crucifixion*, c. 1575, oil on panel.

King Charles I's pale blue silk undershirt worn at his execution, 1649.

Woman's *robe à l'anglaise* ensemble (robe, *fichu* (shawl), petticoat), England, 1780–90, wool crewel embroidery on linen.

James Gillray, *Flannel Armour – Female Patriotism; or, Modern Heroes accoutred for the Wars*, 1793, hand-coloured etching.

A lover bolts the door in his underwear: Jean Honoré Fragonard, *Le Verrou* (*The Bolt*), c. 1778, oil on canvas.

Henry Robert Morland, *A Lady's Maid Soaping Linen*, 1765–82, oil on canvas.

After Élisabeth Louise Vigée Le Brun, *Marie Antoinette in a Chemise Dress*, after 1783, oil on canvas.

John Singer Sargent, *Madame X (Madame Pierre Gautreau)*, 1883–4, oil on canvas.

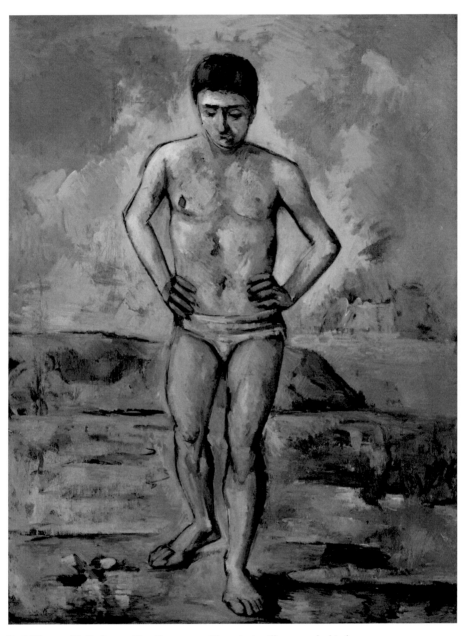

Paul Cézanne, *The Bather*, c. 1885, oil on canvas. The painting illustrates the kind of bathing suit that inspired the creation of the modern brief.

Elizabeth Taylor in the film *Butterfield 8* (dir. Daniel Mann, 1960).

Frightening the natives in *Carry On Up the Khyber* (dir. Gerald Thomas, 1968).

Victoria's Secret store, Union Station, Washington, DC.

Cardrona Bra Fence, Central Otago, 2017, part of a social campaign by the New Zealand Breast Cancer Foundation.

Evan Mock for Calvin Klein billboard, 2021.

'Stop the Sag' billboard, Brooklyn, New York, 2010.

u.s. Army prototype bras for female soldiers, 2022.

Prisoners in the Centre for the Confinement of Terrorism (CECOT) in Tecoluca,
El Salvador, 2023.

Collars and cuffs were often the only features that allowed the quality and style of the shirt beneath to be appreciated. In Charles Dickens's *Barnaby Rudge* (1841), Sir John's too-stylish, too-well-groomed appearance betrays his villainy: 'his linen too, was of the finest kind, worked in a rich pattern at the wrists and throat, and scrupulously white.'[22]

If a clean shirt every day was only available to the well-to-do, then detachable collars and cuffs and dickey shirtfronts served to give the impression of affording regularly laundered underwear. From the nineteenth century and into the twentieth, a poor clerical or shop worker might opt for artificial wipeable celluloid collars and cuffs, designed to look like starched linen. In America celluloid was advertised as a defence against Chinese immigration since the Chinese were closely associated with laundries. One such collar advert proclaims: 'No More Chinese Cheap Labour.'[23] Unfortunately celluloid easily becomes yellow and brittle, curling up and fracturing, giving the game away. Moreover the chemically produced material tended to be even more unforgiving for the wearer than starched linen, cutting into the tender flesh of the neck. Even today the idea of undoing a collar to comfort someone in distress stems from the idea of relieving such restrictive buttoning.

In the 1892 comic novel *The Diary of a Nobody*, the self-important but well-meaning Charles Pooter, keen to dress properly as a gentleman should, is taking his shirts to be mended, his wife Carrie explaining to him that the 'fronts and cuffs are much frayed'. Pooter replies, 'without a moment's hesitation, "I'm 'frayed they are". Lor, how we roared. I thought we should never stop laughing.' Still thoroughly amused by his own wit, he takes the shirts to their local tailor, Trillip, keen to share the joke: 'I said to him "I'm 'fraid they are frayed". He said without a smile: "They are bound to do that, sir." Some people seem to be quite destitute of a sense of humour.' When Pooter returns to pick the mended shirts up, he is outraged by Trillip's bill. The tailor duly responds, referring to the many types of cheaper linen there are, including what was used for a poor man's shroud, and humbling poor Pooter thereby: 'If you wanted your shirt-fronts made out of pauper-linen, such as is used for packing and bookbinding, why didn't you say so?'[24]

We may no longer think of shirts as underwear, with even male prime ministers and presidents happy to be seen as men of the people in shirt sleeves at some official engagements, getting down to business without even a tie at times, and often even lacking a vest beneath. In the United States and some parts of

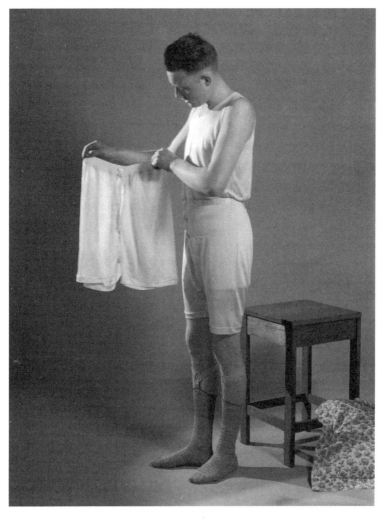

Man in underwear
New Zealand,
c. 1935, photograph
by Gordon Burt.

Continental Europe, certainly in Italy, it is common to wear a spotless white short-sleeved jersey T-shirt as underwear, under a shirt. As the shirt emerged as acceptable male outerwear, the vest, first represented by the sixteenth-century closely fitted and buttoned waistcoat, briefly changed places and became the layer between body and shirt. Modern T-shirts worn as undervests tend to be made of pure cotton, though recent revelations concerning the environmental costs of cotton production have meant a greater willingness to use other fabrics such as bamboo, which requires less water for its production and processing. White continues to be a popular choice for men's underwear in particular, and since it has a shorter life than dyed items, showing up stains more easily and requiring boil-washing if it is to stay white, this puts even more pressure on cotton farmers and manufacturers to keep their prices low.

Herodotus, the Greek historian, writing of his travels in the mid-450s BCE in India, mentions 'trees that grow wild [in India], the fruit thereof is a wool exceeding in beauty and goodness that of sheep. The natives make their clothes of this tree-wool.'[25] The fourteenth-century *Mandeville's Travels* refers to trees bearing 'tiny lambs on the end of its branches'.[26] Cotton remains the most dominant fabric for clothing generally and for underwear in particular. Nothing else quite compares with its ability to absorb moisture and dry out without becoming damaged. For this reason alone some ancient cotton material has managed to survive. Before the discovery of the Americas, Europe had imported its cotton mainly from India. Early cotton clothing fabric has since been found in Peru, Mexico and in the southern states of America, but it was when Columbus found cotton plants growing wild in 1492 that cotton fibre first became available to the Old World, eventually supplying the factories of the Industrial Revolution. Today in the West we source much of our cotton from India and China; what is not made up into clothing there tends to be produced in Turkey and Bangladesh.

Linen comes from the stem of the plant *Linum usitatissimum* and was grown in the hot climates of ancient Mesopotamia, Assyria and Egypt more than 5,000 years ago. It was its light-reflecting sheen and transparency that was so valued by the Egyptians. In the Renaissance it was used for the fine caps and veils that framed a lovely face or might subtly transform a less favoured one. For underwear the more fragile and less absorbent linen was impractical, but again it is this very impracticality that increased its value, and for those of means it would hardly have mattered that it did not last long. Nowadays linen is still produced in northern Europe, although the majority of imports to the West have come from what was the Soviet Union. On account of recent events in Ukraine, it is not only fuel prices that have been hit. The flow of commodities including linen from Russia has been interrupted, and the war has also impeded factory production. Countries like Bangladesh and Turkey are reliant on Russian linen and cotton imports to supply their clothing export trade.[27]

Knitted fabrics allow much greater stretch and therefore comfort. When Coco Chanel adapted men's sportswear shirts for women's use, it was not long before women also sought corsetry that was less restrictive. Latex-based rubber, known as elastic, also known as Spandex, is couched in strips in either cotton or polyester. When it is combined with nylon it can be lightweight enough for delicate lingerie and swimwear. Although elastic initially allowed underpants to be held up more neatly, early examples could abruptly lose their elasticity, sometimes with embarrassing results. The Depression-era American saying used to fill a pregnant pause in conversation – 'sew buttons on your underwear' – was in fact a wise belt-and-braces piece of advice, just in case your elastic were to let you down. Knickers that are cut loose enough to rely on an elasticated waistline to keep them up, made from the many silky, slippery fabrics of the 1930s and '40s, could suddenly and without warning lose their elasticity. But in the words of a limerick, on occasion their sudden removal could be deliberate:

> There was a young lady from Tottenham
> Who'd no manners, or else she'd forgotten 'em,
> At tea at the vicar's
> She tore off her knickers
> Because, she explained, she felt 'ot in 'em.[28]

The American artist Art Frahm was responsible for drawing attention to the unreliability of elastic, which could let you down

Knitted underwear, 1950.

Spandex, from sportswear to leisurewear to everyday clothing.

at the most inconvenient moments, particularly with the additional effects of gravity and sudden gusts of wind. From the 1940s to the 1960s Frahm created a series of images called 'Ladies in Distress'. Blonde bombshells were depicted in everyday situations – boarding a bus or doing the shopping – suddenly finding their knickers down around their ankles. The motif of a stick of celery is a frequent presence among the shopping. One example shows a woman in such a predicament, with a hand at her crotch and a leering 'uniformed man in close proximity, the open fallen purse (consult Freud . . .) and, of course, celery'.[29]

Silk retains a status indelibly associated with high-end luxury. It is valued for its lightness and sometimes light-reflectiveness and for its variety of possible textures. In the context of underwear it can be gossamer fine or come in strong jacquard weaves and lustrous satins or taffetas. As underwear it can be both cool and warm, and modern manufacture means that it can tolerate machine washing, dries fast and requires only minimal ironing. Yet for all this practicality the mystery of its strange origins remains, born of the silken residue of a moth, if you will. It has been associated with magic; Othello, when he demands his handkerchief back from Desdemona, implies that it has spiritual significance: 'The worms were hallow'd that did breed the silk' (III.4). Silkworms here also suggest a form of memento mori, reminding us of the shrouded grave.

Ancient China was producing and wearing silk 4,000 years ago and attempted to keep the secret of its curious provenance, from silkworm cocoon to extraordinary sinuous woven cloth. Production did not begin in Japan and India until 3,000 years later. Emperor Justinian, in 550 CE, had silkworm eggs and mulberry tree seeds smuggled out into Constantinople by two monks, thereby at long last bringing silk fabric to Europe.

Even with modern farming techniques, silk production is a time-consuming process. In commercial production, creating the fabric involves killing the silkworm before it gestates into a moth, or the filaments will break and be spoilt. In order to extract a continuous thread from the pupa, it is either pierced with a needle or the whole cocoon is submerged in boiling water. The earliest and today the best silk fabric stems from China. Pliny the Elder attempts to describe how silk comes about, its sump-tuousness striking him as making it unsuitable for men, describ-ing the silk moths as weaving 'webs, like spiders, that become a luxurious clothing material for women'.[30] Wild or raw silk was produced in Greece as early as the fifth century BCE, and is valued partly for its name alone, which suggests something beautiful but untamed. Harvested from the wild, the pupae have already left their cocoons, which results in the filaments being cut. The resulting fabric frays and is hard to wash successfully, but it has its own textured beauty.

As women's clothing of higher status gradually became less substantial, less layered and buttressed, in the twentieth century 'under-clothing [became] thinner and thinner'.[31] Discussing items of general fashion in the 1920s, Phyllis Cunnington sug-gests a link between the new chemically produced materials and modernity in general, and wonders if they represent aesthetic progress, compared with the wool and linen of the past:

The use of the fabric [artificial silk] for under-clothing
has helped materially to develop the contrast between
the modern attitude towards that part of Woman's
wardrobe and the Victorian, to which, especially,
applied the rules that ugliness was next to godliness.
An immeasurable chasm seems to separate that
conception of sober under-garments from the modern
'amusing undies', imperfectly bridged, psychologically,
by the Edwardian 'fascinating lingerie'.[32]

The Victorian or Edwardian woman's fine lawn camisole
adorned with slivers of silk satin ribbon, miniature iridescent
pearl buttons and clusters of handmade inset lace and embroidery might seem fussy to some modern tastes, but surely seems
far from ugly. Such fine, expensive underwear would of course
have been entirely unavailable to most; new artificial fabrics did
not require the same arduous upkeep and with mass production
clothes were becoming more affordable for all. This meant that
those of lesser means could aspire to a greater choice of wardrobe, including more sumptuous items. In the twentieth century
it must have seemed that new materials such as nylon, viscose,
acrylic/Orlon and polyester/Dacron, and later Spandex/Lycra,
had overcome many of the disadvantages of natural fibres,
making the latter appear largely obsolescent. Scientists were also
experimenting with different blends of natural and synthetic
fibres, so that, for example, the quick-dry qualities of viscose
could be combined with the greater breathability of natural silk.

Knitted goods could now be produced by machine in a continuous tube, making seamless hose possible for the masses. Fine
hand-knitted stockings had been time-consuming to make and
were therefore prohibitively expensive. The knitting machines
of Rouen dating from the Renaissance had only ever served the
few. However, this new tubular method of production could lead
to sagging in wider items – much as a T-shirt can quickly twist
and lose its shape – and failed to satisfy a desire for hosiery to fit

snugly. Warp-knitted fabric could be shaped as it grew on the loom, and the range of new fibres was increasing with 'viscose process rayon, cupra-ammonium [produced from chemically regenerated cotton waste], and acetate and continuing with the hydrophobic group, starting with nylon'.[33] Hydrophobic, or poor-absorbency fibre, which includes polyester and acrylic, needs to be treated to deal with bodily moisture. Natural fibres, on the other hand, are hydrophilic, which is to say wettable or absorbent, and thus are better able to adapt to changing temperatures. Artificial fabrics can cause static electricity and be highly inflammable. On the other hand, some synthetics are more resistant to soiling and wear, and when blended with natural fibres they can give underwear a much longer life. This balance between comfort and practicality means that while many are prepared to wear synthetic mixes for bras and vests, they tend to choose natural fibres for underpants. That said, Lyocell is a semi-synthetic that vies with cotton and silk as a fine-quality lingerie fabric; bamboo is a relatively newly available fabric that is more breathable than cotton, but it does have the disadvantage of shrinking in the wash and taking far longer to dry.

Lycra, developed by DuPont in 1958, has great elasticity and allows many of us to imagine ourselves a smaller or more standard size than we are in fleshy fact. In the alternating effects of fabrics that come in and out of use for underwear, there persists the problem with holding the body in check, squeezing it into conformity. Items may too easily cling to the skin when it is hot or wet and cause chafing, and like bamboo they are easily damaged by too rigorous washing or tumble-drying. The majority of synthetic fabrics have poor ventilation, meaning that underwear put on clean can all too quickly become clammy and malodorous. No wonder some of the most fetching and glamorous items are quickly replaced with breathable, absorbent cotton. Or that someone may hang on to their worn-out jersey Y-fronts rather than don a pair of nippy briefs, however much they flatter.

New cellular fabrics have solved some of these problems, manufactured in a way that is quite different from the traditional knitting and weaving processes. Their interlocking parts are joined together in various geometric patterns that can provide insulation against both heat and cold. The development and range of artificial, synthetic fabrics have dominated the sports clothing market, blended with natural fibres and elastane for high-performance wear.[34] Swimsuits are made in materials that cling without feeling uncomfortable; for men the budgie smuggler, with all its Donald McGill-type comic associations, reduces drag and increases aerodynamism and therefore speed potential in the water. Cycling and running shorts also tend to be worn skin-tight, but not so severely as to cut off circulation for longer periods of exertion. They are designed to be worn against the skin with their in-built lining, known as their chamois, which can protect the groin and buttocks and thus reduce the problem of chafing for the long-distance runner. For water sports such as surfing, neoprene, a synthetic rubbery material, keeps the wearer warm without becoming water-logged or impeding movement.

However, it is the trickle-down effect of inexpensive sports-type clothing that has made its mark on the majority in today's clothing. Versions of the fitted shorts and jockstraps, supportive sports bras and undervests that were developed for various rigorous athletic activities have become everyday leisure wear, known as athleisure. Such clothing expresses an aspiration to be allied with the modern and the athletic, whatever our level of fitness. The quality of the fabric is likely to be inferior to high-performance wear, but such clothing nonetheless makes people to some extent look more toned and certainly feel as if they belong to the tribe of the fit. After all, the same trademarks seen in the professional sphere mark their own more down-market gear.

High-tech wicking fabrics, sometimes still known as thermals, have come to solve the problem of clamminess, letting sweat out and fresh air in without getting wet like cotton and to

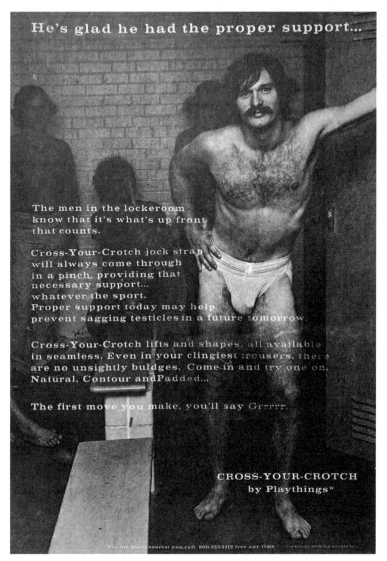

Jockstrap advertisement depicting a locker room of a possibly gay bathhouse, with coded language and imagery, 1970s.

some extent wool-based fabrics. Wool has always been a far better insulator than cotton. Yet lightweight modern materials, though they appear to win out over sweaty cotton in summer or sodden wool in winter, can create new difficulties. The climber Graham Hoyland in 2006 found that wearing what George Mallory and Sandy Irvine had worn to climb Everest in 1924 had unexpected advantages, such as underclothes feeling warm to put on, whereas modern polypropylene underwear feels cold and clammy.[35] Hoyland comments that:

> Like most mountaineers, I am used to synthetic outdoor clothing: polypropylene underclothes and outer fleeces ... They are unforgiving in stretch, and begin to smell unpleasant if worn for more than a couple of days. Mallory's silk, cotton and wool layers were a pleasant revelation.[36]

Edmund Hillary's clothing worn to climb Everest in 1953 included 'a woollen shirt, underwear and Shetland wool pullover'.[37]

The modern fabrics used for sports underpants are lightweight and breathable through tiny pores in their weave, allowing water vapour molecules to evaporate successfully. This is intended to regulate body temperature and to avoid hypothermia and dehydration. However, these pores, smaller than drops of rain, are not large enough to allow bad odours, built up over weeks of wearing, to escape. Such longer-term disadvantages are, of course, less relevant in many less-drawn-out sporting activities. Manufacturers vie with each other to produce the most comfortable and practical combinations of polyester and often cotton to provide improved performance.[38] But watch any high-level running competition and it is clear how important to many of the runners the appearance of their colour-coordinated outfits have become. This in turn goes on to influence the athleisure market designed in far greater numbers for the public at large.

Synthetic artificial fibre has been marketed as durable but also as fine fabric that lends itself to lingerie and hardier types of underwear. Fabric can be manufactured from chemicals or alternatively from regenerated plant fibres, including polyesters, acrylics and viscose from wood bark for high-performance materials such as Kevlar and Nomex. In a study in 1984, it was suggested that while men preferred cotton underwear in everyday life, women said they tended to prefer the smoothness of synthetic fibre.[39] Unfortunately, such smoothness comes at a cost, and many women find themselves returning to cotton for its greater adaptability to varying degrees of moisture.

Cunnington draws attention to a fashion journal entry of 1904 describing what women in England were wearing as underwear before the availability of synthetic fabrics:

> 'Nearly every woman, I presume, wears combinations of wool or silk and wool. Knickers of fine flannel [soft woven wool or cotton] or alpaca with detachable nainsook [fine, soft cotton from India] linings are an economy, but to my mind lack daintiness.' French drawers of mull muslin [lightweight cotton or silk, often used for linings] or washing silk, with flounce and three rows of insertion, threaded with baby ribbon, worn under lace or silk petticoat 'for those who like a froth of frillies beneath their dress skirts'.[40]

Combining different materials can offer warmth, softness and durability, but it also adds texture. In the field of lingerie what sells is not only its appearance but an idea of how it will feel, both to the wearer and also perhaps to an imagined partner.

In her diary the novelist Barbara Pym noted: 'At Marks and Spencer I bought a peach coloured vest and trollies [knickers] to match with insertions of lace. Disgraceful I know, but I can't help choosing my underwear with a view to it being seen.'[41]

The fripperies and gewgaws associated with lingerie can represent an attempt to enter some imagined romantic state. Lace, for example, adds a sense of delicacy and historic craft to modern lingerie, as even though it is likely to be nylon and machine made, it is still associated with the clothing of luxury, of painstakingly handwrought skill, only attainable by those of wealth and taste. The history of underwear continues to involve this see-sawing movement between simplification and the discomfort of a longed-for greater sophistication, often ascribed in some indefinite way to the past. The sweat-soaked bandana won by a workman or knotted at the throat of a Wild West cowboy transmutes into the high-end white linen cravat and travels back again to high fashion looking to the streets for the swagger of a piratical red neckerchief of a French Revolutionary guard.

Blends of artificial and natural fibres appear to be the way to bring about rational, discomfort-free underwear while retaining a sense of sophisticated femininity or indeed masculinity. Lightweight underpants, even with a breathable cotton gusset – a solution adopted by Marks & Spencer in the 1970s – was often not enough to stop the outer nylon-based fabric from becoming clammy and uncomfortable. New mesh and metallic fibres can cause rashes by rasping at delicate skin. Certainly no one in the privileged world attempts to wrap babies in nylon nappies or swaddle them in rayon comforters, for the sake of their drip-dry facility. Moreover, there remains a nostalgia about certain fabric that causes us to savour pure new wool, Irish linen, sea island cotton and shantung silk, not to mention the luxurious, high-status connotations of cashmere.

From early linen and wool, and the development of wrapped and sewn garments, to later cotton and silk and modern-day artificial fibres, rubber underpants and paper throwaways – all their many uses and associations colour our attitudes to underwear. From simple shifts that are shirt, underwear and nightshirt all-in-one, worn by both genders and across many cultures, to a more intricate handmade lace chemise or Liberty bodice, from string vests to six-pack male foundation garments, even to the first bathing outfits of the eighteenth century, all are associated with different textures and qualities of material. The use of stretch jersey fabrics – first used in combination garments, from long johns to baby-grows and back to adult onesies – is a case in point. They were first adopted for sportswear, and later as trouble-free everyday garments, and then back to outerwear in the chic two-piece women's skirt suits introduced by Coco Chanel. The initial shimmering glamour of nylon gradually came to be viewed as cheap and nasty stuff, though, as is the way with fashion, it has lately resurfaced for its vintage nostalgic appeal, gaining a sometimes back-street sexy, sometimes elevated high-fashion allure.

The advent of elastic and all the technological advances of breathable and flexible fabrics such as Lycra have made it possible for underwear to become more flexible and close-fitting. Moreover, there are specialist types of underwear more suitable for menstruation and incontinence and some that filter flatulence. The underwear of the past, of the poor, was traditionally made from worn-out outer-layer clothing fabric, often soft and comforting on account of the fabric having been so often worn and washed. In some Buddhist practice, rags collected from rubbish dumps and shrouds from burial grounds are sewn together and worn as underwear, as if sanctified and cleansed by their modest and ecologically sound reuse.

We might enjoy romantic notions about the history and origins of our clothing – perhaps of gentle sheep in the pasture, the life of the cotton-picking farmer, the marvels of silk production or the ancient craft of linen making. We might even like to think of ourselves as part of an ongoing natural order and want our clothing, in particular garments that come closest to our skin, to reflect these age-old connotations. Even traditional fabric has had to be manufactured, derived from nature but hardly unprocessed; so-called artificial fabrics are merely further along on this trajectory - on fashion's desire for innovation.

6

Medical and Other
Practical Matters

Now we are encouraged not to waste clothing and to avoid throwaway fashion. So should we pay any attention to the idea of the fashion seasons? Should we feel guilty when we scan the rails for a particular colour that is 'in' this winter? I remember as a child being entranced by a series of fashion photographs in a Sunday supplement of waifish models, icy pale in a cloud universe with eerie, frizzy white hair, all kitted out in brilliant orange, pink, lemon and lime neon underwear. Oh, to enter that strange new world.

Today recycled clothing has become hip. No longer a minority enthusiasm, there are market leaders attempting to prove their eco-credentials by using recycled materials; they pronounce their street cred with 'made-from-recycled-polyester' labels. There is always a danger of greenwashing, where a company pays lip service to sustainability, making exaggerated claims about a product and not mentioning, for example, the air miles that have been spent bringing it to market or the wider implications of water requirements on the environment of cotton growing. The designer Katharine Hamnett brought the cost of growing cotton to worldwide attention in the 1980s by promoting organically produced cloth.[1]

This is not a problem born of necessity or availability, as when wedding dresses and underwear in the Second World War were made from reused silk and nylon parachute material, but a shrewd long-term economic decision. As artificial fur used by couture has been a means of drawing attention to the cruelty of factory-farmed mink, say, ecologically conscious high fashion having to some extent encouraged the consumer to consider questions of sustainability.

Economic considerations aside, what of attitudes to recycled underwear? In the affluent West, those who may already buy many of their clothes from thrift shops and online auctions can still seem reluctant to consider second-hand underpants, however unblemished they might be. It is as if any amount of boil washing will never cleanse them of a former crotch, as indelibly defiled as Lady Macbeth's hands. In the novel *Early Morning Riser* (2021) by Katherine Heiny, protagonist Jane claims that she buys virtually everything second-hand. A neighbour, Mr Marshall, asks whether this includes underwear, and she is forced to admit, 'No . . . But I did buy sheets . . . so I suppose I'm only one step away from buying them.'[2] Sheets, the underwear of bedding, we might say, also comes in contact with our undressed bodies.

Thrift shop poster, Kentucky, where everything is welcome except underpants.

The problem of how to keep fabric clean and fresh are particularly relevant to underwear, with beliefs abounding that underclothing should be more hygienic than the other items we wear. Whether or not it is actually germ free, underwear functions as an aesthetic idea and it needs above all to look clean. The use of white and pale colours demonstrate cleanliness, while others colours can suggest cuteness or sophistication but also feral grunge, as with black and red, for instance. Greying white underwear can on the other hand seem grubbier than well-worn black; the popularity of grey underwear is perhaps an attempt to avoid the issue. Certain materials invite similarly diverse readings, so that vinyl and leather and shimmering nylon tend to seem on occasion both appealing and grubby. A dainty nylon baby-doll nightie inhabits a contradictory territory between sugar-sweet babyishness and a knowing play on forbidden desire. A new white crocheted baby shawl, in contrast, is cosy and clean, and would usually have no hidden association with wrongdoing – but wool, since it is more difficult to wash, can in fact more easily harbour disease.

We may want to consider our clothing in clear-cut rational terms, much like the reformers of the late eighteenth century did. Mary Wollstonecraft in the first chapter of her *Vindication of the Rights of Woman* (1792) dismisses 'The air of fashion' as being nothing but 'a badge of slavery', yet with regard to underwear in particular our deeply felt associations are rarely based solely on what seems scientifically or medically proven or happens to be in line with the fashionable ideals of our time and place. For the reformists the question would have become 'entangled ... inextricably in the nineteenth century with organised struggles for the rights of women', whereas today, at least for those who enjoy the luxury of affordable easy-care clothing, we are still encumbered by a range of associations and superstitions about what seems cleanest, or most modest, or allows people to feel more sexually appealing.[3] The market for better-fitting and more attractive male underwear initially grew out of greater rights and freedoms for the LGBTQ+ community in the 1970s, with the limited choices of ill-fitting, baggy post-war high-waisted underwear gradually rejected by the majority of men. Women have, in contrast, been able to experience aspects of underwear that were effectively unavailable to men until well into the twentieth century.

The development of washing soap and powders accelerated during the nineteenth century, when previously it had only been available in the West to those of means.[4] Liquid bleach, or sodium hypochlorite, was used for laundry towards the end of the eighteenth century and it soon became an essential aid for keeping sheets, shirts and underwear white, though an understanding of the need to sanitize cloth was limited. Although the existence of germs had been proved by Louis Pasteur in 1865, for most people it was how fabric and clothing looked and felt that mattered. The fashion for spa bathing, for example, was not always a hygienic one, even if it did feel clean and sanitary to be immersed in waters that were renowned for their health-giving properties. In the naturally heated waters of the Pump Room at Bath you might travel from your lodgings already dressed in waistcoat and drawers if male, or in canvas gown and petticoat if female, the historian Lucy Worsley commenting, 'These outfits were suitably modest for floating around in the warm water in the presence of gentlemen.'5 To maintain modesty lead weights were attached around the petticoat hem – rather as in high-quality curtains – here intended to stop the skirts from floating upwards and causing embarrassment. It may have been modest enough, but since many came to the baths with ailments such as skin disease and wounds that refused to heal, bathing in such waters might well have spread rather than cured their problems. A covering of wet cloth was hardly sufficient protection against infection. In Tobias Smollett's comic novel *Humphry Clinker* (1771), 'one bather is shocked by the sight of a sick child with "scrofulous ulcers" being bathed in the arms of an attendant. "Suppose, the matter of those ulcers, floating on the water, comes in contact with my skin?" he worries.'6

New, less restrictive versions of the corset called on medical evidence to prove their superiority. One of the many producers of 'improved' underclothing in the nineteenth century was Olivia Flynt, who claimed that her approach and her various patents pre-dated the ideas of the Reform Movement. She described how corsets limited mobility, even the ability to climb stairs, and warned that, in her view, some designs could lead to total paralysis. Medical dangers she attested included heart and lung disease, and in children severe curvature of the spine. She produced a manual in 1876 promoting her own designs for both women and children – the looser male corset rarely having done the same degree of damage, so remaining less worthy of her attention. Guided by 25 years of working as a dressmaker, she tells of the horrific consequences of unforgiving corsetry:

> more than half the ills of my sex are the effect of
> the pressure of the corset (even when tight lacing is
> denied), accompanied by many tight overlapping
> bindings, several tightly drawn strings, and the weight
> of heavy skirts, all compressing the form just above the
> hips, creating undue heat in that region, contracting
> and paralyzing the muscles, dragging upon the
> hips, worrying and wearying the victim more than
> excessive toil; producing head-aches and back aches
> that consume more than half one's life, until they get
> sufficient moral courage to discard the old style and
> adopt the new.[7]

Corsets, once thought of as ensuring both female grace and moral rectitude, now are claimed to make the wearer into a coward. As with many such dress 'improvements' the previous high fashion corset became an object of ridicule, and accused of being foreign – appallingly French. At its height a new fashion is extolled as being the newest thing from Paris, but on the wane it is the French that are customarily to blame. It is mothers, sure that tight lacing is essential for fear they might otherwise 'fall to pieces', who strapped up their children from the age of ten, and sometimes from infancy. It was these 'caring' mothers, Flynt insists, who are responsible for bringing about their children's disfigurement and even death. She gives numerous examples of the sad cases she claims to have witnessed in her role as a dressmaker, one example being the beautiful Miss G. Miss G's mother insisted upon reducing her daughter's waist measurement from 24 to 18 inches for her coming-out party, but this desire led to a most melodramatic end: 'The dress was made . . . [she] was engaged before the end of her first season . . . in less

Orthopaedic corset (for an adult male) made of perforated iron and secured by
shoulder straps, 1601–1800.

than another year her corpse was returned to her mother. She could not survive motherhood.'[8]

Flynt insists on wide-ranging repercussions, claiming that traditional corsets were 'the cause of more idiotic, crippled, erratic children than rum drinking'.[9] As with similar new designs for less-confining corsets and more minimal 'waists' which laced the waist area alone, her invention supports the bust from the shoulder, as in most modern-day bras, 'thereby relieving the individual of the discomfort of the weight'. A criss-crossed brace across the back was recommended to avoid the 'protruding abdomen and the cushion-shaped back' of the fuller figure, claiming the additional advantage of stopping the mammary glands from being compressed.[10] 'Fat back' continues to be something of a concern today, when bra straps cut into flaccid and older flesh. Since with the most extreme corseting the arms had to be held at a wide angle, with elbows akimbo, 'if the party is fleshy, the corset steels crowd down the flesh at the bottom of the waist and send it over the hips, to roll up and shake like a jelly.'[11] For a larger person, the excess flesh would result in a shortened waist in front.

Flynt's designs are advertised as being washable since the boning could be easily removed. One can only guess at the state of previous steel-framed corsets that were impossible to launder because of the danger of rusting, worn under layers of petticoats and covered with confining clothing even in high summer. The celebrated actor Sarah Siddons endorsed the Flynt Waist, though at first she was anxious about the professional repercussions of a larger, natural waist: 'My dear madam, will you have me lose my stage figure! You will ruin me!' But she was soon delighted to measure a full 30 inches and to be bursting with new-found energy.[12]

On the subject of laundry, as any reader of crime thrillers will know, it can be a source of information, revealing what appears to be virginity or confirming a suspicion of sexual congress, say. It 'persists as a metaphor for secrets, and tied to its degenerate reputation, is laundry's implicit association with the erotic'.[13] Since many items of clothing were impossible to wash without dye running or fabrics shrinking and distorting, it was customary to avoid the question of cleanliness altogether. Linens were hot washable, but since they tended to be both intimate items of clothing and bed sheets that rubbed up against the body, those who took on such jobs were often tainted by association with the tell-tale filth it was their job to remove.

Bodily stains of hymen, menstruation or semen, not to mention of sweat, urine and excrement, meant that laundresses garnered a disreputable reputation and they were seen to have generally low moral standards. In medieval England even lepers were told to beware of the 'buxom form of the washerwoman'.[14] Laundry was women's work – allowing them time apart from men while at the riverbank, by the village pump or in the washhouse, perhaps. In Spain, the Catalan phrase *fer safareig*, 'to do the laundry', has come to mean 'to gossip': a period of possibly welcome social solidarity is undercut by the suggestion of the meddlesomeness of what surely occurs when women spend too much time together. In England at a wealthy Victorian country house, staffed by a large number of servants, the laundry maid would have come lowest in the pecking order, below both the general housemaids and the scullery maid, who washed the dishes and peeled the potatoes.[15] However, the lady's maid, who came much further up the status ladder, would usually be the only person entrusted with washing her lady's smalls.

Although soap had been produced for millennia, possibly first by the Babylonians in 2800 BCE, throughout the ancient world clothes were cleansed, or at least whitened, with various combinations of lye, salt, animal fat and stale urine. A soap tax in England during the Stuart Restoration (1665–1714) meant that products would have been even more unaffordable to the poor, and friction from a stone or washing board might often have been the sole cleansing method available. Alison Carter points out that in Europe, depending on one's financial position, status could be apportioned by how often one could afford to do the washing, whether weekly, monthly or perhaps three-monthly: 'the wash cycle . . . became a pointer to social class.'[16] Carter quotes the Jacobean play *The Malcontent* by John Marsden (*c.* 1603) in which one character recommends clean underwear: 'use your servants as you do your smocks, have many, use one, and change often, for that's most sweet and courtlike' (IV.I).[17]

Soap remained into the nineteenth century a product that was only available to the well-to-do, and it was not until Lever Brothers in 1886 bought into and developed a small, specialist business that soap for clothes washing became more affordable in England. For centuries there have been various local solutions to the lack of soap, such as the soap pods of the acacia tree, known as the shikakai, still used for washing though mainly for hair in the late twentieth century. The Himalayan and northeast Indian soap pod tree, known as *menangmanba-shi*, contains a high saponin content traditionally used for cleaning, though it has become severely endangered.

Today for many of us with access to a washing machine, laundry has become an easy business. Like putting the rubbish out, it can also be a curiously satisfying activity. The novelist Sue Miller mentions clothes washing as a welcome period of respite, an uncomplicated liminal state that feeds her writing: 'I try to work in the mornings. Usually, I write in my pajamas and slowly assemble myself. I don't get organized and sit down and get dressed. I do the laundry. I drift in and out of writing.'[18] Cate Blanchett sees doing the washing as a way of keeping herself grounded: 'An actress once advised me, "Make sure you do your own laundry – it will keep you honest."'[19]

It seems that those who do the laundry are seen as salacious wantons or may turn into malicious gossips; washing clothes can also be an enjoyable in-between time, used to collect one's thoughts while engaging in a practical activity, and as Blanchett suggests, it can even function as a way of reminding a film star of our common humanity. Hanging out the washing on a

Advertisement for Persil, *Australian Women's Weekly*, 20 January 1951.

Mummy's using
New Persil for
whitest whites
brightest colours

... and she knows
it's *gentle* too!

*Care for your fine fabrics
this easy New Persil way...*

Fine fabrics and washable colours need *gentle* care. And there's no better way of caring for your fine things than by washing with gentle New Persil suds. Simply use enough New Persil in luke-warm water to give a good lather. It's a gentle lather for Persil suds are a special *blend of pure soap and oxygen* which float through the weave removing all the dirt with utmost

gentleness. Squeeze the fine things quickly and gently in the Persil suds—then rinse and squeeze without twisting or wringing. New Persil works so thoroughly, so gently, that dainty things are in the water for the shortest possible time. Washed in Persil they stay soft and new-looking. Try it and see for yourself the difference that Persil makes to your wash!

NEW PERSIL FOR DISHWASHING TOO!

New Persil's busy suds get to work in a jiffy dissolving grease. Your dishes come out gleaming ... what's more, with Persil so gentle, hands are so safe.

HAVE YOU COME AROUND TO NEW PERSIL YET?

Page 56

THE AUSTRALIAN WOMEN'S WEEKLY – January 20, 19

clothesline can be a surprisingly breezy pleasure, too. In the days before disposables, a row of dancing towelling nappies could read as evidence of domestic cleanliness and parental care. Now, with increasing concerns about the effects of disposable nappies and sanitary towels on the environment, cloth versions are beginning to return. In our towns and cities there are companies who collect dirty nappies, returning them in fine good order. However, even on an otherwise unproductive day, hanging out the washing to dry can seem like a small accomplishment.

The designer Stella McCartney has suggested that we cut back on washing clothing because it wears fabric out and wastes water; she recommends instead that we brush the dirt away.[20] However, this is less useful advice when it comes to underwear, which needs to be wet washed. Anyone who has ever tried to revive dirty sweat-stained vintage clothing will know how difficult it is to make it smell sweet again, something that chemical dry cleaning rarely achieves, and anyway few would choose to dry clean underwear.

Even when washing machines are available, more delicate underwear should be laundered by hand, since it can easily get damaged. Modern bras and corsets may be more comfortable, but their elastic and latex content coupled with any boning and metal hooks and eyes means that machine washing is unsuitable. In 1957 the *Coventry Standard* reminded its readers:

> manufacturers plead to make important points
> clear as to the washing of your foundation garments.
> Use lukewarm water; use good pure soap flakes (no
> detergents); rinse gently in suds; use a small nailbrush

Couple folding nappies, Washington, DC, 1943.

to remove actual dirt and stains; rinse in clear water two or three times; roll in a towel to remove excess moisture; lay over a towel on line or rail to dry.[21]

What is and is not disgusting to us about our bodies varies enormously between cultures and individuals and preferences are difficult to predict, apart from to say that like fashion, matters are unlikely to be entirely stable. A sense of longing or desire may suddenly be born of the slightest detail of dress. The Cavalier poet Robert Herrick spoke of 'A sweet disorder in the dress', that is, the allure of a ribbon coming undone or a petticoat in a state of dishevelment. All can bewitch, but just as suddenly the passionate interest can dissolve. For Herrick the clothing itself becomes seductive, even wanton. It is perhaps only in the first throes of passion, on the first morning perhaps, that another's dirty underpants strewn on the floor can fail to irritate. A baby's excrement is perhaps less likely to be distasteful to the new parent, but this is a response that is also unlikely to last for long, a change coming about when the child begins to consume solids. At the other end of life, a beloved parent who requires intimate care may not evoke disgust at all, which would be unlikely to be the case were they less unwell and still able to look after themselves. A sense of what we should do to keep certain unassailable facts about our functioning bodies to ourselves can temporarily, magically, disappear. Presumably nurses and other professional carers learn to put aside a response of disgust in order to change someone's fouled underwear. Perhaps it is fair to say that we all have different thresholds. Apart from matters concerning urine and excrement, similar if less extreme concerns can apply to changing others' sheets. Would you reach for the latex gloves when changing a stranger's sheets, to avoid direct contact with traces of their bodily presence? A similarly visceral response is hopefully less likely with a new sexual partner. These suggestions about our most intimate responses to the emanations of others is peculiarly relevant to the material that covers the naked body.

Night-clothing can evoke an equally extreme response. I might have little problem wearing a friend's outer clothing, but to borrow a nightshirt they had worn might feel more troublingly intimate. To be acutely sensitive to the faint smell of someone else's body is of course a position of economic privilege, when many have no choice but to ignore such precious sensibilities.

The wearing of nappies in the West compares with open crotch garments for babies and small children in some Eastern and Far Eastern historical custom. Split underpants are termed *kai dang ku* in China, where the child is trained to relieve itself through a central open seam. They were in use into the late 1980s, when China began to produce and promote its own disposable nappies. The gradual breakdown of the extended family and the pressures of city living have made the old system hard to manage without a grandmother or someone else with time enough to follow the child around and hold the pants apart when needs be. This situation has in turn brought about a tender notion: to *ha* a baby is to gently hold and press down the legs into a squatting position so that the child learns to relieve itself through the gap. The process requires a great deal of adult attention, both to recognize the signs that the infant needs to relieve itself and to deal with the clear-up afterwards. It is claimed that such intensive nappy-free training allows a baby a far more active role in its own development, with the result that Western babies take as long as eighteen months to become potty-trained, whereas the split-pant child can manage the feat in as little as four to six months. Lately there has been interest in returning to this method, especially because of concerns about the environmental damage caused by discarded disposable nappies. As more people are now working from home as a result of the COVID-19 pandemic, this type of training for babies has become practicable again.[22]

The nightgown for those of means, loose cut and sometimes lined with fur for warmth, was a garment that underwent relatively little change for centuries. It was the twentieth century when pyjamas – a form of clothing worn as outerwear in the Indian subcontinent – began to be worn in bed. Today both genders may wear pyjamas or combined jersey onesies at home, but it is rarer to see a man out and about in his sleepwear, and more unusual still in the West if he were wearing a nightshirt. Men are still expected to be more active and formal. Even the not-uncommon male casual dress of baggy knee-length drawstring shorts and sweatshirt are likely to be in unobtrusive neutral colours, usually light grey.

The choices open to women for nightwear have been many in recent times. Pre-nineteenth century it would have been a matter of sleeping in your chemise or petticoat, and for those of greater means a designated nightdress – white, long-sleeved linen, later cotton, and worn down to the ankle. The Museum of Wales at St Fagans possesses an item catalogued as a maternity nightdress, which during the 1930s was loaned out by a midwife to mothers for their lying-in. It is gathered at the neck and made of thick white cotton, with a deep extra border added to the hem, so that in total it measures 148 centimetres (58 in.), sufficiently generous to allow a birthing mother to remain modestly covered during childbirth. The curator Elen Phillips explained to me during a visit to see their clothing archive that the nightdress was a repurposed item adapted from a choir surplice.

Samuel Pepys in the seventeenth century mentions in his diary that it was unusual to go to bed without a nightshirt, but he took it in his stride, as you might expect. Following the Great Fire of London in September 1666, his friend Sir W. Pen offered him a bed for the night, 'So here I went the first time into a naked bed, only my drawers on, and did sleep pretty well.'[23] By the end of the eighteenth century and certainly in the prudery of a Victorian England household servants would have been expected to wear some form of nightwear. The relaxations of outerwear in the 1920s, with skimpier fashions for both genders, had a knock-on effect on what someone wore in bed. Fashions that required a gamin or waif-like figure soon gave way to a more curvaceous ideal silhouette and in turn to the bias-cut long-length siren nightdresses of the 1930s. The 1950s brought the thigh-length baby-doll nightie and teddy lingerie, like abbreviated, gussied up combinations. Men were still in pyjamas, but of a looser, less slinky variety, usually in manly winceyette stripes or checks. The 1960s and '70s gave us not only fitted nylon sheets, which caught on the toenails, but nylon pyjamas, which could not breathe and crackled with static electricity. Nightwear can be comfortable and modest or in a negligee transparent and deliberately fragile; it can be cute enough to infantilize; sexy as on actress Carroll Baker, or sweet and homely in gingham on Doris Day.

In the medical field an orthopaedic corset of the eighteenth century could be adapted to correct deformities of the spine, and a substantial iron frame could be hinged at either side for easy access. The importance of keeping patients warm, but not too warm, was beginning to be better understood in the nineteenth century, and layers of wool and flannel underwear were worn both in hospital and by those convalescing at home. However, new ideas also abounded about the need for invalid clothing to be both absorbent and breathable, meaning that wool became less used and cotton, silk and linen were preferred. The fabric of underwear for the infirm was intended to rid the body of 'excrementitious fluids and vapours', and thus, for example, address the scourge of widespread tuberculosis: 'No material is "warm" per se. The warmth is necessarily derived from the body, so that a warm material is merely one which does not allow the heat to escape rapidly, a material which is, in short, a bad conductor.'[24]

Some treatments for tuberculosis seem to have been in favour of the free flow of fresh air and thus underclothing that was well ventilated:

The skin must be trained by cold baths and exposure to other cold influences adequately to perform its contractile duties. Under-clothing must be in consonance with physiological principles: that is,

it must be warm, absorbent and ventilated. Nature
did not intend us to live in hot houses . . . linen, cotton
and silk under-garments can be made, and are made,
so as to imprison air in their meshes. Such garments
are every whit as warm as flannel, to which they are
superior in their possession of those absorptive
and ventilating properties with which flannel is so
conspicuously devoid.[25]

The physician Leonard Williams also set great store by maintaining an erect posture, fasting and avoiding the poulticing
of wounds, which he saw as being as stifling as wool flannel,
impeding the flow of curative cool air.

The skin itself was thought to be the best respiratory organ
to fight lung disease. Nonetheless, it was acknowledged if the
skin was too chilled, a person could be put in danger. The physi-
cist Mark Lancaster, discussing a range of new sports fabrics,
made the point that there need to be at least two layers of clothing to trap air if the intention is to modify body temperature:

All these fancy materials used to make sports
underwear are really glorified string vests; Michael
Hunt went up Everest in a string vest and a shirt,
so they can't be all that bad. The holes in the fabric
channel out the sweat, while the remaining fibres
trap warm air next to your skin . . . On a string vest,
the fibres are further apart, so it only works if you
wear a shirt on top.[26]

Turning to other practical difficulties, rags made from worn
clothing were used for centuries to soak up a woman's period.
They were often held in place by a length of cloth attached to a
cord around the waist, like an apron caught up at the back, much
like the ancient loincloth. The Egyptians used papyrus not only
for their documents but for menstrual napkins, which would

have been highly absorbent, like blotting paper. Pliny the Elder, in his *Natural History* of 77 CE, warns that a sensible man would be well advised to avoid period blood, since:

> Contact with [menstrual blood] turns new wine sour, crops touched by it become barren, the edge of steel and the gleam of ivory are dulled, hives of bees die, even bronze and iron are at once seized by rust, and a horrible smell fills the air; to taste it drives dogs mad and infects their bites with an incurable poison.[27]

Such a taboo could work to a woman's advantage; the first female mathematician we know of, Hypatia (d. 415 CE), successfully defended her virtue by throwing her bloodied cloth at a predatory man, who duly ran away in horror, all ardour spent.

In the nineteenth century ideas flourished in the field of underwear, including new designs to hold these menstrual cloths in place. Sanitary belts proved less bulky than the loincloth-like system, and involved a narrow elastic band with clips fore and aft to which handmade or commercial pads could be attached. In 1894, in order to improve the absorbency of the sanitary and surgical napkin, one example alternated the pattern of warp and weft on the loom so that the pile could be cut or raised where absorbency was most required. The centre part of the cloth was raised, or 'flaneletted', like a fine grade of bath towel that is more absorbent than fluffier but coarser towelling.[28]

However, a story from the First World War is perhaps most poignant. Nurses who had served on the front noticed that the cellulose cotton wadding provided to check the flow of wounds was much more absorbent than the woven cloth pads with which they had been issued for their periods. They began to use the wadding instead. You might say that new developments to staunch trench injuries were the inspiration for women's greater practical comfort. The firm Kotex began to market pads made from surplus high-absorbency fibre from 1921 and by the early 1930s were

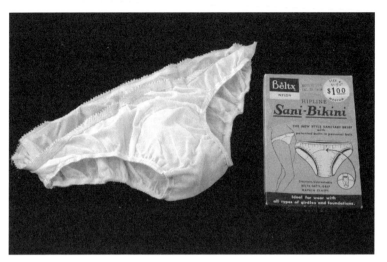

Sani-Bikini, 1954–65, sanitary brief with built-in personal belt synthetic fibre, nylon elastic.

producing the tampon, initially referred to as the internal sanitary napkin. These were made of the same absorbent cotton and rayon, and liberated women from the inconvenience of pads, which could slip out of place and become odorous. Menstrual cups were first made of aluminium or rigid rubber but later of more acceptable silicone, the idea being that it was more hygienic to be able to empty such receptacles rather than allow bloody dressings to fester whether inside or outside the vagina. More recently plastic, virtually indestructible tampon applicators and waterproofed disposable pads, along with babies' nappies, have added to the pressure on our oceans and landfill sites.[29]

As early as the 1950s underpants that held pads in place were beginning to be advertised, though with considerable discretion. Hygiac underwear, for example, was described in a advertisement as providing 'elegance, comfort and security for the busy modern woman'.[30] In the late 1960s a sticky strip on the back of disposable pads meant that additional fixings were no longer required. Though there may seem to be a clear line of development in these menstrual products, it does not follow that women necessarily eschewed older methods. However useful such a product proves, they can be too expensive for some or may be completely unobtainable. In rural Africa, for example, many women

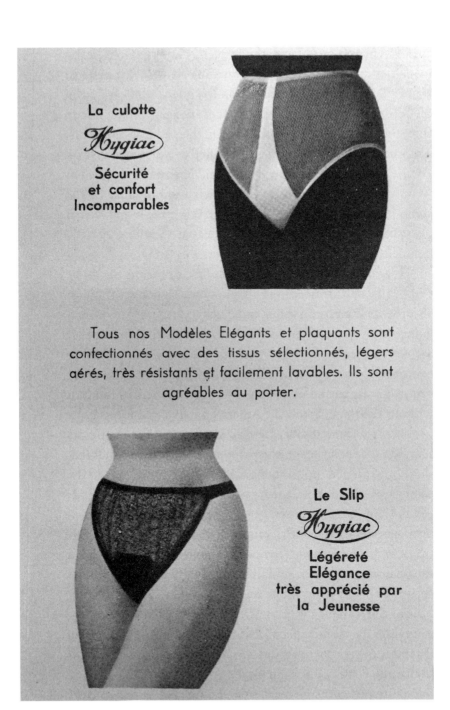

La culotte

Hygiac

Sécurité
et confort
Incomparables

Tous nos Modèles Elégants et plaquants sont confectionnés avec des tissus sélectionnés, légers aérés, très résistants et facilement lavables. Ils sont agréables au porter.

Le Slip

Hygiac

Légéreté
Elégance
très apprécié par
la Jeunesse

Hygiac advertisement for menstrual knickers, claiming to provide elegance, comfort and security for the modern woman, 1950s.

are forced to rely on older methods, such as using 'leaves, sheep's wool, newspaper, grass, even cow dung'.[31] UNESCO in 2016 reported that it is not uncommon for girls to be kept from school during menstruation for want of adequate products, and since this amounts to one week in four, their education suffers. The scholar Helen King makes the point that women in classical Greece were held to be more leaky and absorbent than men: 'Women absorb more fluid from their food because of the spongy texture of their flesh.' This could result in menstrual blood becoming trapped and it was believed that those who did not menstruate regularly risked mental illness.[32]

Few younger women today of sufficient means would be without the new artificial fibre underpants designed with built-in absorbency, easy to rinse out and quick to dry. The firm Wuka, launched in 2017, offers eco-friendly period underpants that are 'Strong. Brave. Fearless. Powerful' and also vegan, so easy to compost when they eventually wear out. The first advertising campaign for period underpants took place in 2019, but not without resistance from the American networks, forcing the firm Thinx to cut out scenes showing an actual bloodstain; CBS refused to be persuaded to accept the adverts on the grounds that the glimpse of a tampon string was shockingly graphic.[33] The campaign created an imaginary world in which men get periods too and have to manage their 'MEN-struation'.[34] They are shown turning to a mirror to see whether any blood is showing on their trousers, asking a pal for a tampon and suffering from cramp. In the finale the man and woman kiss. He pulls away and admits shyly, 'I'm on my period.' She replies, 'Me too.'

For the fearless a 'free bleed' policy has been championed, to counter the taboo aspects of menstruation and demonstrate that bleeding is a beautiful natural process, indicating a state of health and fertility. Incidentally, Pepys mentioned that among the many measures he used to make his wife pregnant was insisting she wore 'cool holland drawers', as well as ensuring that she did not 'go too straight-laced'.[35]

At the height of each wave of corseting fashion, both pregnant and would-be pregnant women are advised to loosen their clothing. However, for the latter at least, tighter clothing has sometimes proved an inducement to congress. It is often held that sperm count is affected by the temperature of the scrotum, some claiming that there is a 25 per cent higher sperm count in men who wear boxer shorts. A study in 1998 threw doubt on this finding, however, concluding that 'the hyperthermic effect of brief style underwear has been exaggerated . . . [there is] no difference in scrotal temperature . . . [and] no significant effect on male fertility.'[36]

Many of the super-absorbent underpants used for menstruation can also be used for incontinence, the advice desk for Tena products, for instance, explaining that though they might have rather different advertising campaigns for the two uses, the products were essentially exactly the same.

Attitudes to period products are a marker of age and social pressure: a pack of tampons in a supermarket trolley might embarrass a younger person perhaps, but at the same time represent that person's continuing youth and fertility. In the Lebanese film *Caramel* (dir. Nadine Labaki, 2008), Jamale (Gisele Aouad), concerned about her age goes to great lengths to suggest she is still in her menstruating prime by secretly dabbing red ink onto the back of her white skirt, then feigning embarrassment when one of her younger friends points it out. Tampons have also been seen as a marker of a sexually active woman, as using one risks rupturing the hymen. Someone might well still be a virgin yet use a tampon, but in some contexts virginity is only proved by the issuing of hymen blood.

Underpants made by firms such as Shreddies claim to 'flatulence-filter' using a carbon-absorbing cloth, similar to the fabric used in chemical warfare overalls. Today textiles have been developed that can monitor a patient's health, adapted to an individual's specific needs. Researchers at the University of California have developed a textile-based, printable electrochemical sensor, which has the capacity to be used for a variety of medical and safety applications. When worn in a waistband it has the ability to pick up and read chemical substances secreted from the skin. Such devices can detect glucose and pH levels in our sweat, and are thus useful for monitoring diabetics; some can even detect cancer cells.[37]

Underwear can be a talisman, like familiar old underpants worn for an important event. They may in contrast suggest the dishabille of someone solitary and depressed. The Finnish state of 'pantsdrunk' describes a man who drinks on his own at home dressed only in his underwear, a theme taken up by actor Steve Martin and the band Steep Canyon Rangers for the song 'Atheists Don't Have No Songs', in which unbelievers sit about in their underwear forlornly watching football on TV.

Swimwear along with much sportswear has become a form of hybrid under/overwear for all in our own time. It had been thought acceptable for men to bathe naked but as soon as sea-bathing became something of a cult activity in the nineteenth century, clothing had to be negotiated for men and women to be able to bathe together – or at least within sight of each other. The nineteenth-century bloomer suit was designed to conceal the body and was often made in dark wool flannel. Even when made in lighter-weight linens and cottons, the amount of material meant that the suits were bulky even before they had become wet. By the early twentieth century swimwear was becoming more streamlined, using man-made fabrics that combine nylon and elastine.

In the novel *Eleanor Oliphant Is Completely Fine* (2017) by Gail Honeyman, a character remarks on the irony of street clothing that mimics professional sporting gear: 'I have often noticed that people who routinely wear sportswear are the least likely sort to participate in athletic activity.' There is some truth in this, yet the more people are inclined towards the easy uniformity of the tracksuit the less it remains associated with sport. Garments such as the seamless pull-on bra and yoga shorts are worn because they are affordable and comfortable, and it is often merely an added advantage that they can make people feel fitter by association. The habit of wearing what was once termed sportswear for all manner of occasions greatly increased during the COVID-19 lockdowns of 2020–21, when people were forced to spend so much time at home.

What is acceptable for Hollywood film stars and in fashion magazines is often harder to accept in the flesh. Local rules have been put in place to limit too much exposure, but, rather like attempts to police the length of schoolgirls' skirts, it can be difficult to legislate. An above-the-knee restriction that seems reasonable on someone of average height could seem unfair for someone with longer legs. Nonetheless officers such as Bill Norton, a swimsuit policeman for Tidal Basin, a reservoir in Washington, DC, that was once a bathing beach, explained that he was only following the orders of the Superintendent of Public Buildings and Grounds by measuring women's bathing suits to ensure they were no more than 15 centimetres (6 in.) above the knee.[38]

By the 1940s pin-ups were exposing a section of their midriffs, even if uncovering the navel was still considered shocking

Victorious English
100-metre women's
relay swimming
team at the
Summer Olympics,
Stockholm, 1912.
From left to right:
Belle Moore, Jennie
Fletcher, Annie
Speirs and Irene
Steer.

Bathing 'cop' measuring the distance between a woman's knee and the bottom of her bathing suit, 1922.

in the flesh. Louis Réard launched the bikini in 1946 in Paris, naming it after Bikini Atoll, the site of American nuclear weapons testing, which had taken place only four days before. The daring new two-piece costume was seen as both modern and dangerous, and so racy that Réard had to use a showgirl, Micheline Bernadini, rather than a model, to advertise his design. The bikini was worn once, and only once, at the Miss World Pageant in 1951, gaining the Swedish winner, Kiki Håkansson, the crown but also international censure, with future contestants having to wear one-piece costumes. Pope Pius XII described the garment as sinful.[39] Brigitte Bardot wore an itsy-bitsy number to advertise *Manina, the Girl in the Bikini* (dir. Willy Rozier, 1952, not released in the USA until 1958, and in the UK in 1959) on the beach at the Cannes Film Festival. Later Ursula Andress as Honey Ryder in *Dr. No* (dir. Terence Young, 1962) wore a plain white two-piece accessorized with a knife at her hip.

As with many features of high fashion, the bikini was not entirely new. The actor Jane Wyman had been pictured wearing a two-piece in 1935, though with waist-high bottoms that covered the navel. The exposure of the midriff was one thing, but to reveal evidence that someone was once 'of woman born' seems to have been for some too much to stomach. In 1964 Rudi Gernreich designed the notorious monokini, a one-piece that left the breasts uncovered, the first topless swimsuit. A sling-style mankini that leaves the bottom cheeks exposed was popularized by Sacha Baron Cohen in *Borat* (dir. Larry Charles, 2006). Alas, while a man appears merely a little ludicrous, a woman in a monokini seems far more undermined.

Bikini-like clothing appears on vases and mosaics of the ancient world. While the Greeks stopped wearing the *perizoma* loincloth, derived from Minoan fashions, its female acrobats and performers wore a form of high-cut briefs.[40] The fourth-century Villa Romana del Casale, near Piazza Armerina in Sicily, has a mosaic floor depicting women practising running, weight-lifting and discus throwing, all wearing what look remarkably like modern-day bikinis. They have become known as the Bikini Girls. The ancient history scholar Charles Seltman in the 1950s devised a dual image of an ancient female athlete alongside a mid-twentieth-century woman in what appears to be identical two-pieces.[41] Ancient Roman women are shown on vases in bikini-style underpants, apparently formed from a tightly wrapped *subligar* loincloth, with breasts bound by a band of cloth or leather, referred to as a *fascia*, literally a bandage. It is possible that these women were slaves or prostitutes, as citizen women would have been unlikely to allow themselves to be exposed in this manner.

One of the aims of environmentally aware fashion today is to question our perceived need for constant change. Yet those who enjoy clothing would perhaps admit that it is this aspect of fashion that can hold the most delight: the excitement of the slim, light Empire-style white dresses of the 1810s, airy muslin replacing the previous generation's heavy brocades and velvets; the new-fangled crinoline and the feel of it ebullient bouncing from side to side as if you were about to become airborne; the exciting new elegance of the figure-hugging bustle; the restriction-free slip dresses of the jazz age; the New Look, with its lavish use of fabric in full skirts at mid-calf and tightly corseted waists after years of meanly cut utility fashion – with breasts and bottom and wasp waist centre stage all over again. The cycle rolls on and on.

Considering the production of what we wear from raw fibre to cloth to manufacture, and the individuals involved in these processes and the companies that purchase their labour, there remain opportunities to limit its wastefulness. While it seems unlikely that many, once they have the means to buy new clothing, can be convinced to stick with garments that are made to last, it is possible to combine the forces of recycling clothing and upcycling discarded materials. In practice it is difficult to assess and compare all the different processes involved, such as laundering, drying, ironing and dry cleaning, and their impact both on our own lives and that of the world at large. Various models have been developed, such as the EcoMetrics calculator, which is an industry tool intended to measure the carbon

Weaving looms in 't Katoentje, a modern cotton spinnery in Bruges, 1970.

impact on the environment of marketing campaigns across digital and offline channels. The Higg Index looks at the environmental effects of the clothing and footwear industry across the supply chain, including matters such as water usage, which is a particular problem in cotton production.[42] As in the Utility Clothing scheme of the Second World War, zero-waste pattern cutting is promoted as a means of reducing the material wasted in offcuts. But in terms of long-term effects on the environment, there is a risk of deceiving ourselves. Such measures cannot do much without an understanding of the leviathan of our competing global economies. Moreover, small-scale measures, however well intended, fail to factor in the seductive lure of fashion.

Two women collaborators, partially stripped, with burns on their faces and heads shaved, are paraded through the streets of Paris, summer 1944.

7

Economic and Religious Concerns

The status and potential stigma of underwear has persisted into modern times, despite our appetite for innovation. From a fourteenth-century simple underskirt to the copious layers of Victorian petticoat and then forward and back again to the slim figure-hugging bias-cut under-slips of the 1930s, what we wear unseen can denote privilege or its absence. Despite the effects of two world wars on the wearing of underwear and the many attempts at its democratization, there has repeatedly been a prompt return when means allow to styles that are expensive and impractical. Wearing underwear that is clean and of good quality, perhaps trademarked on waistband elastic or bra strap where it can be noted by others, is an indicator of economic class and the relation between wearer and their private body.

Following the exodus of German troops from Paris at the end of the Second World War, brutal newsreel film displayed the so-called horizontal collaborators accused of having had relationships with or who had otherwise co-operated with the occupying Germans. There is footage of women having their heads shaved and being paraded in their underwear through the streets of Paris past jeering crowds on their way to prison or summary execution. Underwear when forcibly exposed denies the wearer the privacy it should allow.

Both the unmentionable and conspicuously expensive aspects of these mostly hidden items of dress reveal our attitudes to individual choice. They also imply aspects of our shared nature, embarrassed by our bodies or eager to be seen as prosperous or daring. Being in underwear alone when others are dressed can be shaming for all but the most resilient, or in less confrontational circumstances by the confident or the deranged. The superior quality of and expenditure on expensive items, and in today's context, the designer labels of underwear, betray its fashion *griffe*, the claw that grapples with our acquisitive desires. The UK has been described as 'a nation fluent in the translation of the subtlest of class indicators', but clues to a person's economic status that can be found in one's clothing applies in various degrees to all cultures.[1] An active interest in fashion is common if not universal. Tastes may veer from the influence of subculture trends on the affluent to the trickle-down effects of high fashion on the majority. What is seen on the street as a trend among the young and economically less privileged is taken up by designers who see it as an amusing quirk, and who then combine it with more high-end items so that customers can again separate themselves from those of slender means.

This interplay is common, as for instance with the working man's knotted red neckerchief once worn to soak up the sweat of labourer and sailor alike. It indicated a more carefree indigent life where collar and tie were not required, perhaps coming to suggest a life on the open road. The kerchief was noted for its roguish effect when worn off-centre and adopted as a small feature of relaxed dress by the leisured classes in the West, a jaunty relative of the sublime Beau Brummell precisely centred cravat. Scouts and Girl Guides adopted them as part of their uniform, again suggesting the healthy outdoor life, and Nazi Germany's youth movements also wore a scarf, but smart, black and folded neatly under the collar, positioned strictly centre front.[2] In Communist states a red neckerchief was worn by Pioneer movements, sometimes the only part of the uniform available, and today it is still worn in Vietnam and China. Even a small square of cloth that became a sign of belonging can signify very different shared principles.

How much can underwear as ritual express an unspoken idea? Members of the Church of Jesus Christ of Latter-Day Saints, for example, wear modest, antiquated underclothing. In the 1940s this consisted of long-sleeved and long-legged suits, with a buttoned hatch, or 'fireman's flap', at the crotch, a form of long johns or union suit, which was claimed to 'strengthen the wearer to resist temptation'.[3] A number of small slashes in the fabric at chest, knee and navel, later embroidered rather than cut, are there to remind the wearer of the sacred covenants laid down by their founder, Joseph Smith. This clothing was strictly never to be discussed with outsiders, and as underwear it was kept safely out of sight. Some claim it follows early Masonic designs. The compass symbol over the left chest, for example, was meant to represent 'an undeviating course leading to eternal life; a constant reminder that desires, appetites and passions are to be kept within the bounds the Lord has set'.[4] Since the 1970s a reformed version, with shorter arms and legs and made in two pieces, underpants and undervest and with a camisole for women, has been adopted by some Saints. Fundamentalists denounce such changes as going against the unchanging (since the 1940s) nature of these temple garments, which are 'worn day and night to be a constant reminder to the adherent of their commitment to the faith/church, and they also believe it provides protection to the individual, when worn properly, from evil and temptation in the world'.[5] Greater convenience and comfort are considered to be trite, worldly concerns. The reformed and now gendered underwear has an opening fly front for men's underpants and a fashioned cup and supportive breast seam for women. It should be noted that the Bible, revered by Latter Day Saints, does appear to be against unisex clothing of any kind, so in this respect the reform measures might be seen as more seemly: 'A woman shall not wear anything that pertains to a man, nor shall a man put on a woman's garment; for whoever does these things is an abomination to the Lord your God.' (Deuteronomy 22:5) Apparently the USA supplies camouflage versions of LDS underwear to enlisted soldiers.[6]

The transvestite – literally one who dresses in other garments – was not entirely uncommon in the Middle Ages, though in some cases the practice appears to have had little to do with sexual preference. Joan of Arc, for example, was seen as wholly female, her male apparel a means of both gaining trust as a leader of men and her willingness to take the same risks as men:

> The male clothing set her apart from other women,
> whereas her transparent femininity distinguished her
> from the men with whom she fought. By distancing
> her from her sex without concealing it, cross dressing
> became Joan's trademark, so to speak; it was the
> outward sign of transcendence and uniqueness.[7]

Havelock Ellis argues that Hildegund von Schönau (1170–1188), who lived as a Cistercian monk by the name of Joseph, expressed by her lifestyle a deep admiration for the opposite sex rather than a denial of her own.[8] The distinction is confusing. She was only discovered to be female upon her death, her naked body having been so convincingly strapped up and hidden beneath tunic and habit that no one had suspected her of the deception.

Our view of cross-dressing males has, at least of late, often been influenced by bawdy songs and football chants. In the music hall tradition, while women dressing as men can take on a stylish swagger that might otherwise be denied them, the pantomime dame with her mammoth bosoms and frilly drawers is an exaggerated version of the female. Cross-dressing may be a secret activity, as for example in Monty Python's lumberjack skit. As the lumberjack's song gradually reveals his tastes, his girlfriend and fellow tree fellers become increasingly appalled by his habit of frequenting bars dressed as a woman. The more he reveals, the more they recoil from him.[9]

We may laugh at what embarrasses or even at times disgusts us. The drag queen appears to present women in a sexualized and sometimes grotesque parody, adjusting her bra strap, wriggling her breasts, hitching up her knickers and sashaying her hips in exaggerated seduction. This guffawing style of humour is quite distinct from the private desire of some men to don female underwear. There are those for whom wearing female under-pants, say, is a secret and serious expression of sexuality, and for many it remains shameful, and fear of discovery may form part of the compunction. In Bob Rivers and Twisted Radio's song 'Walkin' 'Round in Women's Underwear' (1993) the attraction lies in the fussy detail of lingerie, in the dainty spaghetti straps and lace.

The wearing of cilice or sackcloth, a garment made of scratchy haircloth, has been worn in various Judaic and Christian trad-itions for centuries, as a means of repentance and mortification of the flesh. In Jewish culture a hair shirt is also worn for mourn-ing, grief mitigated by physical pain. Whereas covering the body with modest underwear might make a person feel more virtuous and less sexual, and from a practical point of view possibly pro-tect intimate parts from injury or from being observed by others,

Healthguard
advertisement
for luxurious and
comfortable lingerie,
Woman magazine,
18 September 1948.

a hair shirt involves the self-infliction of pain as a good in itself. It was considered to be a means of cleansing the body, as in flagellation.[10] In the Catholic tradition hair shirts were worn for the Lenten period for the remission of past sins, and by the most hard-line at all times, as a constant reminder of humanity's sinfulness. Old Testament women are upbraided and ordered to take up penitential clothing without delay: 'Tremble, ye women that are at ease; be troubled, ye careless ones: strip you, and make you bare, and gird sackcloth upon your loins' (Isaiah 32:11).

In the New Testament John the Baptist wears a 'raiment of camel's hair' when preaching in the wilderness (Matthew 3:4). The undershirt is designed to irritate the skin, sometimes with twigs or even wires and spikes of metal added. Today the shirt is still being produced by monks and nuns, and it is said that the process of making the shirts 'involves a great deal of prayer and contemplation, as well as physical labor'.[11]

The list of those who have chosen to wear the cilice is lengthy. James IV, king of Scotland (1488–1513), wore the penitential garment to gain forgiveness for the indirect role he played in his father's death at the Battle of Sauchieburn in June 1488, where rebels fought in his name. The saints Francis of Assisi, Ignatius of Loyola and Catherine of Siena, for example, all chose to wear them. Even Ivan the Terrible wore a hair shirt, explaining that he wanted to die like a holy monk, even if he had not quite lived like one. Thomas More's goat-hair shirt was worn 'as he contemplated a martyr's death in the Tower of London'.[12] He had worn one while testing his vocation to the monastic life as a young man and had continued to wear a hair shirt in private as a means of self-mortification beneath his robes of office as Lord Chancellor of England. Before his execution in 1535 the garment was significant enough for him to bequeath it to his adopted daughter Margaret, and subsequently it was left to an exiled community of Augustinian nuns in Belgium. Later still it was passed on to the Benedictine monastery at Buckfast Abbey, where it can still be seen today, framed in a side chapel as a form of secondary – because it is not a body part – but nonetheless revered holy relic. Today, about 30 per cent of the influential Opus Dei organization within the Catholic Church are said to wear hair shirts, as well as practising celibacy.

An old joke enjoyed by students of Latin, *semper ubi sub ubi*, literally means very little, 'always where under where', but is, of course, heard as a recommendation to 'always wear under-wear'.[13] To return to where this enquiry began, underwear in its most basic form came to be worn by all classes yet was not con-sidered significant enough to be included in sumptuary laws during the Middle Ages. Those shirts that did attract the atten-tion of the arbiters tended to be too ornate to be strictly termed underclothing, and at any rate items that were hidden would have been difficult to forbid, and would hardly have satisfied the desire for public admiration sufficient to justify the paying of such a tax. Clothing was a primary marker of class and wealth, and as such needed to be seen – which suggests that underwear would have been considered to have less status.

In Jewish medieval life nakedness was considered to be a disgrace, and thus the more someone hid their body from view the more respectable they were, a person's 'natural contours bec[oming] totally invisible'.[14] Simple loincloths and braies can suggest humanity stripped down to basics and yet still be considered as decently and modestly covering the more private parts of the body. Maimonides, the medieval Jewish philosopher, argues against material concerns, as if we should put aside such trivial matters. However, a consideration of clothing is arguably an essential aspect of modesty: 'there is a material aspect of reli-gion and then the spiritual core or essence. It is not difficult to see which is more significant, or so it seems. What does it matter what people wear compared to what they are and how they think? It might be argued though that if the point of clothing is modesty, for a group of people, then it does matter, since it is not easy to be modest in immodest clothes.'[15] The aesthetic and the symbolic value we attach to clothing is reliant on how we individually think and feel. The Persian philosopher Avicenna's floating man, entirely separated from the sensory world and yet still self-aware, only not through sensory experience, is an unimaginable state for most of us.[16] We come to know the world through our perception of it. How we see the fabric of our clothing, how we feel its softness, slipperiness or perhaps dry woolly roughness, and recognize the stiff crackle of starched linen or rasp of taffeta and so on, is part of what it means to be alive. Of course, without clothing we might still have an appreciation of our bodies and of the world beyond, but clothing in all its various purposes, the foundation of underwear and its unstable relation to outer clothing, could be said to act as a bridge between us and the outside world.

The priests and high priests of Judaism wore linen braies, which covered them from waist to knee and were further hidden by an undertunic: 'You shalt make them linen breeches to cover their nakedness; from the loins even unto the thighs they shall reach' (Exodus 28–42). The *tallat katan* is still worn in the orthodox community beneath a billowing white shirt, shaped like a poncho with tassels at each corner. As an instance of early recycling policy, the Talmud recommends that worn-out underwear should be made into torch wicks for use in the Temple. Linen underwear is held to symbolize a distinction between the heavenly and the earth-bound, whereas the divine is a constant and unifying state. Like outer clothing, underwear should be modest and follow the example of the past rather than the lure of future-focused fashion. The philosopher Oliver Leaman makes the point that in the orthodox community, this sartorial modesty 'generally means displaying only a limited amount of flesh' and masking the body beneath.[17] Just as one who habitually dresses casually, wearing little more than a T-shirt and shorts, would seem eccentric in wintery conditions when others are warmly dressed, the traditionally dressed orthodox Jew is at their most evident in the heat of summer, cocooned in dark modest clothing, when others are in contrast only sparsely covered.

Islamic Sharia Law similarly holds that underwear that exposes the structures of the body beneath is wrong and that it is a believer's duty to avoid *tashabbuh*, in this context imitating the clothing habits of unbelievers. In Sikhism the *kachera* is a form of underpants much like boxer shorts, which is the only dress requirement for men and women (apart from the turban for men), and similarly intended to be modest and avoid lust. The *kachera* is usually made of lightweight white cotton, with a drawstring, or *nara*, at the waist, the latter acting as a means of controlling sexual desire: 'as a reminder that while one takes the time to untie the drawstring one is given time to think about what one is about to do'.[18] Zoroastrians wear the *sedreh* undershirt, tied with a sacred girdle at the waist, known as the *kushti*, which are similarly intended to instil a sense of responsibility for contemplated actions.

Adam and Eve after the Fall are ashamed of their nakedness, of which they had previously been unaware: 'And the eyes of them both were opened, and they knew they were naked; and they sewed fig leaves together, and made themselves aprons' (Genesis 3:7). These aprons are in effect rudimentary underpants, a strip of cloth with ties for securing it around the waist. When Christ is shown on the cross with the thieves on either side of him, the good and the unrepentant one, all three are usually depicted in paintings, stained-glass windows and illuminated manuscripts wearing such loincloths, reflecting the sensibilities of later times. A crucifixion would in fact have been carried out with the victims stripped naked, in order to maximize their public humiliation. Similarly martyrs are frequently depicted in their bruised and battered agonies yet with their genitals covered by pure white linen, which seems an unlikely delicacy on the part of their persecutors.

The Buddhist *antarvāsa* is a loose inner robe that covers the lower body. Monks are allowed only two sets of these robes, to allow for one to be in the wash, though neither is held to belong to any one individual. Fabric in India was and is a valuable and sometimes scarce commodity, so that Buddhist monks are encouraged to collect rags from burial grounds that can then be patched and sewn together for their clothing. The resulting patchwork is said to resemble the prevalent landscape of small rice paddy fields. Buddhist nuns were once allowed two spare items of traditional underwear, presumably because of the practical difficulties concerning menstruation, although nowadays they wear simple cotton underpants. Nonetheless there remain rules concerning how to go about drying washed underwear, making sure that knicker gussets are hidden on the washing line or risking severe reprimand.

In Japan the question of underwear appears to have been a class-ridden one historically. After the Satsuma takeover of the Ryukyu Kingdom of circa 1609, the Ryukyuan people were forbidden to wear Japanese-style underpants, the *fundoshi* or *mawashi*, in case this gave away Satsuma advances to the Chinese. The Ryukyu archipelago lies between the East China Sea and the Pacific Ocean and there was a risk that Chinese envoys might catch sight of the tell-tale Japanese-style garments and raise the alarm.[19] Both styles are forms of loincloth, like an apron that is sometimes loosely wrapped or otherwise twisted up at the back between the buttock cheeks. *Mawashi* are worn by sumo wrestlers either beneath more elaborate aprons or on their own for practice bouts; *fundoshi* are still worn at festivals such as the Hadaka Matsuri, or Naked Festival. The saying *fundoshi o shimete kakaru* translates literally as 'tighten your loincloth', not unlike the English encouragement to 'gird your loins' for the task ahead.

By the middle of the nineteenth century the rapid introduction of Western-style clothing in Japan necessitated Western-style underwear, and in particular underwear that did not bunch up under more revealing styles. The kimono itself had been 'an outgrowth of a kind of under-garment called *kosode*',[20] and was worn by the upper classes from the eighth to the twelfth century. It had only gradually become an outer garment. As in Western sumptuary laws, which were intended to inhibit the growing merchant classes' aspirations, accompanying disapproval and taxation tended to make out-of-reach goods seem, contrarily, even more desirable. In Japan, silk, for example, was meant to be restricted to the samurai and noble classes. However, the more affluent farmers and merchants became adept at getting round the regulations. Western underwear was being advertised for both genders and for women as 'a symbol of sexual equality'.[21]

One of the strangest forms of underwear, in the sense of being clothing that not only covers the naked body but incorporates the nakedness of another, is the necropant or *nábrók*, which translates as corpse britches. In Iceland in the seventeenth century the idea of witchcraft was empowering and terrifying by turns. When life was one of hard toil to survive the harsh extremes of climate and being at the mercy of an overlord, certain superstitious beliefs would have been persuasive. One such involved two men making a pact, so that he who lived longest would gain the means to accrue great wealth. You would wait until your friend had been buried, then dig up his corpse and most carefully skin it from waist to toe. Any accidental holes or tears would render the potential clothing useless. The resulting footed skin long johns would then be eased on over your own naked legs. As a pièce de résistance perhaps, you had to steal a coin from a destitute widow woman and place it in the empty scrotum of your new leggings, along with the magical symbol for Nábrókarstafur, indicating the magical ritual. An endless supply of coins would be the result, spilling from the scrotum, for ever and ever more.

Unusually it was predominantly men who were accused of witchcraft in Iceland, which this particular manifestation of the occult would seem to bear out. However, there is only one known example of this underwear in existence, in the Strandagaldur, the museum of Icelandic sorcery and witchcraft, and it has been found to be a reproduction. Yet the idea survives and there are plentiful supplies of T-shirts and tattooing possibilities available that use the *nábrók* symbol. It might strike one as an ugly idea, although the practice of putting the skin of a dead lamb over an orphaned newborn to persuade the former's mother to accept it as her own is equally bloody and strange. The necropant ritual might be said to bring to life the metaphor of getting under someone's skin.[22]

During the Middle Ages Catalan women accused of witch-craft – more than a thousand women faced trial during the period – were believed to have the supernatural ability to see through solid objects.[23] Inquisitors were frightened that witches under interrogation would have the power to see through their cloth-ing, including underwear, and ogle their shameful nakedness.

Sometimes it is what underwear misrepresents or disguises that matters. Nakedness can be humiliating. One response to the inherent threat of sexuality was adopted by the Russian Skoptsy religious sect, founded by Kondratii Selivanov in the late 1760s. It promoted extreme measures to remove the stain of original sin in order to obtain salvation and do away with lust, practis-ing "'fiery baptism" – castration for men and the cutting off of breasts for women'.[24] Gaining some popularity in the eight-eenth century, a small number of adherents are said to have sur-vived into the twenty-first century, but the sect has unsurprisingly been repressed throughout its history. One punishment during the Russian Empire was being made to display themselves naked in public, scars and all, or men were sometimes forced to wear female clothing. Under Stalin photographs of their mutilated bodies were circulated to humiliate them. Christ himself, believ-ers claimed, would have been such a castrato. One might expect them to have been proud of their deformities, in bodies now cleansed of certain potential sin, but the habit of wearing cloth-ing to mask one's private parts was and is deep-rooted. Removing the genitals and breasts failed to remove a sense of indignity and perhaps shame at being seen unclothed, no doubt heightened by the prurient curiosity and animosity they triggered. They might feel proud and defiant about such a decision, involving both extreme pain and future danger from the authorities, but it does not follow that one would not be embarrassed to be seen naked or for a man to be forced to wear women's clothing. An amputee, for example, with every right to be unashamed, might nonetheless prefer their impairment to be a private matter, with even a cotton covering between them and the world feeling necessary and right.

When prisoners are forced to remove their clothing by their guards, who are dressed in the higher-status clothing of their uniform, the intention is in part to humiliate, to demonstrate who is in control and who is not. While a common response might appear to be shame, such a prisoner, at the mercy of the guards, might well experience rage, but is forced into a position of slave-like obedience to survive. Recently indiscriminate policies purporting to solve the problem of street gangs and the drug trade in El Salvador have resulted in grossly overpopulated prisons. President Nayib Bukele has ordered mass arrests, often based on unreliable evidence such as the accused having tattoos or being young, male and happening to live in an area where gang members are reported to operate. Looking as if one might be a criminal – *cara de malandros* – is sufficient to justify incarceration, recalling the scant proof that had been required before a person could be arrested in the European witch trials. Bukele has built a vast new prison complex for more than 20,000 prisoners, the so-called Centre for the Confinement of Terrorism. There is provision of dining rooms and even tennis tables, but these are for the guards. Amnesty International reports that the prison is divided into 100-metre (330-ft) cells, each intended to house one hundred inmates.[25] The prisoners lack the most basic sanitary facilities, with each cell provided with only one basin and one lavatory. A framework of metal bunks, without mattresses, form a nightmare metal beehive, and to up the ante still further, there are only eighty metal bunks provided for each cell. The decision deliberately invites bullying, putting the weakest in the most vulnerable position. Images have been disseminated worldwide with apparent pride, showing these

Maurice Becker,
*Conscientious
Objectors in
Leavenworth Prison,*
1919, drawing.

young men and boys with shaven heads, hands shackled behind, barefoot and all wearing loose boxer shorts. They are pictured sitting en masse, closely packed together, with bent 'legs on either side of the man in front of him', their heads lowered in abasement.[26] The underwear is presumably to suggest the prison is run by righteous rule, though the clean underwear was surely put on especially for the photographer and unlikely to remain so pristine in such pitiful conditions.

In modern-day Turkey there has also been an attempt to use underwear or its lack as a means of enforcing control over prisoners who are still on remand. As a boy in 1989, the novelist Haydar Karatas visited one of his brothers in Metris Prison. There he witnessed a protest by the prisoners against wearing uniforms: his brother along with the other remanded prisoners refused to wear anything but their underwear.[27] To stem this type of protest the Turkish government attempted to remove all underwear from incoming prisoners. They thus had a choice: appear naked or agree to wear the uniform. Selahattin Demirtas, leader of the pro-Kurdish People's Democratic Party, appeared in court in 2016 wearing nothing but a shroud.

Prisoners in the West are provided with clothing including basic underwear. The Standard Minimum Rule for the Treatment of Prisoners in America was updated in 2015 with the Mandela Rules, which include the principle that 'All clothing shall be kept in proper condition. Underclothing shall be changed and washed as often as necessary for the maintenance of hygiene.' There is evidence that many female prisoners yearn to wear lingerie rather than merely functional items. Prison authorities at East Sutton Park, Kent, England, have confiscated underwear brought in by day-release inmates that they considered 'did not meet the basic standards of modesty and decency'. Images of this contraband are underwhelming: sets of bras and knickers in pretty pastel colours, lacy and somewhat demure. The idea that incarcerated women might want to wear pretty underwear seems hardly immodest or indecent. A source explained that there were 'enough security risks without a prison having to worry about frilly drawers', but this fails to explain what the risk represented by the frilly items might be.[28] The Prison Service more formally states that 'clothing purchased by prisoners must be approved by the prison before they can wear it or it will be confiscated,'[29] shifting the grounds for objection from aesthetics to a question of their authority being challenged. Modern-day female prisoners are not meant to wear what they prefer, not unless it is formally approved, even when it is hidden beneath outer clothing.

THE VIRTUES OF UNDERWEAR

Some prisons provide paid work for inmates. The *Washington Post* describes how the garment manufacturer Third Generation outsourced its lingerie production to various women's prisons in the 1990s on behalf of companies such as Victoria's Secret. The work is seldom well paid, but still the women were shocked by the high price their underwear sold for compared with the 10 cents per hour they were earning. Although some did manage to secure sewing work after they were released, inmates dubbed the scheme the 'panty mill'.[30]

Whether or not monks should wear underwear at all was a controversial issue in the Middle Ages, since the question arose as to underwear's possible worldly associations and also whether it threatened vows of celibacy. One argument was that underpants were associated with pagan custom whereas the history of Christianity was better represented by the Roman underpants-free tunic. Augustine favoured the greater purity of linen over woollen braies since wool is obtained from sheep, and sheep copulate, so it was therefore better not to have such stuff close up against one's genitals. The Cistercian order considered braies altogether unwholesome for its monks, encouraging lust. This position was lampooned by the twelfth-century clergyman Walter Map, who took a more down-to-earth view:

> If, however, the Cistercians can endure scarcity
> of food, rough clothing, hard toil, and such single
> inconveniences as they describe, but cannot contain
> their lust, and need the wind to act as a check for
> Venus, it is as well they do without breeches and are
> exposed to the breezes . . . perchance, the goddess
> hurleth her attack more boldly against those enemies
> whom she knoweth are more firmly guarded.
> However this may be, the fallen monk would have
> risen with more dignity if his body had been more
> closely confined.[31]

Map relates an incident at court when Henry II, accompanied by some courtiers and priests, was walking outside in windy weather. A monk who was attempting to get out of their way fell and his habit blew up around his neck, exposing his private parts to royal view. Henry politely pretended he had seen nothing but a Master Rericus took the opportunity to quip: 'a curse on this bare-bottomed piety'.[32]

Under the rule of St Benedict monks could borrow a communal pair of braies when venturing outside the monastery so long as they were washed and returned to the monastic wardrobe on their return, though later they were permitted their own underpants. In the French medieval poem *Moniage Guillaume* a knight, Guillaume d'Orange, has retired to a monastery under the rule of an abbot. Since he has promised not to fight, the knight submits to robbers stealing his habit, but he roundly refuses to give up his braies, as he considers his modesty more important than a vow of non-violence.[33]

There is an ongoing debate as to whether underwear is pagan or Judeo-Christian, since Jewish and Christian tradition is associated with Roman and eastern tunics, whereas ancient Germanic tribes wore a form of underpants. At his coronation in 2023, before British king Charles III could be anointed with holy oil, a wall of screens was erected behind which he was quietly disrobed. It was intended as a private moment of reflection, but one which the cameras were permitted to film. We had already seen him in the splendour of his robes, but for a brief time he was left in a plain white undershirt. The *colobium sindonis*, or sleeveless shroud tunic, was then put on to symbolize simplicity. For a ceremony that can be traced back for more than a thousand years this formal undressing and redressing stands for a monarch's pledge of allegiance, that otherwise the grandeur of the *subatunica* coat of gold cloth might undermine.

The press reported that the royal robes were sewn by skilled craftspeople, as if there were intrinsic value in a garment that had not been adulterated by the shallow convenience of machine production, suggesting that there is virtue in the time-consuming hand stitch. A comparison between hand and machine stitchery is both functionally, and in terms of its effects on people's lives, a complex question. Sewing machines are faster and also create a stronger stitch, and underwear, because it is often worn close and tight to the body, requires strength under tension.

As the Industrial Revolution gathered pace, a significant proportion of women's lives was still taken up with making and mending a family's clothing, either by their own labour or by employing others for the task. Mrs Beeton points out, delicately, in her *Book of Household Management* of 1861, that although a visiting seamstress, or in a less affluent household the maid of all works, might carry out the sewing tasks required, certain articles of clothing were better sewn 'by the lady of the house'. A sewing machine offered greater freedom for women, but they were expensive items. The bulk of production still tended to be carried out in sweatshops, with hand-finishing carried out as poorly paid piecework by those who could not leave the home because of childcare or other responsibilities. In Thomas Hood's 'Song of the Shirt' of 1861, the wretched home worker is said to sew 'at once, with a double thread, A shroud as well as a shirt'.34

With ever more sophisticated robotic machines available today, boasting circuit boards and computer chips able to cut and finish in one continuous process in state-of-the-art low-staffed factories, in the battlefield of competitive seasonal production the sweatshop survives. And it is thriving not only in Ethiopia, India and Bangladesh, but here in the West. The many small, backstreet factories in Leicester, Birmingham and Wolverhampton, the heartland of the British clothing industry, were in part responsible for a surge in England's COVID cases during the pandemic, where, much as in the nineteenth century, 'tiny sweatshops were crammed into crumbling old buildings and legally compliant factories using expensive machines were being outcompeted by illegally underpaid humans.'35

The first successfully manufactured machine was designed by a French tailor, Barthelemey Thimonnier, in 1830, sewing with a top-feeding chainstitch, and principally used on tough, rigid materials such as leather and canvas. Underwear required a bobbin-fed stitch that would not unravel so easily under tension.[36] Relative to other items of dress, very little yardage is required for basic underclothing, but it often involves intricate designs. Bras in particular are unstraightforward in their complex shapes and assembly, and require strong but non-bulky seams that allow sufficient stretch. In a study in 2019 setting out to find ways of reducing the amount of thread required for bras and underpants, factors that were examined included the tensile properties of thread under tension and a comparison of the amounts used in bobbin-fed as opposed to needle-fed thread. It was found that there was a far greater proportion used in the manufacture of bras over knickers. Questions such as a fabric's thickness and the number of layers involved were considered, as well as the importance of stitch density and strength. Such a study, ostensibly on economic grounds, to help detect the most efficient means of production, assumed that underwear also required less practical qualities:

> to attempt the translation of a sexy psychological
> feeling . . . the garment should reach a relevant
> compromise between quality (comfort, lowest
> defaults, good shape, high quality sewing threads,
> sexy and original patterns, and so on) and low sewing
> thread consumption.[37]

Apart from a number of graphs and diagrams, the only illustration in the study was of a woman's cleavage, in full soft-focus rosy hue, wearing a revealing push-up lace bra. We are told to note the 'scalloped elasticated edge trimmings', but the intention is claimed to evoke a 'sexy psychological feeling'. Unseen costs play a large part in determining what ends up in the shops – as was evident in the seam left open in women's underpants to save time and therefore money – but what is being referred to here, subliminally at times, is a connection between our underwear and how we see ourselves.

8

The Underwear Drawer

In all but the most impoverished circumstances many harbour what never quite comes to be worn. This is particularly true of underwear. Certain items stand for possibility, and can represent a version of ourselves that has never quite materialized, not quite yet. In the future we may be bolder, slimmer, less self-conscious, more desirable, truer to our own hidden nature.

In the 1920s, for instance, you might have come by a gossamer-fine handkerchief bra that merely required you to transform yourself into the sleek, androgynous snaky figure of the fashionable day. Perhaps today there are articles of shape-wear rolled up at the back of a wardrobe and ready for the day when you might be able to wear that unforgiving silk jersey wrap-around dress if only you had the right occasion to wear it. Perhaps you have a pair of underpants designed to flatter your rear, but have yet to find an opportunity or sufficient courage to wear them. A lace basque ordered by post but now too late to return has since languished, never even tried on.

If you have ever had the task of deciding what to do with someone's clothing after their death, items can resonate with their lost presence, tucked away, rolled in tissue paper or maybe just stuffed unceremoniously into a boot. Is there a shell pink satin nightdress of a sort you cannot imagine your aunt ever having had occasion to wear? In my father's drawer I found a rugby jockstrap, unworn for at least 25 years, the elastic perished; in my mother's a pair of black silk seamed stockings with tiny coloured hundreds-and-thousands up the heel. A box of wool work came to me after an uncle's death, smelling strongly of his cigars. Underneath the tapestries, I came upon a cache of soft pornography, of sultry girls in minimal lingerie.

There is a wide range of medieval stockings, those made of coarse fabric, cut and seamed, and some closer-fitting because they are bias-cut, which took more material and therefore tended to be for the more affluent. There were foot cloths and leg bindings and the intricately hand-knitted, later frame-knitted stockings that had been made in Spain since the eleventh century. Edward VI of England was presented with a fine pair of 'long Spanish silke stockings'. Henry VIII had 'six pairs of black silk hose knit', and his daughter Mary I had her own source of Spanish stockings, on account of her marriage to Philip II of Spain.[1] Elizabeth I gloried in fine apparel and vowed she would never wear anything other than silk after being given a present of English silk stockings by her 'silk woman', Alice Montagu, in 1560.[2] Elizabeth explained, 'I like silke stockings so well because they are pleasant, fine and delicate and henceforth I will wear no more cloth stockings.'[3] In practice, such was their value and so chilly the unheated residences, that those fortunate enough to own them would probably have worn their silk stockings over coarser wool, both for added warmth and to protect the fragile material from sweat damage. Elizabeth first wore them with 'a paire of Taphata garters being edged at the endes with depe golde fringe'. In her wardrobe accounts she is documented as acquiring twenty pairs every year until 1577, when at the age of 44 she switched to warmer but finely textured worsted stockings from Norwich, also supplied by Montagu. These accounts represent a transition from cut-out and sewn-together woven cloth to fashioned silk and then on to frame-knitted fine wool, which might also be said to follow the stages of a queen's reign, from youthful grace to stalwart monarch.

In 1589 Elizabeth refused to back her subject the vicar William Lee in his plans to produce mechanized knitting frames in England. She claimed that it would threaten the livelihood of hand-knitters: 'I have too much love of my poor people, who obtain their bread by the employment of knitting, to give money toward an invention which will tend to their ruin, by depriving them of employment and thus make them beggars.' If only he had come up with a machine to produce silk stockings, for she mentions that in that case she would have been in favour, as they 'would have affected only a small number of my subjects'.[4] Hmmm.

The idea for his prototype frame had come to Lee when observing his soon-to-be-wife 'absorbed in knitting a neat heel by hand'. Disappointed by the queen, he took his invention to Rouen, which was already a centre for textile production, where his business prospered and duly provided employment for French weavers instead. When skirts rose in the early twentieth century, stockings began to be made in a range of scintillating colours. Those who could afford it wore silk, but they also came in new more affordable rayon, although unfortunately the new textile did have a tendency to stretch and pucker.[5]

Ecclesiastical clothing required high standards of hosiery, initially worn only to the knee, but for the self-respecting prelate it was essential to be seen to wear beautifully fashioned black for the everyday, red and or purple stockings for special occasions and high office. One explanation for this practice is that the colour purple represents the blood of Christ, though there is no contemporaneous evidence about when the colour purple was first adopted and it may simply have been a washed-out version of bright red. Rosemary Hawthorne refers to a thirteenth-century painting of the kings Caspar and Melchior, two of the Magi visiting the new-born Christ, wearing thigh-length stockings supported by French suspenders.[6]

In John and Emery Bonett's 1959 crime novel *No Grave for a Lady*, a woman arrives home after an evening out, in stockings and in all likelihood high heels, and 'automatically she [undoes] her two back suspenders to spare her nylons', a small matter of fashion good-housekeeping.[7] With the advent of tights in the 1960s and women's increasing use of trousers, stockings have become marginalized fashion, often seen as raunchy or at times as ultra-feminine, worn once and perhaps never again . . . unless it be of the elasticated support variety. Stockings are frequently chosen for wedding apparel with accompanying suspender belt or lucky garters.

When suspender belts took over from garters at the end of the nineteenth century, they were at first worn over a corset and later sewn onto the corset itself. Later, in the 1920s, the brassiere was often separated from the girdle with the suspenders sometimes left attached. Nonetheless many a flapper found the garter a more appealing accoutrement and, while her figure allowed, stuck to that most inconvenient method of keeping her stockings up. The suspender had been marketed as a practical solution, and championed by the British National Health Society in the 1880s.[8] By the 1950s the suspender belt and stockings had become a staple feature of erotic clothing – along with the feather boa, perhaps.

In the past a woman's trousseau might indicate her status but also her aspirations for a new life through marriage. A magazine article of 1880 remarks that, 'In no item of dress has there been more change in fashion of late years than in underwear. The chief aim now seems to be to minimize such items.'[9] In nineteenth-century Britain, for example, there were no specified rules for what should be in a trousseau, but they were intended to represent a bride and her hopes for her new life ahead. Along with the tablecloths and sheets, the items of underclothing and nightwear were intended to honour the bride's femininity and good husbandry, its linens and maybe silks often handsewn by herself and the other females of the family.

Anton Chekhov's short story 'Trousseau' has a flurry of earnest needlewomen preparing for a marriage, which the reader gradually discovers may never take place. Their claustrophobic little home is surrounded by a beautiful garden, though they hardly notice it. They live for the daughter Manechka and her

Lingerie model
in bra and girdle,
demonstrating
sophistication with
a cigarette, 1949,
photograph by
Stanley Kubrick.

hoped-for romantic future, and have no time for appreciating anything in their present. When a visitor enquires about all the paper patterns strewn about on the floor, assuming the clothes are being made for a definite purpose, the mother declares: 'Oh ... as though we were thinking of wearing them! They are not to be worn; they are for the trousseau.' On another occasion the visitor discovers, hidden away in a storeroom, 'five large trunks,

Korean *sok-jeoksam* and *noreunbaji*.

and a number of smaller trunks and boxes'. The girl insists, un-convincingly, that she really has no expectation of getting married. The female members of her family know better, it seems: "'This is her trousseau", her mother whispered; "we made it all ourselves."' Seven years later the visitor returns and yet again he finds the women still busily sewing away, but now the daughter is absent, for they are preparing mourning clothes for her funeral.

A Turkish documentary novel by Kemal Yalçm, *Emanet Çeyiz – Mübadele İnsanlan* (The Entrusted Trousseau: Peoples of the

246

Exchange), describes the author setting out to find the rightful owners of two trousseaux that had been left in the safekeeping of Yalçm's grandmother. Eventually he does manage to find the Greek neighbours who had been forced to leave their home in 1923 in the compulsory population exchange between Turkey and Greece. They had had to leave behind their daughters' trousseaux, the sheets and nightdresses and the underwear. Yalçm's journey turns into something of an odyssey, gathering the many stories of the dispossessed, but the idea of a trousseau comes to stand for hope against the unlikely odds of ever locating the lost clothing, of regaining something that had been lost.

Korean age-old precepts of virtue and modesty mean that a woman was expected to be well covered, particularly on her wedding day: 'Usually a woman wore at least four sets of undergarments, but she wore even more for the wedding.'[10] Her breasts would be covered by layers of fine linen, *sok-jeoksam* and *sok-jeogori*, and she would also wear put on several pairs of underpants and linings, the *sok sokgot*, *baji* inner layerings and the nappy-like cotton *darisok got*. Over these, for her wedding itself, if she were a noblewoman she might wear an additional pair of wide-cut underpants, the *noreunbaji*, and these would be yet further covered with petticoats in white silk, or sometimes in vividly contrasting alternating colours. This distinctive padded skirt is as extensive as a Victorian crinoline, but unlike the crinoline, it is not hollow beneath, the weight and quantity of petticoats making it less liable to upturn and expose the wearer. The traditional Korean bride is weighed down securely by her underpinnings. This layering is meant as an auspicious symbol of the solid foundations of her marriage, to prepare her for her new life.

How you keep your matched sets of underclothing, whether neat and ordered or stored in an untidy tangle, can be revealing. For some the job of tidying one's underwear is a small, private pleasure, even if the results turn out to be short-lived. One might also keep secret or even shameful items in an underwear drawer. A bottom drawer might house a trousseau, of special underwear for a future marriage or even a hoped-for romance, though the latter is more often a female habit. In a trousseau that forms part of a dowry gift for a future husband's family, underwear is considered as capital. In the medieval period in Jewish marriage arrangements, clothing needed to be long-lasting. It was, moreover, important not to wash garments that might lose their dye, for example, because: 'Washed clothes (*ghasil*) lost much of their value. Nevertheless, washed garments do appear in trousseau lists and were even traded overseas.' The historian Miriam Frenkel goes on to describe such stored clothing as a major metaphor: 'dress was the additional layer that exalted the carnal body and made it human, just as tropes and poetic devices turned prosaic writing into elevated poetry.'[11]

Part of a women's preparation for marriage might may involve a decision about what is suitable to wear for this new carnal role. The right nightwear needs to be alluring but also suggest wifely qualities. When a bride is less likely to be sexually unknown to her new husband, it can be tricky to decide on exactly what approach to take, wide-eyed virgin in diaphanous white lawn or woman of the world in slinky black lace. A Kate Atkinson novel, *Shrines of Gaiety* (2022), has a character, Gwendolen, choosing to dodge the issue; she enjoys the sensual pleasures of fine nightwear without seeing the necessity of getting married first:

> She reached for her dressing gown, not her felted woollen one that had seen her through the war and its aftermath but a lovely silk peignoir, courtesy of Liberty's. It was a partner for the nightdress beneath it, silk garments fit for a bridal trousseau. Gwendolen had no intention of ever honeymooning but she didn't see why she shouldn't have the trousseau.[12]

Contrary to the notion that women dress and undress the way they do for an audience, many – even those who might categorize themselves in one of the many gendered positions from binary to non-binary – may still wear fine and flimsy layers of underwear as a private pleasure. Where once women in particular may have sought frilly items to satisfy a desire for something of opulence in their clothing, from the later 1920s when 'creaseless perfection [could] only be acquired by wearing a minimum of clothing underneath',[13] tiny details of style and adornment came to replace the love of excess:

Wynne Gibson wearing black lace underwear in the film *If I Had a Million* (dirs James Cruze, H. Bruce Humberstone and Ernst Lubitsch, 1932).

The breach with Victorian tradition was fundamental. Under-garments became lingerie. The immense importance of 'frillies' as an instrument of sex appeal cannot, of course, be appreciated by a generation which has practically discarded this weapon, and is content that undies should be merely 'amusing'. The Edwardians took them very seriously indeed.[14]

The business of matching underwear came to the fore in the more luxurious sphere, though with today's fast fashion it is easy to find coordinated sets of lingerie at all levels of quality and price. Some find the idea of such sets too obvious, much as you might prefer separates to suits of outer clothing.

With greater choice now offered to fashion-conscious men for their underwear the same concern may become more of a dilemma, to satisfy a desire for fine clothing, but also counter the continuing pressure not to seem too aware of fashion in order to maintain their masculinity. Colour in male underwear is rare. The confident metrosexual apart, many men appear unconcerned about such matters, whether or not they harbour a secret interest in what they wear.

For the eighteenth- and nineteenth-century man of means the dressing gown was able to answer such a hidden desire. Cut in a T-shape like many Eastern robes, it could be made of richly ornate damasks and velvets, and was sometimes worn as informal outerwear. The option of colour and exotic trimmings such as contrasting cuffs and lapels, fancy cord-work and tassels must have been a relief from the increasingly sombre requirements of respectable male dress. The twentieth century brought the dressing gown into the bedroom again, becoming a less formalized and less heavyweight garment. Rudolph Valentino, the Latin Lover himself, is pictured in an orange and black satin gown, but worn demurely over shirt and trousers. He is casually posed beside his new wife, with the slinky, shiny garment somehow suggesting the smouldering lover at bay. In contrast, figures such as Fred Astaire and Noel Coward bring 'urbane elegance' rather than sexiness into play.[15] More recently, for all genders, the dressing gown seems to have become a far less sumptuous item, intimating a relaxed lifestyle, often in machine-washable cosy fleece fabrics. Neither formality nor sexiness nor elegance seem to fit the modern bill.

Women's nightwear in the Edwardian period was still influenced by the disapproval surrounding anything too whimsical. In an Elinor Glyn novel, *The Vicissitudes of Evangeline* (1905), the heroine refuses to understand that there might be anything wrong with her flighty choice of night attire. Her friend Mary, and Mary's mother Lady Katherine, visit Evangeline in her bedroom and are astonished by what they see:

'Oh, Lady Katherine, I am afraid you are wondering at my having pink silk.' I said, apologetically, 'as I am in mourning, but I have not had time to get a white dressing gown yet.'

'It is not that, dear,' said Lady Katherine, in a grave duty voice, 'I – I – do not think such a night-gown is suitable for a girl.'

'Oh! But I am very strong,' I said. 'I never catch cold.'

. . . Mary Mackintosh held it up, with a face of stern disapproval.

'Evangeline, dear, you are very young, so you probably cannot understand', Mary said, 'but I consider this garment not in any way fit for a girl – or for any good woman for that matter. Mother, I hope my sisters have not seen it!'

I looked so puzzled.

She examined the stuff, one could see the chair through it, beyond . . .

'Of course it would be too light for you', I said, humbly, 'but it is otherwise a very good pattern, and does not tear when one puts up one's arms.'

'I hope, Evangeline, you have sufficient sense to understand now for yourself that such a – a – garment is not at all seemly.'

'Oh! Why not Lady Katherine?' I said. 'You don't know how becoming it is.'

'Becoming!' almost screamed Mary Mackintosh. 'But no nice-minded women wants things to look becoming in bed!'[16]

Along with all the sports bras and cosy dressing gowns, we also inhabit an era of raunchy underwear, with designers vying to produce sexy styles that often hint at the sadomasochistic. Corsets and bustles have returned to impede our movement, but now they are for all manner of genders. The love token carved wooden staybusk becomes a fetish feature in metal, designed to look as painful as possible, its original purpose of equalizing pressure on the abdomen long forgotten. To pull the busk free of a corset bodice was once considered a form of daring flirtation, 'to gesture with it' enticingly, no doubt.[17] 'Theyr breasts they embuske', which is to say, place their breasts in a form of ambush for the unsuspecting.[18] Worn up against the skin and close to the heart, the metaphorical seat of our emotions, once it was a simple love token that even the poorest could afford to give, often carved with the names of a couple and adorned with romantic symbols; now it has become an instrument of feigned brutality.

Although the erotic resonance of underwear has seldom been absent, the thrust of advertising to make us consider what covers our bodies as sexually provocative seems like a simplification in relation to underwear. A baby's layette prepared by a mother for her child's birth would hardly come into this category. Items that are often retained long after the baby has grown up, and kept at the back of an underwear drawer, can become an only sometimes sensual reminder of the past.

Underwear is largely a private matter, whatever the fashion. When exposed, it reveals its putative hidden nature, its call for

modesty. On the other hand, underwear can transform us, pinched or swollen, into the silhouette of the moment. Comfort continues to be valued, but discomfort can be acceptable too. When underwear is removed, we feel exposed, laid bare in more ways than just our physical body. This examination of the history and nuance of underwear has been an attempt to undress how we feel about our most intimate clothing and the body that lies beneath.

Knitted doll's
underwear, 1962.

GLOSSARY

Braies or bruches: From late Middle Ages worn as undergarments, loose
to knee or mid-calf

Breechcloths: loincloths, dhotis, strips of fabric worn around the loins
and buttocks

Cache-fesse: small apron-like anus cover

Cellulose fabrics, human-made: acetate, Lyocell, rayon, Tricel

Chausses: medieval leggings

Chemise: undergarment with short sleeves, late eighteenth century,
which became a simple shift dress in the early nineteenth century

Chiton: ancient Greek woollen tunic shift

Cotillion: a mid-eighteenth-century underskirt, becoming a term for an
elaborate dance

Drawers, underpants, knickers: worn from the sixteenth century in
Holland and Germany

Fundoshi: traditional Japanese undergarment, a form of loincloth

Hose: stockings

Jaconet: eighteenth-century strong cotton cloth from India

Kalasiris: ancient Egyptian fitted sheath dress, possibly cut on bias

Lawn: fine woven linen or cotton

Liberty bodice: child's brushed-cotton-backed vest with reinforced
seams, sometimes with suspenders attached

Linen/flax: from the stem of *Linum usitatissimum*. The plant fibres
are very long, 15–102 centimetres (6–40 in.); stronger than cotton,
lint-free and has a lustre when newly ironed

Nainsook: very fine, soft cotton fabric

Necropants/*nábrók*: underpants made from the skin of a dead person;
Icelandic

Peascod, or goose belly: sixteenth- and early seventeenth-century
padded male stomach

Ramie: like linen, made from the fibrous stem of a plant, but softer so
well suited to underwear. Because it creases even more than linen,
it is usually blended with other natural fibres or with polyester

Rayon: made from cellulose organic fibre, so although manmade it is
produced from natural products

Silk: produced by the silkworm in a continuous filament
Spandex/elastane: used in shapewear and sportswear since 1958, lightweight and very stretchy
Synthetic fabric, non-cellulose human-made: acrylic, nylon, polyester
Thread count: the number of warp threads in a square inch of fabric, expressed either as, for example, 50 × 75, or as a total, as 125
Warp and weft: in woven fabric, the warp goes vertically and the '*weft* goes from *left* to right'

REFERENCES

Introduction

1 Curtis Sittenfeld, *Rodham* (London, 2020), p. 121.
2 Ibid., p. 122.
3 Kerry Olson, 'Roman Underwear Revisited', *Classical World*, XCVI/2 (2003), p. 201.
4 Alison R. Drucker, 'The Influence of Western Women on the Anti-Footbinding Movement, 1840–1911', *Historical Reflections*, VIII/3 (1981), pp. 179–99.
5 Frank Armer, an American Depression-era publisher, cited in Peter Haining, *The Classic Era of American Pulp Magazines* (New York, 2000), p. 55.
6 'Lingerie Lovelies Lure Drinkers to Austrian Wine', www.wine-searcher.com, 13 September 2014. The advertising scheme was the brainchild of Ellen Ledermüller-Reiner, in Burgenland.
7 Sanchez Manning, Molly Clayton and Sophie Macdonald, '"Stop Making Women Share Changing Rooms with Men": Feminist Campaigners Demand Change amid Growing Reports of Traumatic Encounters at Stores from Primark to M&S', *Mail on Sunday*, 1 October 2022. Debbie Hayton, 'M&S's "Gender Inclusive" Changing Room Policy Is a Mess', *The Spectator*, 26 August 2022, www.spectator.co.uk.
8 Russell A. Davis, 'Creating Spaces: A Letter to the Editor about Transgender Students and Their Right to Space on College Campus', *Journal of Black Sexuality and Relationships*, II/3 (2016), pp. 93–8 (p. 94).
9 Casey Finch, '"Hooked and Buttoned Together": Victorian Underwear and Representations of the Female Body', *Victorian Studies*, XXXIV/3 (1991), pp. 337–63 (p. 340).

1 What Is Underwear For?

1 Geoffrey Chaucer, 'The Pardoner's Tale', 662–4, the host berating the pardoner, at www.librarius.com.
2 Hilary Mantel, *Wolf Hall* (London, 2009), part II, chap. II, p. 84.
3 In central Italy in 1375 a law was passed to prevent *pandos* being worn, because of their indecency.

257

4 *The Diary of Samuel Pepys*, Friday, 15 May 1663, www.pepysdiary.com.
5 Ibid., Thursday, 16 June 1664.
6 See C. Willett and Phillis Cunnington, *The History of Underclothes* [1951] (London, 1992), p. 65, or more recently Lucy Worsley, *Jane Austen at Home: A Biography* (London, 2017), p. 199.
7 See 'The Georgians', Historic Royal Palaces, www.hrp.org.uk, accessed 14 May 2023.
8 John Harvey, *Men in Black* (London, 1995), p. 23.
9 Jonathan A. Allan, 'Impossibly Erotic Things: On Men's Underwear in *Brief Encounters* by Suzanne Forster', *Critical Studies in Men's Fashion*, IX/2 (August 2022), p. 209.
10 Cecil Saint-Laurent, *A History of Ladies Underwear* (London, 1966), p. 8.
11 Shaun Cole, *The Story of Men's Underwear* (London, 2010), p. 13.
12 John Donne, 'To His Mistress Going to Bed', in *John Donne: The Complete English Poems*, ed. A. J. Smith (London, 1971).
13 Thomas Hardy's *The Well-Beloved* quoted in Casey Finch, '"Hooked and Buttoned Together": Victorian Underwear and Representations of the Female Body', *Victorian Studies*, XXXIV/3 (1991), pp. 337–63 (p. 338).
14 Manuela Morgaine, *En Slip* (Paris, 2021), pp. 20–21, 23.
15 Cole, *The Story of Men's Underwear*, p. 7.
16 Ibid., p. 50.
17 Mireille M. Lee, 'Antiquity and Modernity in Neoclassical Dress', *Classical World*, CXII2 (2019), p. 84.
18 Sam Wollaston, 'The Splashback Scandal: Should All Men Sit Down to Urinate?', *The Guardian*, 20 August 2010.
19 For macaronis see Willett and Cunnington, *The History of Underclothes*, p. 15.
20 'Dear Sexy Knickers', *Are You Being Served?*, series 1, episode 2, BBC1.
21 C. Willett Cunnington, *English Women's Clothing in the Present Century* (London, 1952), pp. 88–95; p. 94, referring to the year 1909.
22 Lauren Windle, 'Mind-Blowing Truth about Why Women's Underwear Have Bows on Them', *The Sun*, 11 May 2021.
23 Christina Patterson, 'The Real Villain in Alice Sebold's Tragic Tale Has Yet to Be Caught', *The Telegraph*, 1 December 2021.
24 Ska and pop band Madness, 'In the Middle of the Night', Chris Foreman and Graham McPherson, *One Step Beyond* album, 1979.
25 Caroline Lowbridge, 'Cat Steals Hundreds of Pounds of Items from Neighbours', www.bbc.co.uk, accessed 3 May 2023.
26 Alison Carter, *Underwear: The Fashion History* (London, 1992), p. 11.
27 Miranda Cowley Heller, *The Paper Palace* (London, 2022), p. 15.
28 Eric Gill, 'Epilogue on Trousers', in *Fashion: Critical and Primary Sources*, vol. IV: *The Twentieth Century*, ed. Peter McNeil (Oxford, 2009), p. 57, from Eric Gill, *Clothes: An Essay upon the Nature and Significance of the Natural and Artificial Integuments Worn by Men and Women* (London, 1931).
29 Marilyn Yalom, *A History of the Breast* (London, 1997), p. 161.

30 Rosemary Hawthorne, *Knickers: An Intimate Appraisal* (London, 1994), p. 9.
31 Ibid., p. 12.
32 Kassia St Clair, *The Golden Thread: How Fabric Changed History* (London, 2018), pp. 241–2, citing Chris Hadfield as quoted in Mary Roach, *Packing for Mars: The Curious Science of Life in Space* (Oxford, 2011), p. 46.
33 Robert Frost's comments in answer to the question 'Do female astronauts wear bras in space?' were upvoted by Jonathon Miller on www.quora.com, accessed 9 November 2023.
34 Philippe Naughton, 'Scottish Tradition Hit by Cover-Up Ruling', *The Times*, 2 August 2004.
35 See the definitions of the terms at www.urbandictionary.com.
36 City of Myrtle, ordinance number 2013 – 28 6-11-13, www.cityofmyrtlebeach.com, accessed 3 January 2024.
37 Information on this is available in the Ryan Report, a 2009 commission that looked into institutional child abuse in Ireland, www.gov.ie.
38 Giovanni Boccaccio, *The Decameron*, trans. John Payne, Day 9, story 2, at www.gutenberg.org.
39 Daniel Miller, *Stuff* (Cambridge, 2010), p. 39.
40 Kristin Romey, 'Here's What the Iceman Was Wearing When He Died 5,300 Years Ago', *National Geographic*, 18 August 2016.
41 Brenda Fowler, 'Forgotten Riches of King Tut: His Wardrobe', *New York Times*, 25 July 1995.
42 Frances Boucher, *20,000 Years of Fashion* (New York, 1987), p. 157.
43 Nina Edwards, *Pazazz: The Impact and Resonance of White Clothing* (London, 2023), p. 141.
44 Sally A. Hastings, 'The Empress' New Clothes and Japanese Women, 1868–1912', *The Historian*, LV/4 (1993), pp. 677–92.
45 Tatsuichi Horikiri, *The Stories Clothes Tell: Voices of Working-Class Japan* (London, 2016), p. 17.
46 Ibid., p. 57.
47 Isabella L. Bird cited in Horikiri, *The Stories Clothes Tell*, p. 76.
48 Aoife Hanna, 'The Purpose of Pockets in Underwear Explained and Women are Loving It!', *Woman and Home*, 30 November 2021, www.womanandhome.com.
49 Smriti Daniel, 'Why Some People Are Soiling Their Underwear to Help the Earth', www.aljazeera.com, 29 April 2021.
50 Ibid.
51 Mario Perniola, 'Between Clothing and Nudity', in *Fashion: Critical and Primary Sources*, vol. 1: *Late Medieval to Renaissance*, ed. Peter McNeil (Oxford, 2009), part 2/8, p. 95
52 Mark A. Wrathall, ed., *The Cambridge Heidegger Lexicon* (Cambridge, 2021), pp. 792–6.
53 'Wonderjock', at https://vocla.com, accesssed 2 January 2024.

2 Codpiece and Corset

1 Marilyn Yalom, *A History of the Breast* (London, 1997), p. 161.
2 Siu-wai Hibarly Sham, 'An Analysis of Ladies' Normal Dressing and Their Appreciation of Clothes and Accessories in Song Dynasty', MA thesis, Hong Kong, 2017.
3 Constance Larymore, *A Resident's Wife in Nigeria* (London, 1908), p. 199, at https://archive.org.
4 Leigh Summers, 'Yes, They Did Wear Them: Working-Class Women and Corsetry in the Nineteenth Century', *Costume: The Journal of the Costume Society*, 2 (2002), p. 65.
5 Writing under the pseudonym Luke Limner, *Crinoline Mania of 1862: Madre Natura versus the Moloch of Fashion – A Social Essay* (London, 1870), p. 6.
6 See 'Abkhazians', *World Culture Encyclopedia*, www.everyculture.com, accessed 14 December 2023.
7 Quoted in David Kunzle, *Fashion and Fetishism: A Social History of the Corset, Tight-Lacing and other Forms of Body Sculpture* [1982] (London, 2006), p. 111.
8 Thomas Nashe cited in Yalom, *A History of the Breast*, p. 163.
9 Shaun Cole, *The Story of Men's Underwear* (London, 2010), pp. 16–18.
10 Grace Vicary, cited in Dan Piepenbring, 'A Brief History of the Codpiece, the Personal Protection for Renaissance Equipment', *New Yorker*, 23 May 2020.
11 Albrecht Classen, *The Medieval Chastity Belt: A Myth-Making Process*, cited in Maris Fessenden, 'Medieval Chastity Belts Are a Myth', www.smithsonianmag.com, 20 August 2015.
12 Thorstein Veblen, *The Theory of the Leisure Class* [1899], ed. Candace Ward (Oxford, 2007).
13 Ibid., p. 106.
14 Cited in C. Willett and Phillis Cunnington, *The History of Underclothes* [1951] (London, 1992), p. 180.
15 A German fashion for low male necklines at the beginning of the sixteenth century. Women of fashion started the century with revealing necklines, but gradually the chest and then neck were covered, ultimately with the ruff.
16 Philip Stubbes, 'Stubbes on Fashion: Excerpts from *Anatomie of Abuses*, 1583', at www.elizabethancostume.net/stubbes.html, accessed 20 March 2022.
17 *The Scarlet Pimpernel* is a novel set in 1792 during the Reign of Terror. The chivalrous Sir Percy Blakeney rescues aristocrats from the guillotine, his frivolous, fashionable appearance helping to deflect suspicion.
18 Thomas Creevey quoted in Willett and Cunnington, *The History of Underclothes*, p. 106.
19 Felix M'Donogh, *The Hermit in London* (London, 1819), footnote, in Willett and Cunnington, p. 106.

20 Thomas Creevey, *The Creevey Papers* (New York, 1904) at
   https://archive.org, chap. XII.

21 Robert Elms, cited in Charlie Thomas, 'Street Smarts: Mods,
   Rudeboys, Teddy Boys and Punks', www.therake.com, accessed
   12 May 2021.

22 *The Rational Dress Society's Gazette* (London), January 1889, issue 4.

23 Joan Nunn, 'Anti-Fashion; or, Victorian Attempts at Reform
   of Male and Female Dress', at www.victorianweb.org, accessed
   20 March 2023.

24 Marna Jean Davis, 'Mother Hubbard Dresses Not Prairie Dresses',
   www.marnajeandavis.com, 30 December 2021.

25 Carolyn D. Taratko, MA thesis, Nashville, TN, 2014, p.9,

26 Stella Mary Newton, *Health, Art and Reason: Dress Reformers of the
   Nineteenth Century* (London, 1974), p. 41.

27 Casey Cadwallader, creative director of Mugler, cited in Jessica
   Testa, 'Nothing Says Fashion in 2023 Like a Corset Hoodie', *New
   York Times*, 3 May 2023.

28 Cally Blackman, *One Hundred Years of Menswear* (London, 2016),
   p. 80.

29 John Carl Flügel, *The Psychology of Clothes* (Madison, CT, 1971).

30 David Kunzle, *Fashion and Fetishism: A Social History of the Corset,
   Tight-Lacing and other Forms of Body Sculpture* [1982] (London, 2006).

31 Edwina Ehrman, *Undressed: A Brief History of Underwear* (London,
   2015), p. 95.

32 Norbert Elias, *The Civilizing Process* [1939] (London, 2012), p. 174.

33 Anne Hollander, *Seeing through Clothes* (New York, 1975), p. xiii.

34 Yalom, *A History of the Breast*, p. 201.

35 Lidewij Edelkoort, *Fetishism in Fashion* (Amsterdam, 2013), p. 6.

36 Valerie Steele, *The Corset: A Cultural History* (New Haven, CT, 2003),
   referring to the corsetier Fakir Musafar, p. 47.

37 Abbé de Choisy, François-Timoléon, *The Travestite Memoirs of the Abbé
   de Choisy*, originally published in French 1737, trans. R.H.F. Scott
   (London, 1973), p. 36.

38 Ibid., pp. 48–9.

3 Modesty and the Immodest Torso

1 *The Oracle* newspaper, cited in Keith Eubank and Phyllis G. Tortora,
   Survey of Historic Costume, 5th edn (New York, 2009), p. 315.

2 See Jane Taylor, 'Beyond the Trivial: Austen's Narratives of Fashion',
   PhD thesis, University College London, 2016. Taylor quotes Jane
   Austen's letters to her sister Cassandra, 15–16 September 1813,
   p. 220, and 8–9 January 1810, p. 70. Deidre Le Faye, ed.,
   Jane Austen's Letters, 3rd edn (Oxford, 1996).

3 Plato, *The Republic* (London, 1955), p. 230.

4 Ibid., p. 229.

5 Chris Belcher, *Pretty Baby: A Memoir* (London, 2022), p. 167.

6 Lianne Aarntzen, Belle Derks, Elianne van Steenbergen and Tanja van der Lippe, 'When Work-Family Guilt Becomes a Woman's Issue: Internalized Gender Stereotypes Predict High Guilt in Working Mothers But Low Guilt in Working Fathers', *British Journal of Social Psychology*, LXII/I (2023), pp. 12–29.

7 Jessica Wright, 'Victorian Vogues to Kardashian Culture: Nineteenth Century Perceptions of the Female Body and the Modern Media', *Historian Journal*, 20 May 2017, www. thehistorianjournal.wordpress.com, citing '"Hooked and Buttoned Together": Victorian Underwear and Representations of the Female Body', *Victorian Studies*, XXXIV/3 (1991), pp. 337–63 (p. 341).

8 Madeleine Aggeler, 'When a Bra Won't Cut It', *New York Times*, 6 July 2022.

9 Alison Lurie, *The Language of Clothes* (London, 1981), p. 46.

10 Jennifer Lynne Matthews-Fairbanks, *Bare Essentials: Underwear Construction and Pattern Drafting for Lingerie Design* (Los Angeles, CA, 2011), p. 9.

11 Barbara Pym, *Excellent Women* [1952] (London, 2008), p. 94.

12 Ibid., p. 117.

13 Ibid., p. 174.

14 Jennifer Lee, 'Feminism Has a Bra-Burning Myth Problem', *Time Magazine*, 12 June 2014, https://time.com.

15 Kassia St Clair, *The Golden Thread: How Fabric Changed History* (London, 2018), p. 258.

16 Susan K. Cahn, 'Coming On Strong', *International Journal of the History of Sport*, XXXIV/3–4 (4 March 2017), pp. 293–5 (p. 296).

17 James Forsyth, quoting Kevin Maguire, in 'Is This the New "John Major Tucks His Shirts into His Underpants"?', *The Spectator*, 11 October 2007.

18 Lauren Aadhar and Alexis Bennett, '8 Ways to Disguise Panty Lines Without Going Commando', *Cosmopolitan*, 28 April 2020, www.cosmopolitan.com.

19 Maureen Lee Lenker, 'The Billionaire's Bra Brouhaha: How Jane Russell and an Undergarment Made *The Outlaw* a Hit', www.ew.com, 20 March 2022.

20 Cited in Marlen Komar, 'All the Unbelievable Times in History that Your Bra Was a Big Freaking Deal', www.bustle.com, 29 October 2017.

21 Lucy Mangan, 'Beware the Cold, Hard Truths of Your Underwear Drawer', *The Stylist*, 2016.

22 Mary Quant, *Quant by Quant: The Autobiography of Mary Quant* (London 1966), p. 37.

23 'Valentine Underwear: The 11 Worst Gifts You Can Buy Your Significant Other', *HuffPost*, 8 February 2013, www.huffpost.com.

24 Malu Halasa and Rana Salam, *The Secret Life of Syrian Lingerie: Intimacy and Design* (San Francisco, CA, 2008), introduction, p. 7.

25 Ibid., p. 8.

26 Castro, 'To Strip or Not to Strip? Egyptian Clerics Debate Sex',
    9 January 2006, www.somaliaonline.com.
27 Shereen El Feki, *Sex and the Citadel: Intimate Life in a Changing Arab
    World* (London, 2013), cited in Malu Halasa, 'No Sex Please, We're
    Syrian: On Syrian Sexual Humor During War', https://themarkaz.
    org, accessed 3 January 2024.
28 Juliette Morel, *Lingerie Parisienne* (London, 1976), p. 10.
29 Joyce Bedi, 'Ida and William Rosenthal', *Lemelson Center for the Study
    of Invention and Innovation*, www.invention.si.edu, 3 June 2021.
30 Guy Trebay, 'Suddenly It's Bare Season', *New York Times*,
    22 July 2021.
31 Ibid.
32 Patricia Marx, 'Is the Army's New Tactical Bra Ready for
    Deployment?', *New Yorker*, 19 June 2023.
33 J. D. Salinger, *Catcher in the Rye* (New York, 1951), cited in Moira
    Redmond, 'Lingerie, Literature's Little-Seen Layer', *The Guardian*,
    5 December 2013.
34 Shaun Cole, *The Story of Men's Underwear* (London, 2010), p. 41.
35 Theodore Richards, 'A Brief History of the T-Shirt', www.medium.
    com, 6 January 2021.

4 Outer to Under and Back Again

 1 John Evelyn, Tyrannus pamphlet of 1661, at https://archive.gyford.
    com.
 2 Arthur Grimble, *A Pattern of Islands* [1952] (London, 1981), p. 19.
 3 Marianne Thesander, *The Feminine Ideal* (London, 1997), p. 51.
 4 In the collection of St Fagans, Museum of Wales. See also www.vads.
    ac.uk/digital/collection/POCKETS.
 5 Nina Edwards, *Pazazz: The Impact and Resonance of White Clothing*
    (London, 2023), p. 127.
 6 Thesander, *The Feminine Ideal*, pp. 50–51.
 7 Judith Flanders, *Inside the Victorian Home* (London, 2003), p. 306.
    The Regency shift weighed only about 450 grams (1 lb).
 8 Friedrich Theodor Vischer, cited in Ludmila Kybalová, Olga
    Herbenová and Milena Lamarová, *The Pictorial Encyclopedia of
    Fashion*, trans. Claudia Rosoux (London, 1968), p. 271–2.
 9 Tamami Suoh, '18th Century', in Akiko Fukai et al., *Fashion from
    the 18th to the 20th Century: The Kyoto Costume Institute* (Kyoto, 2002),
    p. 25.
10 Thesander, *The Feminine Ideal*, p. 91.
11 Cited in Kate Eschner, 'Although Less Deadly than Crinolines,
    Bustles Were Still a Pain in the Behind', *Smithsonian Magazine*,
    21 April 2017.
12 Benjamin Black, *A Death in Summer* (London, 2011), p. 173.
13 Paul Poiret, *My First Fifty Years*, trans. Stephen Haden Guest
    (London, 1931), pp. 265–6.

14 Quentin Bell, *On Human Finery* (London, 1976), pp. 64–5.
15 Michel de Montaigne, *The Complete Essays*, vol. 1, trans. Donald Frame (Stanford, CA, 1965), part 14, p. 41, cited in Marilyn Yalom, *A History of the Breast* (London, 1997), p. 162.
16 Flanders, *Inside the Victorian Home*, p. 309.
17 Alison Carter, *Underwear: The Fashion History* (London, 1992), p. 16.
18 Robert Crowley, 'Epigrams of Nice Wives', in *The Selected Works of Robert Crowley* (London, 1550), cited in Carter, *Underwear*, p. 18.
19 A point made by curator Elen Phillips at St Fagans, Museum of Wales, 2023 during a visit to the St Fagans clothing archive, Cardiff.
20 J. Ramsay Kilpatrick and Felicity Kilpatrick, *Down the Memory Lanes of My Hafod*, (Brecon, 2009).
21 Yalom, *A History of the Breast*, p. 174.
22 Cited ibid., p. 164.
23 Luke Limner, *Crinoline Mania of 1862: Madre Natura versus the Moloch of Fashion – A Social Essay* (London, 1870), p. 12 and notes p. 4 and p. 6.
24 Ibid., p. 17.
25 Shaun Cole, *The Story of Men's Underwear* (London, 2010), p. 45.
26 Jennifer Craik, *Face of Fashion: Cultural Studies in Fashion* (London, 1993), p. 128, and cited ibid., p.8.
27 Patrick Mauriès, *Androgyne: Fashion and Gender* (London, 2017), p. 117.
28 Cally Blackman, *100 Years of Menswear* (London, 2012), p. 236.
29 Plutarch, *The Life of Lycurgus*, 22.2.
30 See Edwards, *Pazazz*, p. 141.
31 Alison Lurie, *The Meaning of Clothes* (London, 1981), p. 258.
32 Jane Austen, *Pride and Prejudice* [1813] (London, 1972), p. 82.
33 Keith Eubank and Phyllis G. Tortora, *Survey of Historic Costume*, 5th edn (New York, 2009), p. 550.
34 Peggy Moffitt and Marylou Luther, *The Rudi Gernreich Book* (New York, 1999).
35 Susie Rushton, 'Unravelled! The Death of the String Vest', *The Independent*, 8 December 2007.
36 Lorinda Cramer, 'Rethinking Men's Dress through Material Sources: The Case Study of a Singlet', *Australian Historical Studies*, LII/3 (2021), pp. 420–42.
37 Jordan Tembo and Patricia Mambwe, 'Underwear Exposure through Sagging: Unearthing Women and Girls' Perception of Young Males' Modern Style of Dressing in Zambia', *Research Inventy: International Journal of Engineering and Science*, 11/9 (2021), pp. 30–35.
38 Gene Demby, 'Sagging Pants and the Long History of "Dangerous" Street Fashion', www.npr.org, 11 September 2014.
39 Ibid.
40 M. McMillan, 'Saga Bwoys, Rude Bwoys, and Saggers: Rebellious Black Masculinities', *Critical Arts*, XXXI/3 (2017), pp. 72–89.
41 Tatsuichi Horikiri, *The Stories Clothes Tell: Voices of Working-Class Japan* (London, 2016), p. 54.

42 Alexandra Jones interview with Johnny Flynn: 'Rehearsal Spaces Can Be Very Toxic', *Evening Standard*, 3 May 2023.

43 For the Christian Dior Fall Collection of 1959, cited in Claire B. Shaeffer, *Couture Sewing Techniques* (Newtown, CT, 2011), p. 217.

44 Vanessa Friedman, 'Hey, Whatever Happened to the Half-Slip?', *New York Times*, 5 February 2021.

45 Ibid.

5 Fabric and Fit

1 Daniel Miller, *Stuff* (Cambridge, 2010), p. 23.

2 Karl Marx quoted in Djurdja Bartlett, *Fashion and Politics* (Yale, CT, 2019), pp. 12-13.

3 Rosemary Ingham and Liz Covey, *The Costume Technician's Handbook*, 3rd edn (London, 2003), p. 66.

4 Stella Mary Newton, *Health, Art and Reason: Dress Reformers of the Nineteenth Century* (London, 1974).

5 Nina Edwards, *Dressed for War: Uniforms, Civilian Clothing and Trappings* (London, 2015), p. 79.

6 For scarcity during the war see John E. Vollmer, ed., *Berg Encyclopedia of World Dress and Fashion*, vol. VI: *East Asia* (Oxford, 2010), p. 367.

7 *Brassières and Belts Scrapbook*, Wellcome Library, https://wellcomecollection.org/works/wmfsbmmx, accessed 15 May 2024.

8 Alice Newbold, 'From Cashmere Bras to Kit-Flops, How Katie Holmes Became a Stealth NY Influencer', 26 August 2020, www.vogue.co.uk. The Khaite bra cost $520.

9 Susannah Conway, 'The History of . . . Cashmere: The Golden Fleece', *The Independent*, 6 September 1998.

10 James Boswell, *The Journal of a Tour to the Highlands 1785*, p. 70, at https://classic-literature.co.uk.

11 Gustave Jaeger quoted in Edwina Ehrman, *Undressed: A Brief History of Underwear* (London, 2015), p. 13.

12 Newton, *Health, Art and Reason*, p. 100.

13 C. Willett Cunnington, *English Women's Clothing in the Present Century* (London, 1952), p. 65.

14 Mrs Gaskell, *Cranford* (New York, 1853), p. 14. Captain Brown on Miss Betsey Barker's Alderney cow.

15 Andrew Combe, *Principles of Physiology Applied to the Preservation of Health and to the Development of Physical Education* [1834], cited in Newton, *Health, Art and Reason*, p. 20.

16 Alison Carter, *Underwear: The Fashion History* (London, 1992), p. 15.

17 Vogelsang-Eastwood, textile archaeologist, in Brenda Fowler, 'Forgotten Riches of King Tut: His Wardrobe', www.nytimes.com, 25 July 1995.

18 C. Willett and Phillis Cunnington, *The History of Underclothes* [1951] (London, 1992), p. 18.

19 Grace and Philip Wharton, *Wits and Beaux of Society* (1861), cited at www.dandyism.net.
20 Robert Cruikshank, *The English Spy* (London, 1826)
21 Grace and Philip Wharton, *Wits and Beaux of Society*.
22 Charles Dickens, *Barnaby Rudge: A Tale of the Riots of Eighty* (London, 1841), chap. 10, at www.gutenberg.org.
23 Robert Friedel, 'A White Collar with a Message', https://americanhistory.si.edu, 4 October 2018.
24 George and Weedon Grossmith, *The Diary of a Nobody* (London, 1892), 25 and 26 May.
25 Benjamin Aldes Wurgaft, 'Animal, Vegetable, or Both? Making Sense of the Scythian Lamb', www.laphamsquarterly.org, 5 August 2019.
26 Ingham and Covey, *The Costume Technician's Handbook*, p. 64. Popular in its time, the fantastical travelogue purports to be the diary of Sir John Mandeville, 1357–1371, which was admired by and influenced Christopher Columbus.
27 'The Russia Ukraine War to Weigh on Textile Sector', www.textiletoday.com, accessed 11 January 2023.
28 Limerick supplied by a friend's father, Geoffrey Thomas Floyd.
29 James Lileko, 'The Art of Frahm: An Artistic Study of the Effects of Celery on Loose Elastic', www.lileks.com, accessed June 2022.
30 Pliny the Elder, *Natural Histories*, 11. xxvii.76.
31 Cunnington, *English Women's Clothing*, p. 76.
32 Ibid., p. 23.
33 F. F. Hubach, 'Knit Goods', *Industrial and Engineering Chemistry*, xliv/9 (1952), pp. 2149–51.
34 Marie O'Mahony and Sarah E. Braddock, *SportsTech: Revolutionary Fabrics, Fashion and Design* (London, 2002).
35 Janine Ainley, 'Replica Clothes Pass Everest Test', http://news.bbc.co.uk, 13 June 2006.
36 Kassia St Clair, *The Golden Thread: How Fabric Changed History* (London, 2018), p. 198.
37 Ibid., p. 198.
38 David R. Hooper et al., 'Synthetic Garments Enhance Comfort, Thermoregulatory Response, and Athletic Performance Compared with Traditional Cotton Garments', *Journal of Strength and Conditioning Research*, xxix/3 (March 2015), pp. 700–707.
39 S. L. Paek, 'Subjective Assessment of Fabric Comfort by Sensory Hand', *Journal of Consumer Studies and Home Economics*, viii/4 (December 1984), pp. 339–49.
40 Ibid., p. 65.
41 Barbara Pym, *A Very Private Eye: The Diaries, Letters and Notebooks of Barbara Pym*, ed. Hazel Holt and Hilary Pym (London, 1985), diary entry 8 January 1934.

6 Medical and Other Practical Matters

1 Alison Gwilt, *A Practical Guide to Sustainable Fashion* (London, 2014), pp. 24–6.
2 Katherine Heiny, *Early Morning Riser* (London, 2021), p. 14.
3 Stella Mary Newton, *Health, Art and Reason: Dress Reformers of the Nineteenth Century* (London, 1974), p. 59.
4 Nina Edwards, *Pazazz: The Impact and Resonance of White Clothing* (London, 2023), pp. 125–47.
5 Lucy Worsley, *Jane Austen at Home: A Biography* (London, 2017), p. 198.
6 Ibid., p. 198.
7 Mrs O. P. Flynt, *Manual of Hygienic Modes of Under-Dressing for Women and Children* (Boston, MA, 1876).
8 Ibid., p. 3.
9 Ibid., p. 25.
10 Ibid., p. 15.
11 Ibid.
12 Ibid., p. 17.
13 Aritha Van Herk, 'Invisible Laundry', *Signs*, XXVII/3 (Spring 2002), pp. 893–900.
14 Carole Rawcliffe, *Leprosy in Medieval England* (Woodbridge, 2006), p. 280.
15 Mrs Beeton, *The Book of Household Management* (London, 1861).
16 Alison Carter, *Underwear: The Fashion History* (London, 1992), p. 37.
17 Ibid., p. 17.
18 Sue Miller, interview with Elizabeth Berg, 2020, www.youtube.com.
19 Daisy Grenwell, 'A List Stars Set Out for a Clean Sweep', *The Times*, 1 March 2012, www.thetimes.co.uk.
20 Hannah Furness, 'Stella McCartney: Don't Wash Clothes, Just Brush the Dirt Off', *Daily Telegraph*, 7 July 2019.
21 *Coventry Standard*, 18 April 1957.
22 Vittoria Traverso, 'The Split Pants that Are China's Alternative to Diapers', www.atlasobscura.com, 21 September 2017.
23 Diary of Samuel Pepys, Friday 7 September 1666, www.pepysdiary.com.
24 Leonard Williams, *Tubercle and Underwear* (London, 1908), p. 15.
25 Ibid.
26 Mark Lancaster, cited in Susie Rushton, 'Unravelled! The Death of the String Vest', *The Independent*, 8 December 2007.
27 'The Modern Menstruation Conversation', www.thepranaproject.com, accessed 3 January 2024.
28 See Dugald Scott's patent of 1895 for the 'Improved Sanitary Towel, Napkin, Surgical Bandage, or Similar Appliance, and the Manufacture of Textile Fabric for such Purposes'. Patent reference: 1894/20701.
29 See Jennifer Kotler, 'A Short History of Modern Menstrual Products', www.helloclue.com, 20 November 2018.

30 The Wellcome Collection, Print, A. Mulcey (Paris, 1950–59).
31 Helen King, 'From Rags and Pads to the Sanitary Apron:
   A Brief History of Sanitary Products', www.theconversation.com,
   25 April 2023.
32 Helen King, *Hippocrates' Woman: Reading the Female Body in Ancient
   Greece* (London, 1998), p. 69.
33 Alexandra Steigrad, 'CBS Bans TV Ad That Depicts Menstruating
   Men', *New York Post*, 8 October 2019.
34 Moya Lothian-McLean, 'Thinx Rolls Out National Campaign
   Where Men Get Periods Too', *The Independent*, 10 October 2019.
35 Diary of Samuel Pepys, Tuesday 26 July 1664, www.pepysdiary.com.
36 Robert Munkelwitz and Bruce R. Gilbert, 'Are Boxer Shorts Really
   Better? A Critical Analysis of the Role of Underwear Type in
   Male Subfertility', *Journal of Urology*, CVX/4 (October 1998),
   pp. 1329–33.
37 Alana Clifton-Cunningham, 'From the Loincloth to Thinx:
   A Brief History of Undies', 21 July 2018, https://qz.com.
38 'Swimsuit Police Check the Length of Swimmers' Ensembles
   in Amazing Recolorized 1922 Photo', *HuffPost*, 6 August 2013,
   www.huffpost.com.
39 'The Fabric of Your Life', in *Selvedge* (London, 2005), p. 39.
40 Larissa Bonfante, *Etruscan Dress* (Baltimore, MD, 2003), p. 21.
41 Charles Seltman using the parallel images at the beginning of a
   chapter, 'The New Woman', in his *Women in Antiquity* (London,
   1956) p. 138.
42 Gwilt, *A Practical Guide to Sustainable Fashion*, p. 39.

7 Economic and Religious Concerns

1 Susie Rushton, 'Unravelled! The Death of the String Vest',
   The Independent, 8 December 2007.
2 Jennifer Craik, *Uniforms Exposed: From Conformity to Transgression*
   (Oxford, 2005), p. 39–40.
3 *The General Handbook: Serving in the Church of Jesus Christ of Latter-day
   Saints* (2010), at www.churchofjesuschrist.org.
4 David McKay, 'Apostle', quoted in David John Buerger, *The Mysteries of
   Godliness: A History of Mormon Temple Worship* (Salt Lake City, UT, 2002),
   at www.ldsendowment.org.
5 Ralph Brickley, 'Vague Dogma: Holy Magic Underwear',
   https://dividetheword.blog, 20 August 2018.
6 Ibid.
7 Valerie R. Hotchkiss, *Clothes Make the Man: Female Cross-Dressing in
   Medieval Europe* (New York, 1996), p. 51.
8 Ibid., p. 4.
9 Terry Jones, Michael Palin and Fred Tomlinson, 'The Lumberjack
   Song', first appeared in *Monty Python's Flying Circus*, episode 9,
   'The Ant: An Introduction', BBC1, 4 December 1969.

10 See Ian Hodder, *Çathlhöyük: The Leopard's Tale: Revealing the Mysteries of Turkey's Ancient Town* (London, 2006).

11 George Ryan, 'The Lost Art of Catholic Hair Shirt Making', https://ucatholic.com, 28 February 2023.

12 Simon Caldwell, 'Thomas More's Hair Shirt Enshrined for Public Veneration', *Catholic Herald*, 22 November 2016.

13 Carla Tilgham, 'Semper Ubi Sub Ubi: Braies and Meaning', https://hugovanharlo.com, accessed 11 November 2023.

14 Miriam Frenkel, 'Material Culture in the Jewish Medieval World of Islam: Books, Clothing and Houses', in *Handbook of Jewish Ritual and Practice*, ed. Oliver Leaman (London, 2022), pp. 125–36 (p. 130).

15 Oliver Leaman, 'Clothes', in *Handbook of Jewish Ritual and Practice*, pp. 335–44 (p. 338).

16 Nina Edwards, *Darkness: A Cultural History* (London, 2018), p. 22.

17 Leaman, 'Clothes', p. 340.

18 'Kachera', www.sikhiwiki.org, accessed 3 January 2024.

19 Kristine M. Kamiya, 'Overview of the Ryukyus', in *Berg Encyclopedia of World Dress and Fashion*, vol. VI: *East Asia*, ed. John E. Vollmer (Oxford, 2010), pp. 423–4.

20 Toby Slade, *Japanese Fashion: A Cultural History* (Oxford, 2009), p. 53.

21 Ibid., p. 58.

22 Regína Hrönn Ragnarsdöttir, 'The Museum of Icelandic Witchcraft and Sorcery at Hólmavík in the Westfjords Region of Iceland', see 'The Necropants', https://guidetoiceland.is, accessed 3 January 2024.

23 'The Witch-Lore of Catalonia', Perennial Pyrenees – Archaeology and Traditions of the Pyrenean Peaks, https://perennialpyrenees.com, 22 May 2017.

24 Oleg Skripnik, 'The Skoptsy: The Story of the Russian Sect that Maimed for Its Beliefs', www.rbth.com, 25 August 2016.

25 'El Salvador: President Bukele Engulfs the Country in a Human Rights Crisis After Three Years in Government', www.amnesty.org. 2 June 2022.

26 'Another 2,000 Gangsters Herded Like Animals into World's Worst Prison', www.news.com.au, 16 March 2023.

27 Pinar Dinc, 'Turkish Decree on Coloured Uniforms for Coup Suspects Could Sow Seeds of Future Unrest', www.theconversation.co.uk, 11 January 2018.

28 Stian Alexander and David Flett, 'UK Prison Cracking Down on Female Lags Smuggling in "Inappropriate" Lingerie', *Daily Star*, 26 February 2023, www.dailystar.co.uk.

29 Stian Alexander, 'Sexy Lingerie Confiscated from Female Prisoners Smuggling It in on Day Release', *The Mirror*, 25 February 2023.

30 Emily Yahr, 'Yes, Prisoners Used to Sew Lingerie for Victoria's Secret – Just Like in "Orange is the New Black" Season 3', *Washington Post*, 17 June 2015.

31 Walter Map, *De nugis curialium* (Courtiers' Trifles), cited in Viktor Athelstan, 'Medieval Monastic Clothing Part 3: A Medieval Monk's

Underwear (and Lack of It!)', www.themedievalmonk.wordpress.
com, 13 December 2020.
32 Ibid.
33 Elizabeth Howard, *The Clothes Make the Man: Trangressive
Disrobing and Disarming in Beowulf* (Youngstown, OH, 2007),
pp. 18–19.
34 Nina Edwards, *Pazazz: The Impact and Resonance of White Clothing*
(London, 2023), p. 120.
35 Sarah O'Connor, 'Leicester's Dark Factories Show Up a Diseased
System', *Financial Times*, 3 July 2020.
36 Charles Frederick Wiesenthal, a German working as an engineer
in England, developed the chainstitch machine in 1755, for tough,
resistant materials. Cited in Joan Perkin, 'Sewing Machines:
Liberation or Drudgery for Women?', *History Today*, LII/12 (12
December 2002), pp. 35–41.
37 B. Mariem et al., 'A Study of the Consumption of Sewing Threads for
Women's Underwear, Bras and Panties', *Autex Research Journal*, XX/3
(2019), pp. 299–311.

8   The Underwear Drawer
1   It is worth noting that men's hose did not become known as
stockings until the mid-seventeenth century.
2   Jeremy Farrell, *Socks and Stockings* (London, 1992), p. 9.
3   John Nichols, ed., *The Progress and Public Processions of Queen Elizabeth*
(London, 1823), vol. II, p. xlii.
4   Rosemary Hawthorne, *Stockings and Suspenders: A Quick Flash*
(London, 1993), p. 20.
5   Ibid., p. 89.
6   Ibid., p. 10.
7   Cited in Moira Redmond, 'Lingerie, Literature's Little-Seen Layer',
The Guardian, 5 December 2013.
8   Dana Wilson-Kovacs, 'From Petticoats to Suspender Belts: A Brief
History of Women's Underwear', www.theconversation.com,
18 April 2016.
9   *The Queen Magazine*, cited in Shelley Tobin, *Inside Out: A Brief History
of Underwear* (London, 2000), p. 28.
10 John E. Vollmer, ed., *Berg Encyclopedia of World Dress and Fashion*,
vol. VI: *East Asia* (Oxford, 2010), p. 326.
11 Miriam Frenkel, 'Material Culture in the Jewish Medieval World of
Islam: Books, Clothing and Houses', *Routledge Handbook of Jewish
Ritual and Practice*, ed. Oliver Leaman (London, 2022), pp. 125–36
(p. 131).
12 Kate Atkinson, *Shrines of Gaiety* (London, 2022), p. 358.
13 C. Willett Cunnington, *English Women's Clothing in the Present Century*
(London, 1952), p. 179.
14 Ibid., p. 30.

15 Cally Blackman, *One Hundred Years of Menswear* (London, 2012), p. 134.
16 Elinor Glyn, *The Vicissitudes of Evangeline* (London, 1905), pp. 102–3.
17 Marilyn Yalom, *A History of the Breast* (London, 1997), p. 162.
18 Quote from Thomas Nashe, *The Unfortunate Traveller; or, The Life of Jack Wilton* (London, 1594), cited ibid., p. 163. The work follows the protagonist's travels in Germany and Italy during the reign of the English king Henry VIII.

BIBLIOGRAPHY

Anthony, P., 'Underwear with Particular Reference to the Development
    of the Bustle', 1968, www.euppublishing.com, accessed 10 January
    2022
Barbier, Murcel, and Shazia Boucher, *The Story of Underwear: Male and
    Female* (London, 2010)
Baumgarten, Linda, *What Clothes Reveal: The Language of Clothing in
    Colonial and Federal America* (New Haven, CT, 2012)
Benson, Elaine, and John Esten, *Unmentionables: A Brief History of
    Underwear* (London, 1996)
Blackman, Cally, *100 Years of Menswear* (London, 2012)
Bremner, Geoffrey, 'Rousseau's Realism or a Close Look at Julie's
    Underwear', *Romance Studies*, 1/1(1983), pp. 48–63
Cahn, Susan K., 'Coming On Strong', *International Journal of the History
    of Sport*, XXXIV/3–4 (4 March 2017), pp. 293–5
Campbell, Emily, *Inside Out: Underwear and Style* (London, 2001)
Carr-Gomm, Philip, *A Brief History of Nakedness* (London, 2010)
Carter, Alison, *Underwear: The Fashion History* (London, 1992)
Choisy, Abbé de, *The Transvestite Memoirs*, trans. R.H.F. Scott
    (London, 1973)
Clifton-Cunningham, Alana, 'From the Loincloth to Thinx,
    a Brief History of Undies', www.qz.com, 21 July 2018
Cole, Shaun, *The Story of Men's Underwear* (London, 2018)
—, 'Underpinnings: The Next Best Thing to Naked', in *Fashioning
    Masculinities: The Art of Menswear*, ed. Rosalind McKever
    and Claire Wilcox, with Marta Franceschini (London, 2022)
Cunnington, C. Willett, *English Women's Clothing in the Present Century*
    (London, 1952)
—, and Phillis, *A History of Underclothes* [1951] (London, 2000)
Davies, Andrew, *Thermal Underwear, 1936–c. 1987* (London, 2016)
Daynes, Katie, and Nilesh Mistry, *The Revealing Story of Underwear*
    (London, 2006)
Dolan, Quinn, *Sexy Underwear and Hot Pussy: Panties, Bras, Thongs,
    Stockings, Lingerie* (London, 2021)
Edelkoort, Lideroy, *Fetishism in Fashion* (Amsterdam, 2013)

Eden, Diana, *Stars in Their Underwear* (London, 2020)

Ehrman, Edwina, *Undressed: A Brief History of Underwear* (London, 2015)

Engel, Birgit, *Male Underwear* (London, 2003)

Eubank, Keith, and Phyllis G. Tortora, *Survey of Historic Costume* (New York, 2009)

Ewing, Elizabeth, *Dress and Undress: A History of Women's Underwear* (London, 1986)

—, *Fashion in Underwear: From Babylon to Bikini Briefs* (London, 2012)

Farrell, Jeremy, *Socks and Stockings* (London, 1992)

Farrell-Beck, Jane, and Colleen Gall, *Uplift: The Bra in America* (Philadelphia, PA, 2002)

Finch, Casey, 'Hooked and Buttoned Together: Victorian Underwear and Representations of the Female Body', *Victorian Studies*, XXXIV/3 (Spring 1991), pp. 337–63

Flynt, Mrs O. P., *Manual of Hygienic Modes of Underdressing for Women and Children* (Boston, MA, 1882)

Fury, Alexander, 'Why Vivienne Westwood Still Rules', *Financial Times*, www.ft.com, 5 April 2022

Gao, Xia, et al., 'Shape Controllable Virtual Try-On for Underwear Models', *arXvLabs* (Ithaca, NY, 2021)

Goodkind, Nicola, 'Is a Recession Coming? Alan Greenspan Says the Answer Is in Men's Underwear', www.edition.cnn.com, accessed 4 April 2022

Halasa, Malu, and Rana Salam, eds, *The Secret Life of Syrian Underwear: Intimacy and Design* (San Francisco, CA, 2008)

Hansen, Karen Tranberg, and D. Soyini Madison, eds, *African Dress: Fashion, Agency, Performance* (London, 2013)

Hartnell, Jack, *Medieval Bodies: Life, Death and Art in the Middle Ages* (London, 2018)

Harvey, Barbara, *Monastic Dress in the Middle Ages* (Canterbury, 1988)

Hawthorne, Rosemary, *Knickers: An Intimate Appraisal* [1985] (London, 1991)

—, *Stockings and Suspenders: A Quick Flash* (London, 1993)

Hill, Daniel Delis, *The History of Men's Underwear and Swimwear* (London, 2022)

Hollander, Anne, *Seeing through Clothes* (New York, 1975)

Horikiri, Tatsuichi, *The Stories Clothes Tell: Voices of Working-Class Japan*, trans. Rieko Wagoner (London, 2016)

Hotchkiss, Valerie R., *Clothes Make the Man: Female Cross-Dressing in Medieval Europe* (New York, 1996)

Jenkins, David, ed., *The Cambridge History of Western Textiles* (Cambridge, 2003), vol. I

Kemp-Griffin, Kathryn, *Paris Undressed: Secrets of French Lingerie* (London, 2017)

Keyser, Amber J., *Underneath It All: A History of Women's Underwear* (London, 2018)

Lattimore, Deborah Nourse, *I Wonder What's Under There? A Brief History of Underwear* (London, 1998)

Lee, Mireille M., 'Antiquity and Modernity in Neoclassical Dress: The Confluence of Ancient Greece and Colonial India', *Classical World*, XII/2 (Winter 2019), pp. 71–95

Lewis, Dulcie, *Casting Off the Corsets: A Brief History of Underwear* (Newbury, 2011)

Lim, H., 'Smart Underwear for Diabetic Patients', *Journal of Textile and Apparel Technology and Management*, VI/1 (11 March 2009), pp. 1–11

Lynn, Eleri, *Underwear: Fashion in Detail* (London, 2014)

MacDonald, Margaret F., et al., *Whistler's Woman in White: Joanna Hiffernan and James McNeill Whistler* (New Haven, CT, 2020)

McKever, Rosalind, and Claire Wilcox, eds, with Marta Franceschini, *Fashioning Masculinities: The Art of Menswear* (London, 2022)

Mangan, Lucy, 'Beware the Cold, Hard Truths of Your Underwear Drawer', *Stylist Magazine*, 14 March 2016

Matthews-Fairbanks, Jennifer Lynne, *Bare Essentials: Underwear: Construction and Pattern Drafting for Lingerie Design* (Los Angeles, CA, 2011)

Mauriès, Patrick, *Androgyne: Fashion and Gender* (London, 2017)

Metzger, Rainer, *London in the Sixties* (London, 2012)

Miller, Daniel, *Stuff* (Cambridge, 2010)

Morgaine, Manuela, *En Slip* (Paris, 2021)

Newton, Stella Mary, *Health, Art and Reason: Dress Reformers of the Nineteenth Century* (London, 1974)

Piepenbring, Dan, 'A Brief History of the Codpiece, the Personal Protection for Renaissance Equipment', *New Yorker*, 23 May 2020

Rantanen, Miska, *Pantsdrunk: The Finnish Art of Drinking at Home. Alone. In your Underwear* (London, 2018)

Reddy-Best, Kelly L., et al., *Visibly Queer and Trans Fashion Brands and Retailers in the Twenty-First Century*, 26 October 2021, at www.researchgate.net

Reynolds, Helen, *A Fashionable History of Underwear* (London, 2003)

Robinson, Dwight E., 'The Economics of Fashion Demand', *Quarterly Journal of Economics*, LXXV/3 (1961), pp. 376–98

Ross, Geoffrey Aquilina, *The Day of the Peacock: Style for Men, 1963–1973* (London, 2011)

Ruby, Jennifer, *Underwear* (London, 1995)

St Clair, Cassia, *The Golden Thread: How Fabric Changed History* (London, 2018)

Salazar, Ligaya, ed., *Fashion v Sport* (London, 2008)

Sang, J. S., and M. J. Park, 'A Study on the Use of Underwear as Outerwear', *International Journal of Costume Culture*, XII/1 (2009), pp. 1–12

Seleshanko, Kristina, *Bound and Determined: A Visual History of Corsets, 1850–1960* (London, 2013)

Shaeffer, Claire B., *Couture Sewing Techniques* (Newtown, CT, 2011)

Simmel, Georg, 'The Philosophy of Fashion', in *Simmel on Culture*,
    ed. David Frisby and Mike Featherstone (London, 1997)
Smith, Desire, *Irresistible: The Art of Lingerie, 1920–1980s* (London, 2012)
Sorge-English, Lynn, *Stays and Body Image in London: The Stay-Making
    Trade, 1680–1810* (London, 2011)
Steele, Valerie, 'Appearance and Identity', in *Men and Women: Dressing the
    Part*, ed. Claudia B. Kidwell and Valerie Steele (Washington, DC,
    1989)
—, *The Corset: A Cultural History* (New Haven, CT, 2003)
Thompson, O. M., *Held Up By Clothes: Dress and Underwear in Victorian
    Novels* (Melbourne, 2009)
Tobin, Shelley, *Inside Out: A Brief History of Underwear* (London, 2000)
Watts, Madeleine, 'Slip: An Essay of Sorts, about Women's Underwear',
    The Lifted Brow, 28 December 2013
Whitty, Helen, *Underwear* (London, 2001)
Williams, Leonard, *Tubercle and Underwear* (London, 1908)

ACKNOWLEDGEMENTS

I want to thank the many historians of dress on whose in-depth knowledge and imagination I have relied; with many thanks to the Arts Library at the v&a, the British Library, Jackie Clark at Market Lavington Museum, Elen Phillips – who allowed me to explore their splendid clothing archive – and Kay Kays of St Fagans Museum of Wales, Amelia Walker and Maggie Sawkins at the Wellcome Library, the Westminster Arts Library, and to the University of West London Library, who gave me permission to work there. My thanks to friends and colleagues who have kindly put their minds to this pithy subject: Philip Attwood; Anthony Daniels; Brigitte Dold; Peter Edwards; Josie Floyd; Oliver Leaman; Jamil Mar at Honey Birdette; Deborah Newgate; Sheila Perkins; Liz Pilley; Jane Reddish; Marcin Tumidajski; Dick Vigers. To Michael Leaman for his help and advice, and many thanks to Alex Ciobanu, Martha Jay, Helen McCusker, Fran Roberts and all at Reaktion Books. Also to the Pasold Fund for a travel grant, thank you.

PHOTO ACKNOWLEDGEMENTS

The author and publishers wish to express their thanks to the below sources of illustrative material and/or permission to reproduce it. Some locations of artworks are also given below, in the interest of brevity:

Alamy Stock Photo: pp. 166 (© Museum of London/Heritage Image Partnership Ltd), 175 (*bottom*; Associated Press/Robert Mecea), 176 (*bottom*; Associated Press); © Amgueddfa Cymru – National Museum Wales: pp. 58, 73, 85, 113; Art Institute of Chicago: pp. 26, 80, 114, 168 (*top*); Bibliothèque de l'Arsenal, Paris (MS 5070 réserve, fol. 325r): p. 47; Bibliothèque nationale de France, Paris: pp. 24 (MS Français 2663, fol. 164r), 94; British Library, London (Royal MS 2 A XXII, fol. 220r): p. 162 (*bottom*); The British Museum, London: p. 63; Bundesarchiv, Koblenz (Bild 146-1971-041-10, CC BY-SA 3.0): p. 220; Castello della Manta, Saluzzo: p. 163 (*top*); Detroit Institute of Arts, MI: p. 163 (*bottom*); photos Nina Edwards: pp. 194, 253; English Broadside Ballad Archive, University of California at Santa Barbara: p. 14; Flickr: p. 174 (*top*; photo Elvert Barnes, CC BY-SA 2.0); from Inès Gâches-Sarraute, *Le Corset: Étude physiologique et pratique* (Paris, 1900): p. 31; iStock.com: p. 6 (Martyna87); The J. Paul Getty Museum, Los Angeles: p. 142 (photo Eugène Atget); David Kamm, DEVCOM Soldier Center: p. 176 (*top*); Kunsthistorisches Museum, Vienna: p. 129; Lewis Walpole Library, Yale University, Farmington, CT: p. 20; Library of Congress, Prints and Photographs Division, Washington, DC: pp. 99 (photo Angelo Rizzuto), 146, 203 (photo Esther Bubley), 215, 216 (photo Herbert E. French), 234, 245; Los Angeles County Museum of Art (LACMA): pp. 78 (*left* and *right*), 110, 167; Maison de Victor Hugo – Hauteville House, Paris and Guernsey: p. 72; J. Mayer/Shutterstock: p. 175 (*top*); The Metropolitan Museum of Art, New York: pp. 66, 83, 171; Minneapolis Institute of Art, MN: p. 165; Mitchell Library, State Library of New South Wales, Sydney: pp. 152, 182; Musée du Louvre, Paris: p. 168 (*bottom*); The Museum of Modern Art (MOMA), New York: p. 172; Museum of New Zealand Te Papa Tongarewa, Wellington: p. 178; Museum Rotterdam (CC BY-SA 3.0 NL): pp. 98, 210; Museums Victoria, Melbourne: p. 135; National Folk Museum of Korea, Seoul (Korea Open Government License): p. 246; National Gallery of Art, Washington, DC: pp. 69, 170; National Institute of Japanese Literature, Tokyo (CC

INDEX

Page numbers in *italics* indicate illustrations